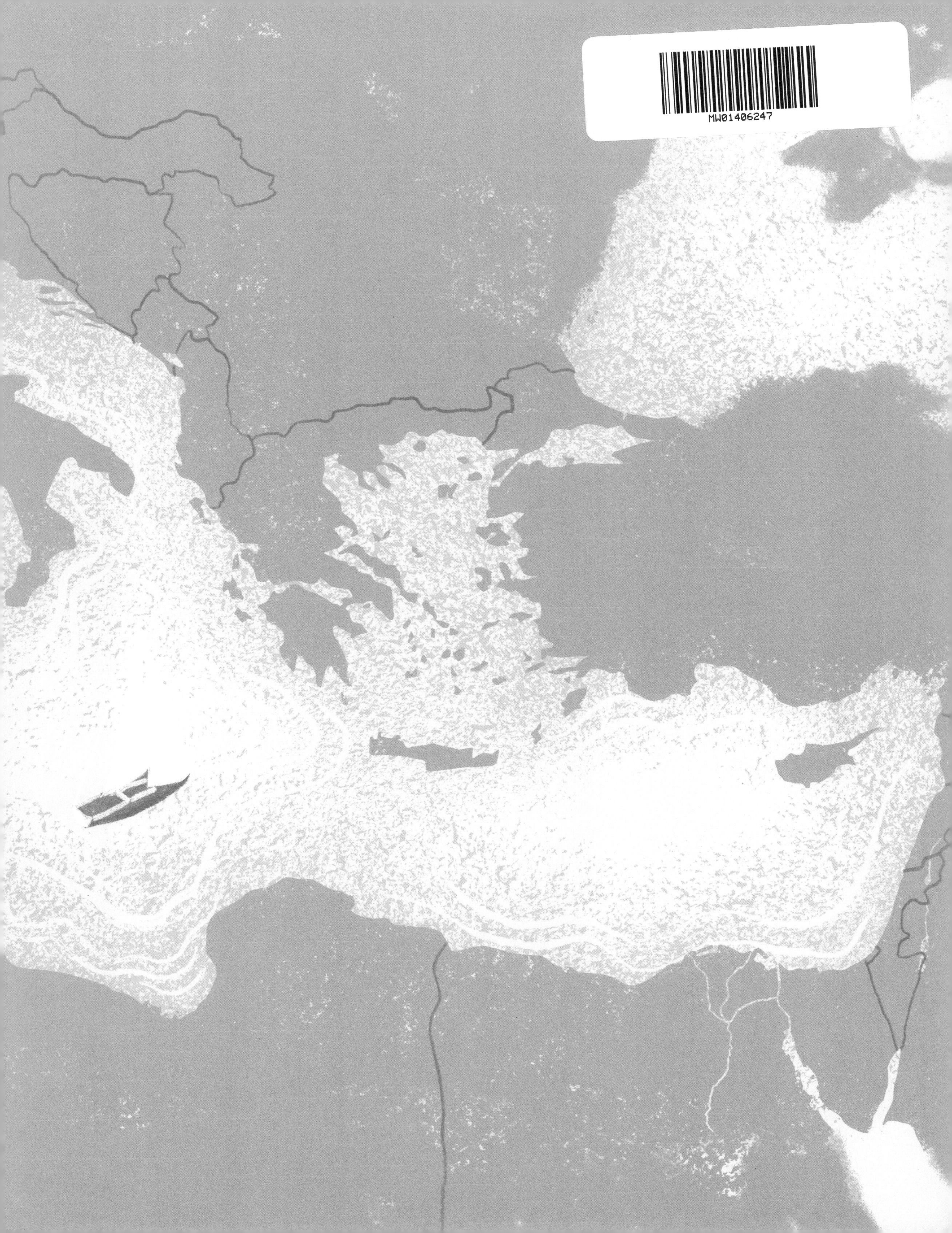

lonely planet

THE MEDITERRANEAN

Discover the stories and secrets
of the Mediterranean coast

CONTENTS

04
INTRODUCTION

248
INDEX

06
Spain
~~

The Strait of Gibraltar is a gateway to the Mediterranean Sea and this trip along 3300km (2000 miles) of Spain's shores. Pass Moorish forts, fertile wetlands, and Modernista architecture. The Balearics await, with their distinct island cultures.

42
France
~~

Discover the biodiversity of the wild Camargue; the wines of the Languedoc; how migration has shaped Marseilles; and the light that draws generations of artists here. Beyond, Monaco and Corsica are each defined by isolation.

120
The Adriatic
~~

Crossing from Trieste into the nations that line the Adriatic Sea, links to Italy linger – dialects, truffle-laden dishes, and relics of the Roman Empire. Limpid waters lap pine-shrouded beaches on the islands of Istria and Dalmatia.

150
Greece
~~

The mainland and islands of Greece are sprawling in the complexity of their topography and history. Traces of ancient civilisations are vividly apparent, from Corfu in the west and Rhodes, the largest of the Dodecanese, near Türkiye.

CONTENTS

251
CREDITS

80
Italy

Sardinia & Sicily. Cinque Terre & the Amalfi Coast. Pompei & Venice. Much of Italy's Mediterranean is over-exposed. But surprises exist. Taste *panissa* along the Ligurian Riviera; explore street art in Naples; join locals on a *passeggiata* in Bari.

184
Türkiye

We depart from where the Dardanelles Strait feeds into the Sea of Marmara – this is in the Aegean, with the Mediterranean region starting from Ölüdeniz. Meander rustic hinterlands on foot, or explore aboard a traditional *gulet*.

212
Cyprus

An island of compelling culture and landscapes steeped in myth and riddled with ancient riches, Cyrpus is also refuge of marine wonders.

218
Egypt and Malta

From the engineering feat of the Suez Canal and Egypt's second city, Alexandria, to the flavours of the Maltese Archipelago.

230
The Maghreb

Onwards into North Africa's Maghreb – in Arabic, 'the place of the setting sun'. Highlights include the Tunisian village of Sidi Bou Saïd; sipping mint tea in Algiers' Casbah; and the art scene of Tangier, Morocco. The Strait of Gibraltar concludes this adventure.

THE MEDITERRANEAN

INTRODUCTION

Picture the Mediterranean and a sea that encompasses far more than its inviting waters reveal. This book carries you on a journey along its shores, taking in their bewildering diversity.

FRANCE

SPAIN

Balearic Islands

MOROCCO

ALGERIA

The ancient Romans knew the Mediterranean as both the Mare Nostrum ('Our Sea') and the Mare Internum ('Internal Sea'). The 2,500,000 sq km (970,000 sq mile) surface area of this totemic body of water is, indeed, mostly surrounded by land, linking Southern Europe, Western Asia and Northern Africa. It only flows outwards to the far west, into the Atlantic via the narrow Strait of Gibraltar, and to the far northeast, into the Black Sea via the Sea of Marmara and the Bosporus.

The Mediterranean is skirted by at least 20 nations, a list that grows if you consider overseas territories of other nations and those disputed. There are over 10,000 islands and islets, along with 15 sub-seas bearing names as evocative as the Adriatic, Aegean, Ionian and Levantine.

For millennia the Mediterranean has been a meeting point of cultures and empires, Egyptian, Greek, Roman, Carthaginian, Umayyad, Byzantine and Ottoman among them. Traces of their legacies still shape the region.

A note on the areas covered in this book: when we began this project, our idea was to follow the coastline of the Mediterranean and transport you on a vicarious journey through this complex, often magical region. Each section would zoom in on the history, culture, food, art, and significant sites at certain stops along the way. As of this writing, political upheaval in certain areas has caused increased travel advisories, devastating and significant loss, and continued and unpredictable impacts to the landscape and communities there. We hope to publish a comprehensive book in the future, one that shows the diverse and unparalleled beauty of the people and places in every region that touches the Mediterranean Sea.

For generations past and generations to come, this is a region of passion, story, and beauty. The Mediterranean's exquisite views and atmosphere have and will continue to deliver inspiration. 'When I realised every morning that I would see this light again,' wrote painter Henri Matisse after moving to the French Riviera in 1917, 'I couldn't believe how lucky I was.'

Ebro

VALENCIA
PARC NATURAL DE L'ALBUFERA
Valencia

ALICANTE

Murcia

Andalucía
PARQUE NATURAL SIERRA DE GRAZALEMA
GRANADA
PARQUE NATURAL DEL CABO DE GATA-NÍJAR
RONDA
MÁLAGA
ALMERÍA
MARBELLA
GIBRALTAR
ALBORAN SEA
TARIFA

Strait of Gibraltar

CADAQUÉS

Catalonia

• BARCELONA
• SITGES
• TARRAGONA

PARC NATURAL DEL DELTA DE L'EBRE

BALEARIC SEA

SERRA DE TRAMUNTANA

Menorca

Mallorca
• PALMA

Balearic Islands

Ibiza
• IBIZA TOWN

CHAPTER ONE

SPAIN

ANDALUCÍA'S PUEBLOS BLANCOS ∼ **BARBECUED SEAFOOD IN MÁLAGA**
MOORISH ALMERÍA ∼ **CYCLING CABO DE GATA** ∼ **CARTHAGINIAN CARTAGENA**
ALICANTE'S FIERY FESTIVAL ∼ **VALENCIA'S MODERN ARCHITECTURE**
MIRÓ'S MALLORCA ∼ **SITGES PRIDE** ∼ **VERMOUTH IN BARCELONA**

THE MEDITERRANEAN

→ The Mallorcan town of Deià lies in the Serra de Tramuntana, a UNESCO World Heritage Site.

Spain's dazzling Mediterranean coast meanders from the jaws of Europe, on the wind-lashed Strait of Gibraltar, all the way to the Catalan town of Portbou near the southern-France border. Flung offshore is the beach-circled paradise of the four Balearic Islands. In total, around 3350km (2081 miles) of coastal drama awaits discovery. Much of the way, craggy mountain ranges cascade down towards the Med's shimmer, bringing forests scented by pines, rosemary and lavender. Hiking trails dip between secluded coves, sweeping promontories and flamingo-roamed wetlands, and echoes of the country's past emerge in Roman theatres, Phoenician ruins, medieval villages, Moorish fortresses and other treasures.

With each hop across into a new region, a distinctive coastal gastronomy steps into the spotlight, with *arroces* (rice dishes), the freshest local seafood and from-on-the-doorstep wines starring on most menus. The A7 highway parallels much of this fabled shore, from Algeciras to north of Barcelona. Weaving along it, on one side there is often nothing but glinting, bewitching cobalt.

SPAIN

THE MEDITERRANEAN

→ Kites flying at Tarifa, one of Europe's best kitesurfing destinations. Two prevailing winds meet here, known as the Levante and Poniente.

↘ The Golden Mile in Marbella, actually 5km of soft sands, a promenade, five-star hotels and Michelin-starred restaurants.

TARIFA, MÁLAGA AND THE COSTA DEL SOL

In Tarifa, on mainland Spain's southernmost point, a salt-white curve of sand looks out on Morocco across the Strait of Gibraltar. Locally known as Playa Chica (Little Beach), this is the westernmost strand of Spain's Mediterranean coast. Beyond unfolds the Atlantic Ocean and the sugar-white Costa de la Luz. A magnet for windsurfers and kitesurfers since the 1980s, Tarifa has a bohemian energy. Its old centre is a swirl of whitewashed homes, cobbled alleys, and overflowing restaurants serving the prized *almadraba* tuna.

Northeast from Tarifa, Cádiz province's Mediterranean shoreline curves 45km (28 miles) to the Rock of Gibraltar. Awash with pastel-coloured streets that evoke its diverse heritage, the British Overseas Territory is one of the two Pillars of Hercules – the other is northern Morocco's Jebel Musa, just 27km (17 miles) away across the sea.

The most famous stretch of Andalucía's littoral begins in Málaga province, where laid-back Estepona (with its revitalised Old Town) marks the western end of the Costa del Sol. It was here, from the 1950s, that Spain's tourism scene kicked off, transforming fishing towns like Fuengirola and Marbella into an epicentre of European beach tourism. There's still a taste of this maritime heritage in the region's mid-July Virgen del Carmen festivities. At the heart of it all, Marbella is a world of sparkling marinas with a charming historic core.

Málaga, 55km (34 miles) further on, is a soulful provincial capital known as the hometown of Pablo Picasso. **CONTINUED ON P16 »**

local angle
Málaga's Art Scene

'Málaga's public institutions, with the support of an extensive network of museums with extraordinary collections and temporary exhibitions, have put art at the centre of a rich, varied cultural offering. This unstoppable process has placed us in a top spot on Spain's museum scene, and we are constantly working to show how Málaga is much more than the city of the great Pablo Picasso.

'Starting with Romantic travellers who, in the early 19th century, discovered in Andalucía fascinating themes for their painting, and who in several cases passed through Málaga, the city has captivated many artists. Many of these are present in our collection at the Museo Carmen Thyssen Málaga. Joaquín Sorolla painted on our beaches, as Francisco Iturrino did at the Jardín Botánico Histórico La Concepción (pictured). Also since the 19th century, Málaga has had a local school of painters, specialised mostly in landscapes and marinas, with standout names awarded in national exhibitions and now especially represented in the collections of local museums. In more recent times, a generation of *malagueño* artists put the city at the vanguard of the national scene between the 1960s and 1980s, such as the Palmo Collective, among many others. Still today Málaga is a hub of artistic creation.

'I can't help but begin by recommending the Museo Carmen Thyssen Málaga, to enjoy its collections of 19th- and early 20th-century Spanish art and its many changing exhibitions. But the Casa Natal de Picasso, the Centre Pompidou, the Museo Picasso Málaga and the Museo de Málaga (in the splendid old Aduana building) are also essential for any art lover.'
Lourdes Moreno, Artistic Director at the Museo Carmen Thyssen Málaga

THE MEDITERRANEAN

THE WHITE VILLAGES

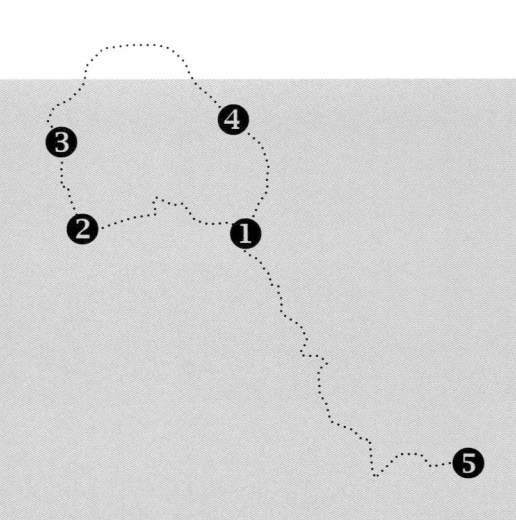

Explore rural Andalucía on a drive via centuries-old *pueblos blancos*

Distance 235km (146 miles)
Duration Three nights
Start Marbella
Finish Marbella

❶ Ronda
Heading northeast of Marbella, the A397 snakes into the Serranía de Ronda, opening up mountain views that become more entrancing with every turn. Continue to Ronda, Andalucía's most famous *pueblo blanco*. It's impossible to overstate the drama of the city's setting, on a gorge high above the Guadalevín River. The Moorish-origin Old Town is linked to modern Ronda by the 18th-century Puente Nuevo, while vineyards and olive groves roll across the countryside. Peaceful hotels here include Molino del Santo, a delightfully restored riverside mill. ***62km (39 miles)***

❷ Grazalema
West of Ronda rises the wild, mountainous beauty of the 534-sq-km (206-sq-mile) Parque Natural Sierra de Grazalema. Among Andalucía's loveliest hiking destinations, it has trails that pass through near-silent forests of rare *pinsapos* (Spanish firs) or up the tallest peak in Cádiz province, El Torreón (1654m). Overlooking the hills, Grazalema village has whitewashed houses, ancient churches, and some fine tapas bars for devouring local Payoyo cheese and crisp sherry. Pause overnight at rustic guesthouse La Mejorana. ***34km (21 miles)***

❸ Zahara de la Sierra
This gleaming-white village sits just north of Grazalema, reached via a drive via the hairpin bends of the narrow CA9104. Shady patios burst with geraniums along Zahara's steeply sloping streets, and a medieval castle high above evokes its history as a key frontier waypoint between Catholic and Islamic Spain. Below the village, a turquoise reservoir is a playground for kayakers, paddleboarders and swimmers. Stay at Al Lago, with a superb restaurant. ***17km (10 miles)***

❹ Setenil de las Bodegas
The A384 skirts around the white town of Olvera as you travel east from Zahara, before taking the CA9120 south to Setenil de las Bodegas. Setenil was built into natural caverns in the rock face above the Trejo River, and is known for its cave houses, which now host buzzing tapas bars and private homes. ***87km (54 miles)***

❺ Marbella
Head 20km (12 miles) south to return to Ronda, then further back down to Marbella's golden shores. ***35km (22 miles)***

↖ Ronda's 98m-high Puente Nuevo (New Bridge) spans the Guadalevín River.

↙ The Zahara-El Gastor reservoir in the Parque Natural Sierra de Grazalema.

MÁLAGA GUIDE

The revitalised city that gave us Picasso

taste
BARBECUED *ESPETOS*

Málaga is defined by its silvery urban beaches, where the air is thick with the scent of sizzling seafood and tangy *espetos* – skewers of sardines – barbecued at fuss-free *chiringuitos* (beach restaurants). This classic *malagueño* bite is said to have emerged from the fishing district of El Palo, east of the Old Town, and lingering over a seafood lunch here is a beloved local pastime.

culture
THE MOORISH ALCAZABA

On the slopes of Gibralfaro hill, Málaga's landmark Alcazaba was built as an imposing fortress under Moorish rule. It dates from around 755 CE and was partly transformed into a palace by the Nasrid Arab dynasty in the 11th century CE. The calming courtyards, especially the Patio de la Alberca, echo Granada's Alhambra with their decorative pools, horseshoe arches and marble columns. In many ways the Alcazaba also recalls the mesmerising, intricately arched Mezquita in Córdoba, a Moorish-era jewel just an hour's train inland from Málaga.

SPAIN

explore
SOHO

Nowhere encapsulates Málaga's creative soul quite like Soho, a revitalised port-side district now bursting with bold street art. It's also home to a crop of boutique-style hotels, cool coffee spots, the city's contemporary art centre, and even a theatre run by Málaga-born actor Antonio Banderas.

buy
LOCAL OLIVE OILS

Andalucía famously produces some of the world's finest olive oil. Córdoba and Jaén might be the most renowned provinces for this liquid gold, but Málaga has exquisite oils of its own made from local olive varieties like *verdial* and *arbequina*. Just off the leafy Alameda boulevard, the 1870s-founded Mercado Central de Atarazanas (below) is a perfect spot for picking up top-tier olive oils (and other local goodies); bottles with 'Sabor a Málaga' stamps are produced locally.

"Lingering over a seafood lunch prepared at fuss-free chiringuitos (beach restaurants) is a beloved local pastime"

nightlife
ROOFTOP SUNDOWNERS

As the sun begins to fade, plan to join gaggles of stylish *malagueños* for a chilled *tinto de verano* (red wine with soda) at one of the city's many hotel-rooftop bars, such as La Terraza de Valeria or AC Hotel Málaga Palacio. Enjoy soaking up the glow of golden hour cast across the cathedral, Gibralfaro castle and the harbourfront promenade. As you bask in the spectacle – most vivid in late summer – it's easy to see how this dynamic city lures fans from all over the world.

THE MEDITERRANEAN

EASTERN COSTA DEL SOL AND GRANADA'S COSTA TROPICAL
In 1959, a group of friends stumbled across an extraordinary subterranean cavern with rock formations dating back five million years, just 60km (37 miles) east of Málaga. Today the Cueva de Nerja (Nerja Cave) is the premier attraction of the Costa del Sol's easternmost stretch, which revolves around the relaxed beach town of Nerja, framed by the Muscatel-growing hills of the Axarquía region.

The area's best beaches, however, lie well beyond Nerja, in places like Cantarriján, a back-to-nature beauty. Hidden within the protected Paraje Natural Acantilados de Maro-Cerro Gordo, Cantarriján is the beginning of Granada province's Costa Tropical. Silver-sand coves huddle beneath craggy cliffs, hot-pink bougainvillea spills over whitewashed walls, and the reliably warm year-round climate makes for superb diving, kayaking, paddleboarding and windsurfing. The low-key towns of Almuñécar and Salobreña are topped by crumbling castles dating back to Moorish times, and feel less developed than the busy Costa del Sol. Beachgoers here tend to be mostly locals or people popping down from Granada. Detour just inland to the mountain haven of the Sierra Nevada, home to mainland Spain's tallest peak, 3479m-high Mulhacén.

Set in Granada, the Moorish marvel of the Alhambra is less than an hour's drive north from the Costa Tropical. This palace-fortress gazing out over the city reveals a wonderland of intricate geometric design, terraced gardens, fountain-bathed courtyards and trickling water channels. With a great array of carved wooden ceilings and mesmerising tilework, the Alhambra's 14th-century Palacios Nazaríes mark a high point of Islamic architecture in Europe. **CONTINUED ON P18 »**

↓ The craggy coastline and azure waters around Nerja. The Moors named the town Narixa (translation: 'abundant spring').

local angle

Granada's Coastal Gastronomy

'Granada's coast has its own special regional cuisine, heavily influenced by the fresh ingredients grown locally and the fish and seafood sourced off its shores. The tropical fruit produced in this warm region is notable, such as mangoes and cherimoyas (custard apples).

'One of the classic local dishes I love is the delicious local shrimp, called *quisquillas de Motril,* which is smaller and sweeter than other shrimp found in Spain. *Pulpo seco* (dried octopus) is another typical dish from this coastline. It is a recipe that requires some time to accomplish, as the drying takes around two days. Bar El Paso in Motril has perfected this dish over four decades. The colourful *ensalada tropical* contains locally grown mango and avocado, as well as other seasonal fruit, all heaped atop fresh green lettuce. A traditional sweet bake is the *torta real,* also from Motril, a delicate sponge made with almonds and light meringue; find the best at Pastelería Videras or Casa Palomares. The local rum, Montero, is also worth sampling.

'My favourite places to dine along the Costa Tropical include Motril's Restaurante Katena for exquisite fish dishes; Sunahra Beach Club for a chilled-out vibe by the sea in Motril; and Almuñécar's Restaurante Lute y Jesús, which specialises in fried fish.'

Molly Sears-Piccavey, Granada blogger and food-tour guide at Spain Food Sherpas

THE MEDITERRANEAN

→ Almería's Alcazaba has featured in TV series and movies, including *Game of Thrones*, *Wonder Woman 1984* and *Indiana Jones and the Last Crusade*.

↘ The Playa de los Muertos (Beach of the Dead) in Cabo de Gata, named after the corpses of mariners shipwrecked off the rocky coast here.

THE ALMERÍA COAST

Wedged into the Spanish mainland's southeast corner, the coast of Almería province is a quieter stretch of Andalusian bliss. In Almería city, the 10th-century Alcazaba fortress recalls a time when this port was a major Moorish stronghold. A wander around its tangled *casco antiguo* (Old Town) takes in lively plazas dotted with palms and olive trees, and ancient chapels built where mosques once stood. Also here are some of Andalucía's finest tapas bars, where ultra-fresh prawns and slices of *tortilla* are paired with Almería-made wines. Around 40km (25 miles) inland lie the plains of the Desierto de Tabernas, where spaghetti westerns have been filmed since the 1960s.

The shining star of this *costa*, however, is Cabo de Gata – a wild, raw, cove-fringed cape swooping southeast from Almería, home to some of the most naturally spectacular beaches in Spain. Protected as the vast Parque Natural Cabo de Gata-Níjar, the area is a vision of secluded golden-white strands (many of them clothing-optional) resting beneath volcanic cliffs, including Playa de Mónsul, Playa de los Genoveses and Playa de San Pedro. Often its loveliest beaches involve a hike to reach, and some of the best views are from offshore aboard a kayak or paddleboard. High above the shoreline, hazy semi-desert landscapes sprawl between white-walled villages, including the main local hub, San José (population: 920).

25km (15 miles) north, Mojácar, a pretty town of cascading white buildings, dates back to Phoenician times. **CONTINUED ON P20 »**

SPAIN

know-how
Active Cabo de Gata

↑ Mountain biking trails circle and cross the Parque Natural Cabo de Gata-Níjar, taking in the driest area in mainland Europe.

Hiking between beaches, enjoying seafood by the sea and swimming in the Mediterranean are key draws for anyone seeking to laze away a few days in Cabo de Gata, but this pocket of coastal wonder is also a rewarding destination for active souls.

There is a whole other side to Cabo de Gata's pristine natural beauty beneath the surface, making the protected waters here among Spain's best spots to dive into the deep. Barracudas, groupers, rays and other underwater creatures flit between gardens of *Posidonia oceanica* (aka Neptune grass), an oxygen-producing sea grass that is the secret behind the intense clarity of the sea here. Local dive schools run an array of courses and excursions, mostly from spring to autumn, including to see ancient wrecks resting on the seabed.

Heading out on two wheels is a richly rewarding way to soak up the eerie sand-dusted expanses, otherworldly rock formations, remote farmsteads and far-flung beaches. It's possible, for example, to cycle all the way from San José to the Faro de Cabo de Gata, an isolated lighthouse on the promontory's southwestern tip; coastal views dazzle along the entire route, particularly those from the 18th-century Vela Blanca watchtower.

Simply casting an eye upwards reveals an immense diversity of birdlife, with both migratory and resident species congregating across the *parque natural*. A series of glittering salt lagoons near San Miguel village pulls in hundreds of pink-tinged flamingos during warmer months, along with egrets and storks. Eagle owls, Bonelli's eagles and European bee-eaters also cruise the blue skies.

THE MEDITERRANEAN

MURCIA'S COAST

Bathed in 3000 hours of Mediterranean sunshine a year, the Costa Cálida (Warm Coast) is aptly named. It marks the beginning of both the understated Murcia region and Spain's eastern shoreline. Roaming around here, distant splashes of pale pink turn out to be flocks of flamingos wading through salt flats, and rainbows of kitesurfers' sails soar across the sea. Sweeps of golden sand wend between headlands, some of them only accessible on foot, such as the wild coves of the Parque Regional Calblanque.

Halfway along Murcia's coast, ancient Cartagena commands attention with its setting on an azure harbour, its historical relics (especially Roman ruins), and its streets filled with Modernista mansions covered in tilework and wrought-iron balconies.

Approximately 35km (22 miles) east of Cartagena, Murcia's 'second' sea looms into view in the Mar Menor, a 140-sq-km (54-sq-mile) saltwater lagoon separated from the Med by a narrow isthmus. Kitesurfers, windsurfers, kayakers and paddleboarders are lured by its warm waters, and divers and snorkellers discover the Reserva Marina Cabo de Palos-Islas Hormigas, just offshore from heavily developed La Manga. In many ways, the Mar Menor's recent story encapsulates Spain's ecological challenges as a coastal-tourism destination: among efforts to protect the lagoon from environmental damage, it has been granted 'legal personhood'.

The regional capital, Murcia, sits 50km (31 miles) inland from Cartagena, surrounded by the *huerta*, a fertile agricultural area with an irrigation system that has existed since Islamic times. It is no surprise that fresh, on-the-doorstep produce fuels a thriving food scene all over the Murcia region. **CONTINUED ON P22 »**

↓ Greater flamingos are the largest of flamingo species, standing at up to 150cm tall, and breed in the wetlands around Murcia.

SPAIN

know-how

Cartagena's Ancient Roots

↑ Cartagena, known by the Romans as Cartago Nova, gained its theatre in 1 BCE. The site was rediscovered under later constructions in 1988.

Millennia of intriguing history hang in the air in Cartagena, a still-prosperous port framed by forested coastal hills, founded in 229 BCE by the Carthaginian general Hasdrubal. It grew into a key outpost for the Roman Empire, and then a flourishing independent emirate during the Moorish era, before falling under Catholic control in the mid 13th century. More recently, it served as the main Republican naval base during the Spanish Civil War, when it suffered intense bombing. A stroll through the city's pedestrianised and now-restored historic centre peels back the centuries.

The Romans conquered Cartagena just 20 years after its foundation, in 209 BCE, and nowhere is the empire's might more evident than in the magnificent 7000-seat Teatro Romano at the heart of the city. Roman Cartagena's mining and fishing wealth is on full display at the 1st-century-CE Casa de la Fortuna, a villa rich with well-preserved murals and mosaics.

Meanwhile a Punic defensive wall on the fringes of Cartagena's Old Town shines as one of few Carthaginian relics still standing across the Iberian Peninsula.

THE MEDITERRANEAN

VALENCIA'S COSTA BLANCA

Just a quick glance at the cerulean sea washing on to silver-shingle coves explains how the southernmost stretch of the Valencia region, the arrow-shaped Costa Blanca, rivals the Costa del Sol as the country's favourite beach destination.

In the capital Alicante, alleys meander uphill through a Moorish-origin Old Town where houses are dressed in bold pastels and oleanders scent the air. High above, the Castell de Santa Bàrbara – a 9th-century Moorish creation rebuilt in the 16th century – keeps watch. The city's tapas bars dish out seafood delicacies like cod fritters and grilled red prawns. Or try one of Alicante's countless *arrossos*, rice dishes mostly made with a smokey *salmorreta* paste of peppers, garlic, olive oil and tomato.

Today's Benidorm, 45km (28 miles) from Alicante, might be undeniably built-up, but this was the first place in Spain to allow bikinis on the beach back in the 1950s, at the height of the repressive Franco dictatorship. There's plenty of charm to laid-back Altea, a short drive further north, with hike-in pebble beaches and a hilly, whitewashed historic core crowned by a tile-domed church.

The shoreline continues past tempting beach towns – like pine-ringed Moraira, or Calp, home to the 332m-tall limestone outcrop of the Penyal d'Ifac – to Cap de la Nau, a wildly beautiful cave-pocked promontory. Bordering the cape to the north, Xàbia, like many towns along these shores, has two personalities: a bougainvillea-filled Old Town and a buzzy beach district a few kilometres away. Around 10km (6 miles) north, castle-topped Dènia is surrounded by powdery beaches and cliff-framed coves, and doubles as one of the major ports for reaching the Balearics. **CONTINUED ON P26 »**

↑ Patio plants line the steep alleys of the Barri de Santa Creu, Alicante; the neighbourhood forms part of the city's Casco Antiguo (Old Town).

Ninots (the Valencian word for puppets or dolls) enter the *cremà* (burning) closing act to the Falles de Cullera festival, Valencia.

know-how
Festival Fever

The theatrical Falles de Valencia in spring may rank among Spain's most famous and beloved festivals, but southern Valencia has its own inspired line-up of local festivities, many of them laying claim to centuries of historical context.

Alicante's premier festival, the Fogueres de Sant Joan, visually recalls Valencia's Falles, and follows an ancient tradition of burning useless objects around the summer solstice each June. Hundreds of elaborate effigies (mostly with a satirical slant) are paraded around the city over several days, before being set alight – in what is known as the *cremà* – at midnight on 24 June, the Nit de Sant Joan.

The colourful Barri de Santa Creu (Alicante's historic core) steps into the spotlight every year during Semana Santa (Holy Week). Those in town at this time can expect to witness elaborate trains of *pasos* (floats) in evocative incense-clouded procession, carried by *costaleros* around the neighbourhood's immensely steep streets. The focal point of activity is the small 18th-century Santa Creu chapel, built atop the city's medieval wall.

In the palm-studded city of Elche, 20km (12 miles) inland from Alicante, a baroque basilica is the unlikely setting for a UNESCO-listed medieval play, *Misteri d'Elx*, still performed annually in mid-August. The two-act chanted drama, with its roots traced back to the late 15th century, sees viewers queue up for hours to bag a spot and is split across two days. It honours the death, Assumption and crowning of the Virgin Mary. Ticketed open rehearsals also allow a glimpse of the performance in the run-up to the main event.

THE MEDITERRANEAN

VALENCIA GUIDE

A city of Modernista wonders and more

culture
LOCAL CERAMICS

buy
MERCAT CENTRAL PRODUCE

It's tricky to know which counter to first make a beeline for at Valencia's fabulous Modernista-style Mercat Central. Pick from giant tubs of olives, cheeses from all over Spain and, in season, plump tomatoes fresh from La Huerta, then enjoy it all as a picnic in the Turia gardens.

Like many other parts of Spain, Valencia has a strong ceramics heritage with its roots dating back to the Moorish era, and today remains a major producer of beautifully handcrafted, geometric-shaped *azulejos* (tiles). Local tilework adorns many of the city's Modernista masterpieces, often visible on balconies and facades from street level. Some local ceramicists, meanwhile, are busy creating chicly contemporary pieces. The Museu Nacional de Ceràmica, housed in a magnificent baroque mansion, celebrates this ancient craft.

explore
RUSSAFA

Whether for a crisp afternoon vermouth, a Valencia-flavoured brunch at an arty third-wave cafe, a browse around the vintage shops or even a stay in a design-led boutique hotel, Russafa (just south of the Ciutat Vella) has become Valencia's most stylish district. The neighbourhood's brutalist market, with its multicoloured decorative panels all over the outside, has been going since 1962 and still has a lively local energy.

> *"In Barri del Carme, plazas spring to life in the early evening"*

nightlife
BARRI DEL CARME

The Ciutat Vella (Old City), especially its northwest quarter known as the Barri del Carme, is sprinkled with pretty plazas that spring to life in the early evening, when terrace tables come out and people gather for catch-ups at lively bars. The chief focal point for meeting up is the Plaza del Tossal, from where you can fan out to explore the always-buzzing Plaza del Mercado, the Plaza del Doctor Collado, set behind the Silk Exchange, and the Plaza de la Virgen, by the cathedral.

taste
VALENCIAN PAELLA

If there's one dish Valencia is known for, it's undoubtedly paella, which is generally believed to have been born in the Albufera wetlands south of the city, possibly as far back as the 15th century. Rice has been grown here since Islamic times, but Valencian-style paella is just one of the many rice dishes cooked up locally. For an authentically delicious rice, head out to El Palmar in the Albufera to dine while overlooking the canals at cherished restaurants like L'Establiment or Bon Aire.

THE MEDITERRANEAN

→ The Via Verda de la Mar passes between pine and carob trees to connect the seaside resort towns of Oropesa and Benicàssim.

↘ The Edificio del Banco de Valencia, developed in 1935 in the Valencian neo-baroque style by architect Francisco Almenar Quinzáin.

VALENCIA TO THE CATALONIA BORDER

In the protected Parc Natural de l'Albufera, 15km (9 miles) south of Valencia city, flat-bottomed boats roam through narrow canals, fields yield an array of prized rice varieties, and sunsets blaze over Spain's largest freshwater lake and a string of sensitively regenerated wild beaches. Local restaurants serve fragrant rice dishes – perhaps laced with rabbit and chicken, as is the Valencian way.

Reaching Valencia, a feast of mostly traffic-free streets, lavishly adorned Modernista buildings and a Gothic cathedral await in the romantic Ciutat Vella. The city might be a sunny coastal hub, but its main urban strands rest 5km (3 miles) east of the centre, bordering the fishing quarter of El Cabanyal. Cycle along the converted Turia riverbed – now a maze of palm-shaded gardens – to eventually reach the sea.

Past coves and the ruined castle at Sagunto, Castelló province unveils Valencia's northern shoreline, the Costa del Azahar. In less-touristed Castelló de la Plana, the El Grau coastal district has a restaurant-filled port and miles of dune-rimmed sands, backed by pine-clad mountains. Benicàssim, just north, traces its popularity as a seaside escape back to the late 19th century. A highlight of this region is biking or walking the Via Verda de la Mar, a former railway track transformed into a 5.7km (3.5-mile) coastal path between Benicàssim and Oropesa, taking in crumbling watchtowers and isolated coves en route.

Approaching the Catalonia border, the walled town of Peñíscola is on a promontory lapped by the sparkling Med. **CONTINUED ON P28 »**

local angle
Architecture and Design in Valencia

'Among the recent architecture of Valencia city, the Ciutat de les Arts i les Ciències complex built in the Jardí del Turia stands out, designed almost entirely by Santiago Calatrava. The Jardí del Turia is a grand, tree-filled longitudinal park stretching for kilometres, the great axis of Valencia city. It's magnificent to visit at any time, in any season, but especially at sunset.

'Other contemporary buildings I'd highlight are La Rambleta cultural centre, devoted to art and entertainment, and the Institut Valencià d'Art Modern (IVAM), the hub of modern Valencian art today. We have extraordinary remodels of earlier buildings, starting with the Mercat de Colom in the Eixample, restored as a shopping and leisure space. Or the transformation of the Teatre El Musical, in the maritime quarter, into a magnificent auditorium with impactful interiors. The recent restoration of the Fundación Hortensia Herrero, in a building on Calle del Mar, is an intervention of maximum respect and integration. And the art deco Bombas Gens building, which dates from the 1930s, has been reinvented as a multipurpose complex.

'In the historic centre, on a journey to the medieval and Renaissance eras, I'd highlight the Torres de Serranos and Torres de Quart, as well as Calle Caballeros.'

Jaime Sanahuja, architect, professor at the Universitat Politècnica de València and business developer at Arqueha

→ A 125m curved pylon supporting the cable stays of the Assut de l'Or Bridge (2008) rises above the Jardí del Turia, Valencia.

THE BALEARIC ISLANDS

A palm-roofed *chiringuito* curled into a tiny pebble cove. A honey-stone village beyond a sea of almond trees in pink-white bloom. Saltpans bathed in a peachy early-morning glow. Welcome to the Balearic Islands, often lauded as the most magical place anywhere on the Spanish coastline.

Mallorca, the largest of the Balearics, dazzles with its 550km (342-mile) coast, along which isolated pebble-strewn *calas* and long, velvety strands are set against windswept capes emerging from the depths.

The easternmost of the Balearics, Menorca, has an irresistibly go-slow pace. Many of its pristine beaches – white-gold on the south coast, rust-red to the north – can only be reached on foot, often via the ancient 185km (115-mile) Camí de Cavalls trail that traces the entire coast through pine forests and bird-rich wetlands. In the elegant capital Maó, colourfully painted mansions overlook a 5km-long (3-mile) natural harbour punctuated by ruined fortresses.

Closer to the mainland, beautiful Ibiza is now just as popular for wellness retreats, glorious Balearic cuisine and hikes to remote coves as for late-night clubbing. Savour a *bullit de peix* – a traditional fish-and-potato stew – followed by *arròs a banda* (rice cooked with leftover fish-stock), overlooking a deep-blue bay for a taste of Ibiza's soul.

Dangling off Ibiza's southeast tip, Formentera is a barefoot-vibe island with some of Europe's best beaches. The salt-white sands of Platja de Migjorn, the Trucador Peninsula and other jewels are washed by cyan waves, below which lie Spain's most important meadows of Neptune grass. Formentera has wonderful coastal hiking and biking, and off-track lighthouses where sunsets burn over the water. **CONTINUED ON P34 »**

↑ Watching the sun setting beyond the islet of Es Vedrà from the nature reserve of Cala d'Hort, on the western edge of Ibiza.

local angle
Creative Balearics

'The Balearic Islands are magic and special. They have a unique light, unique colours, a unique aroma. I think they are an inspiration for all artists because they are so natural and pure that they urge creativity.

'The crafts of the islands capture pieces of nature and history, and the day-to-day life of each artist. I'll highlight the *espardenyes* (espadrilles), allowing us to enjoy walking and living on our islands. Also the *capazos* (palm- or cane-crafted bags) – it feels sublime that today we can carry an open bag like this without fear, when in cities this isn't so possible. The jewellery is magnificent, inspired by our colours, our skies, our air. I'll also strongly highlight local painting and everything that is created with recycled materials, helping to maintain these islands.

'The Mediterranean is unique. The *Posidonia* (Neptune grass) here makes our waters crystal-clear, a home for so many different species. My work in particular pushes me to protect those. The Mediterranean brought my work colour, it brought me life, and transmits that happiness I feel every day for living here. This is what I try to convey in every piece. We take for granted that the sea as we know it will always be there, and every year we notice how it is slowly being affected. So the security we have that future generations will be able to enjoy this natural marvel depends on us and how we care for it.'
Sol Courreges, sustainable artist based in Formentera

THE MEDITERRANEAN

MALLORCA GUIDE

Wander the largest of the Balearics

base
PALMA

Mallorca's capital Palma makes an inspired base. Several centuries-old mansions in the lively Old Town have been reborn as boutique hotels and the local-based food scene is a treat, from bars serving vermouths and *variats* (platefuls of varied tapas) to innovative kitchens for Balearic-rooted tasting menus. Add in a masterful Gothic cathedral (above) and nearby coastal escapes.

explore
FUNDACIÓ MIRÓ

Mallorca has tempted creative minds for centuries, among them the Barcelona-born surrealist Joan Miró, whose enthralling foundation just outside Palma is a Balearics highlight. Miró worked here for almost three decades, until his death in 1983. Exhibitions are now split between the wave-like Taller Sert (above, Miró's 1950s studio designed by Josep Lluís Sert), Son Boter (an 18th-century country house) and the angular 1992 Moneo Building.

beach
CALÓ DES MÀRMOLS

Many of Mallorca's 220 beaches rank among Spain's finest. For something idyllic yet off the beaten path, small Caló des Màrmols – 10km (6 miles) south of Santanyí on Mallorca's southeast tip – is worth the journey. Surrounded by pale-aqua water, it's a sand-and-stone beauty without any facilities, reached by hiking from either Cala s'Almunia or Ses Salines lighthouse (allow at least an hour and bring snacks and water). Dune-backed Platja Es Caragol is another remote, hike-in joy.

activity
TRAMUNTANA HIKING

Rolling across northwest Mallorca, the UNESCO-designated Serra de Tramuntana bursts with limestone crags, pine-scented slopes and villages carved from golden stone. The best way to explore it is by hiking the 140km-long (87-mile) Ruta de Pedra en Sec (Dry Stone Route) – or tackling a shorter section as a day hike. This trail is named for the dry-stone walls that support agricultural terraces across the mountainous landscape. The route weaves between villages like Deià, Sóller and Valldemossa, all with characterful accommodation.

"Many of Mallorca's 220 beaches rank among Spain's finest"

secret
GRIFFON VULTURES

In 2008, an autumn storm blew dozens of griffon vultures off course as they migrated from mainland Spain to Africa. Somehow, they landed in Mallorca. Previously unknown to inhabit the Balearics, griffon vultures have since adapted to this new environment, and there are now around 20 breeding pairs spread over the island, including the Serra de Tramuntana.

THE MEDITERRANEAN

IBIZA GUIDE

An island with natural treasures to the fore

base
IBIZA TOWN

The capital Ibiza Town (or Eivissa) centres on UNESCO-protected Dalt Vila (above), a stylish, cobbled historic core wedged between Renaissance-era ramparts, on the site of what was once the island's main Phoenician settlement. It's an unbeatably evocative place to stay, whether in a boutique old-town guesthouse or a sunny midranger down by the glitzy harbour.

activity
KAYAK AND PADDLEBOARD

Among the most enriching, low-impact ways to get under the skin of this bijou island is to explore its coast by kayak or paddleboard, dipping into distant coves inaccessible by land and snorkelling above underwater gardens of *Posidonia* (Neptune grass). An evening kayak trip with long-established operator Ibiza Outdoors presents the chance to swim in the Balearic Sea as the sun begins to set. Take a three-hour loop out from Sant Miquel beach in the north, via a rocky promontory known as The Finger of God, to Benirras and back again.

secret
SALT FLATS

Ever since Phoenician times, around 650 BCE, Ibiza has been a major producer of salt. Today protected within the UNESCO-listed Parc Natural de Ses Salines, the ancient salt flats hidden away in the southeastern pocket of the island still yield natural salt – free from artificial chemicals – and can be glimpsed on a walk (or drive) inland from gorgeous Ses Salines beach. The nutrient-rich marshes here also serve as an important feeding ground for flamingos.

> *"Cliffs and pine groves encircle remote bays only reachable on foot, but the walk is always part of the appeal"*

explore
LOCAL WINES

Mallorca often steals the spotlight when it comes to Balearic wines, but several small-scale wineries in northwest Ibiza are producing terrific options from specialised local grapes like Garnatxa and Monastrell. Among these is Can Rich, a family-run vineyard that specialises in organic wines, which can be sampled on a small-group tour along with their own olive oils.

beach
NORTHERN COVES

Ibiza's most gorgeous cream-sand strands are dotted around the south and west coasts, but beach-lovers keen to escape the crowds head to the quieter, craggier northern shore. Here, cliffs and pine groves encircle remote bays, such as Cala d'en Serra (below), Es Portitxol and Port de Ses Caletes. Most are only reachable on foot, but the walk is part of the appeal, and in several of these coves you'll spot traditional wooden fishing shacks.

SOUTHERN CATALONIA AND BARCELONA

Each year, the glinting wetlands of the Ebro Delta produce around 120 million kg of rice – 20% of Spain's total. Here in Catalonia's southwest corner, the Parc Natural del Delta de l'Ebre protects golden dunes, untouched beaches beloved of kitesurfers and reed-fringed lagoons patrolled by thousands of flamingos. It is best explored along cycling trails, by sailing to the mouth of the mighty Ebro, or over lunch on a floating mussel farm.

The Costa Daurada, Catalonia's down-to-earth beach playground, extends northeast in a string of buzzing towns like Cambrils and Salou. In Tarragona (once Roman Tarraco), curious relics of the past lie strewn about, including a 14,000-seat amphitheatre overlooking the Mediterranean. Founded in 218 BCE, Tarragona was one of the Iberian Peninsula's major Roman cities, though today it's equally known for its tradition of *castells* (Catalonia's human towers), celebrated with a spectacular biennial competition.

Around 60km (37 miles) east from Tarragona, Sitges has grown into Spain's most-loved coastal hub for the LGBTIQ+ community. The town's palm-dotted seafront promenade is framed by a small historic core bursting with art galleries and Modernista mansions. Along the surrounding coast, dusty paths thread through pine groves and under railway tracks to coves that curve between headlands sprinkled with lavender, thyme and rosemary. Catalonia's crisp cava hails from the Penedès area just inland, easily discovered on a tour or bike trip from Sitges.

Heading northeast, the Garraf Mountains loom over the Med and velvety strands like Castelldefels give way to Catalonia's capital, Barcelona, whose honey-sand beaches were created for the 1992 Olympics. **CONTINUED ON P40 »**

↓ The compact old town of Sitges wraps around Sant Sebastià beach, a particular favourite among locals; it is one of 17 beaches here.

SPAIN

local angle
LGBTIQ+ Sitges

'What sets Sitges apart is its people – the *sitgetans*. Sure, we could dive into its history as a retreat for bohemian artists in the late 19th and early 20th centuries, which naturally attracted those who felt different. But why did they come? The people here are happy, welcoming and open-minded. This joyful spirit is what has made Sitges so popular. Generations of open-mindedness and a "Carnival-like" attitude towards life have shaped the town into the vibrant community it is today. The weather is fantastic, and many say the light here is unlike in any other place.

'Sitges Pride is one of Europe's most unique celebrations. Imagine five days of free open-air concerts in a stunning setting right by the Mediterranean Sea. The Sunday parade is the real showstopper, drawing crowds of all ages – from eight to 80-plus. It's an elegant affair, with local LGBTIQ+ bars and businesses competing to transform traditional Carnival floats into fabulous, over-the-top creations.

'Sitges may be a small town, but it's booming with more than 25 LGBTIQ+ bars and restaurants. No visit is complete without a drink at Parrots, located in the heart of "Judgement Square", where all the seats face outwards. For a quieter escape, slip into La Villa and enjoy a cocktail in the charming garden terrace. For late-night fun, catch a show at Comodin Bar, one of Europe's oldest gay bars. For a truly unforgettable night, grab a seat at Queenz for a dinner show. And, of course, Sitges' number one attraction: the beach! We've got 17 of them.'

Keith O'Reilly, Sitges-based editor of GayTravel4u and founding member of AFGAL, the organisation behind Sitges Pride

↑ Rainbow flags signal the opening of five days of celebration in Sitges Pride, while the Sunday parade sets off from the Passeig Maritim.

35

THE MEDITERRANEAN

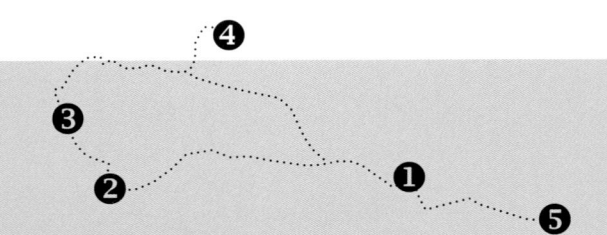

INTO PRIORAT

Top-tier wineries await on a road trip through mountain settlements

Distance 145km (90 miles)
Duration Three days
Start Tarragona
Finish Tarragona

❶ Reus
Around 40km (25 miles) west of Tarragona, Catalonia's DOQ Priorat ranks among Spain's most exclusive wine regions. First up is Reus, famously the birthplace of the great Antoni Gaudí (though some say he was born in nearby Riudoms). Around 80 Modernista buildings cluster here, including Lluís Domènech i Montaner's Casa Navàs with its floral-carved facade. Gaudí himself never worked here (he moved to Barcelona in 1868 to study architecture), but Reus is home to the exquisite Gaudí Centre museum, and also has a thriving vermouth scene. *15km (9 miles)*

❷ Falset
A quick spin further west, Falset, the region's main hub, rests just outside the Priorat border in the adjacent DO Montsant wine region. With bubbly bodegas, a small medieval Old Town and local olive farms to visit, it's a rewarding overnight stop. Lotus Priorat has stylishly rustic rooms in a converted 18th-century home with views across a lush gorge. *30km (19 miles)*

❸ Gratallops
Gratallops, north of Falset, is home to some of Priorat's most esteemed wineries. Prized for its robust and intense reds, Priorat primarily produces Garnatxa and Cariñena grapes, and is one of just two Spanish wine regions (along with Rioja) awarded the prestigious DOQ designation. Get a taste on an expert-guided tour, at pioneering Clos Mogador in Gratallops or organic-driven Bodegas Mas Alta nearby. A 15-minute drive from Gratallops leads to Gran Hotel Mas d'en Bruno, an 18th-century *masia* (farmhouse) turned luxe retreat, overlooking the vines and mountainscapes. *10km (6 miles)*

❹ Siurana
In northern Priorat, the village of Siurana teeters on a cliff face above an aquamarine reservoir. Stroll its streets to discover a rare Romanesque church built in the 12th and 13th centuries. The underrated Parc Natural de la Serra de Montsant a short distance west makes for a worthy detour; with abrupt geography and sheer rock faces, it is a hiking, biking and via-ferrata wonderland. *35km (22 miles)*

❺ Tarragona
From Siurana, an easy hour's drive zips back to Tarragona. *55km (34 miles)*

SPAIN

↖ Social housing in the Barrio Gaudí, Reus, designed in the 1960s by Ricardo Bofill.

↙ The Romanesque church of Santa Maria de Siurana, overlooking the Serra de Montsant.

THE MEDITERRANEAN

BARCELONA GUIDE

A city of architecural masterpieces

explore
L'EIXAMPLE

taste
VERMOUTH

Vermouth first arrived in Barcelona from Italy around the turn of the 20th century, but in the last decade this fortified, botanical-infused drink has had a resurgence. It's enjoyed as a pre-lunch tipple, served over ice with an olive and a slice of orange and, ideally, accompanied by simple tapas like anchovies. To *fer el vermut* (literally, 'do a vermouth'), you can't beat the Gràcia district.

The creations of Antoni Gaudí and his Modernista contemporaries lurk all over the broad boulevards of L'Eixample, from wonders like tile-covered Casa Batlló (above) to less-obvious structures such as Josep Puig i Cadafalch's Casa Serra. An elegant, grid-like neighbourhood, L'Eixample emerged in the late 19th century, soon after Barcelona's medieval walls were demolished. Now this is home to a blossoming accommodation scene taking in swish five-star havens, artsy boutique hotels and sociable hostels.

culture
EL RAVAL

Step into one of Europe's most thrilling street-art hubs on a roam through the shadowy El Raval district, where the scene has been flourishing since the 1980s and some artists even offer tours. Bright faces painted on garage doors, heart-warming messages scrawled across wall-mounted drinks cans and a mural by Keith Haring count among the highlights.

> *"Barcelona has a long, rich literary heritage and over the years has inspired a host of international writers"*

nightlife
COCKTAIL BARS

In recent years, Barcelona has grown into a global hotspot for creative mixology and is now home to a crop of prize-winning cocktail bars celebrated for pushing boundaries. Locals and visitors alike are more than happy to queue up for the chance to sample cutting-edge liquid mixes topped with coffee 'clouds' (at Paradiso) or crafted from seaweed-infused pisco (at Dr Stravinsky), both in El Born, and negronis served over ice that never melts at L'Eixample's Sips.

buy
BOOKS

Barcelona has a long, rich literary heritage, which is intimately intertwined with renowned Catalan-language authors such as Josep Pla, Mercè Rodoreda, Pere Calders and Caterina Albert (who used the pseudonym Víctor Català). Over the years the city has also inspired a host of international writers – Ernest Hemingway, George Orwell, Gabriel García Márquez – and every 23 April people gift each other books for the Festa de Sant Jordi. Excellent bookshops can be found all over Barcelona, many of them stocking translations of Catalan classics.

THE MEDITERRANEAN

→ The 16th-century, Late Gothic-style church of Santa María in Cadaqués, the most easterly town on the Iberian Peninsula.

↘ Diving in the Illes Medes marine reserve, home to underwater meadows of seagrass and caves where groupers breed.

THROUGH THE COSTA BRAVA

When the northerly Tramuntana wind swoops down from the Pyrenees, it can bring gusts of up to 200km/h (120mph) to Catalonia's beautiful Costa Brava. Beginning 60km (37 miles) northeast of Barcelona, beyond the understated Costa Maresme, it is made up of tiny bays where scented pine forests trickle down to the water. Along this coast, restaurants cook up Catalan classics like grilled Roses prawns and seafood-laced *fideuà* (similar to paella but made with vermicelli), served with crisp Empordà wines.

The Costa Brava's southern stretch around Tossa de Mar was developed from the 1950s, but this quickly fades into the distance as the journey continues northeast. Ancient stone towns beckon a hop inland, like castle-crowned Begur and Peratallada. Fishing villages painted in whites and pastels – Sa Tuna, Calella de Palafrugell, Tamariu – buzz with visitors. Divers descend through the Illes Medes marine reserve off the Badia de Roses. And hiking between coves, capes and villages is a treat thanks to the long-distance GR92 trail that runs along the entire coast.

North of Roses, a long hairpin-bend road reaches Cadaqués, huddled into a bay just 30km (19 miles) from Portbou on the French border. Whitewashed houses, stone-flagged alleys and bougainvillea ripple beneath its 16th-century church. The town's sublime Mediterranean light has long lent it a creative edge. The Costa Brava reaches its crescendo in Cap de Creus, north of Cadaqués, where Catalonia's Pyrenees meet the Med. The cape bursts with pebble coves, rock formations and hiking paths.

SPAIN

know-how
An Artists' Paradise

The Costa Brava has attracted, inspired and nurtured artists of all kinds since the late 19th century, and nowhere more so than Cadaqués. The wild drama, unusual glowing light and endless hues of blue to this otherwise pearly-white, Tramuntana-whipped town famously captured the heart of the controversial surrealist Salvador Dalí. His instantly recognisable 1931 masterpiece *The Persistence of Memory* – depicting 'melting' clocks against a cliff-indented coastal backdrop – was painted while living here, among many other works.

Dalí and his Russian-born wife Gala lived in the compact, light-washed fishing village of Port Lligat, just outside Cadaqués, from 1930 to 1982. The extraordinary home they created among delicately fragrant olive groves is today preserved as the Casa-Museu Dalí. Gradually extended from a small and simple fishers' hut, the house feels more like a labyrinth, with views over the Port Lligat bay shown off at every turn.

Beyond Dalí, Cadaqués has lured such art-world greats as Joan Miró, Henri Matisse, Pablo Picasso, David Hockney, Richard Hamilton and even Mick Jagger. The conceptual French painter and sculptor Marcel Duchamp (a friend of Dalí's) first fell for the town's charm in 1933, before spending many later summers here.

The most renowned of Dalí's madcap creations awaits 35km (22 miles) inland from Cadaqués, in his birth-town Figueres. Enormous decorative eggs, Oscar-shaped figurines and plaster croissants burst from an ochre-red fortress at the Teatre-Museu Dalí, which was created by the surrealist himself and opened in 1973. Dalí was buried under the stage here after his death in 1989.

→ Surrealist artist Salvador Dalí, on a photoshoot in 1955, clutches to the walls of the home he built with his wife, Gala.

ORANGE
CÉVENNES
Rhône
Tarn
NÎMES
MONT SAINTE-VICTOIRE
TOULOUSE
MONTPELLIER
AIX-EN-PROVENCE
MARSEILLE
PARC NATUREL RÉGIONAL DE CAMARGUE
Occitanie
NARBONNE
CASSIS
GOLFE DU LION
COLLIOURE

CHAPTER TWO

FRANCE

WINES OF THE LANGUEDOC ~ BIRDLIFE IN THE CAMARGUE
ROMAN ORANGE ~ BOUILLABAISSE IN MARSEILLE ~ PÉTANQUE
CORSICAN SINGING ~ DRIVING THE ALPES-MARITIMES
CANNES FILM FESTIVAL ~ MATISSE'S NICE ~ F1 IN MONACO

PARC NATIONAL DE
MERCANTOUR

Provence-
Alpes-Côte-
d'Azur

• NICE
• MENTON
MONACO

• CANNES

• ST-TROPEZ

ÎLES D'OR

Corsica

• PORTO-VECCHIO

THE MEDITERRANEAN

→ The grey native horses of the Camargue region live a semi-feral life in this wetland, managed by local guardians.

France's Mediterranean coast runs from the craggy russet creeks of the Côte Vermeille to the smooth sands and grey pebbles of Menton at the Italian border. Along the way are the highest cliffs in Europe at Cassis; a saltmarsh paradise for birds in the Camargue; and a combination of cinema, superyachts and sunbathing that have given the French Riviera an air of decadent luxury. So many artists have left a deep trace near France's southern shores, attracted there by the consistent sun, relaxed mentality and clear air. Picasso, Lèger, Ingres and Toulouse-Lautrec have museums entirely dedicated to their art, while the Musées des Beaux Arts in Montpellier and Nice can rival their equivalents in Paris.

The French *art de vivre* is about enjoying life – chatting with friends over a game of *pétanque*, wandering around a fresh-produce market in the morning, then visiting an antiques fair at the weekend – and there is nowhere better to do this than by the vivid blue waters of the Mediterranean.

FRANCE

THE MEDITERRANEAN

→ The Château Royal in Collioure. Earlier fortified structures had been built on this site by the Visigoths and Knights Templar.

ALONG THE CÔTE VERMEILLE
The tiny border town of Cerbère guards the gates of France's Côte Vermeille. At the start of the 20th century this brief section of coast – named for its rust-red rocks – became hugely popular with artists, attracted by the remote coves and bright natural light.

Set back from the sea, among the vines, olives and fig trees of Banyuls-sur-Mer, is La Métairie, the farmhouse where locally-born sculptor Aristide Maillol worked during the winter. On his tomb in the garden is his bronze statue, La Méditerranée, depicting a nude woman seated on the ground, which Maillol himself described as the 'incarnation of the land of light, the region of radiant intelligence, the Greco-Roman zone where she had her birth.'

In 1905, the same year that Maillol finished La Méditerranée, Henri Matisse and André Derain – the Fauves (wild beasts) – arrived in Collioure, setting up their easels all over town and painting the port and landscapes in strident, pulsating colours. You can follow the chemin du Fauvisme around the port, accompanied by the constant jangling of small fishing boats in the harbour and the faint scent of paraffin and salted anchovies.

Collioure is dominated by two austere giants: the Château Royal, founded in the 13th century and used as a holiday home by the Kings of Mallorca; and the Church of Notre-Dame des Anges, whose belfry was originally built as a lighthouse. Much of the rest of the town is taken up with art galleries and the colourful houses of a population of modern-day Fauvists. **CONTINUED ON P48 »**

know-how

The Anchovy

The anchovy has been a staple ingredient of Mediterranean cuisine since Roman times and its 'capital', as all French chefs know, is Collioure. The port once had an anchovy fishing fleet of over 200 boats and 30 salting companies. Today, Anchois Roque, one of only two remaining salters, imports most of its fresh fish but carries out the same process it has done for five generations: hand-filleting, pre-salting, layering, re-salting and ageing the anchovies in barrels for 200 days. Anchovy-based specialities take centre stage at Collioure's Fête de l'Anchois on the first weekend in June. Some of the most popular include:

Anchoïade Crushed garlic, olive oil, egg yolks, cured anchovies and white-wine vinegar, used as a dip or spread.

Assiette de Collioure A plate of anchovies soaked in white-wine vinegar, with lettuce, red peppers, boiled egg and *escalivade* (aubergine roasted with garlic, tomatoes and oil), served with sprigs of parsley.

Pichade A baked pizza-style square covered in cooked-tomato sauce and sliced onion, with anchovy fillets criss-crossed on top and lots of garlic in between.

Pissaladière A flatbread tart topped with anchovy fillets, caramelised onions, tiny black olives and *pissalat*, a paste of crushed anchovies, thyme, black pepper and olive oil.

Tapenade A condiment of de-salted anchovies, capers and black olives, puréed with lemon juice, garlic and olive oil.

THE MEDITERRANEAN

→ Traditional rowing boats moored in the centre of Sète. Both mussels and oysters are cultivated in the nearby Étang de Thau.

↘ Dwellings in Old Gruissan fan out from the Tour Barberrousse (Redbeard Tower), the sole remnant of a 10th-century castle.

NARBONNE AND ITS BEACHES
Before silt clogged the surrounding channel, Old Gruissan was an island, narrow streets winding around the 10th-century Tour Barberrousse. Invaders became trapped in there and were finished off before they could turn back. Modern Gruissan flows onto a vast beach, home to a seaside utopia of hundreds of wooden chalets on stilts – one of which was set alight by Betty Blue in Jean-Jacques Beineix's film of the same name.

Eight miles (5km) inland is Narbonne, a former Roman capital on the Via Domitia that linked Italy to Hispania. Spared the summertime coach parties that pass through the medieval gates of nearby Carcassonne, Narbonne is known for its gargantuan Archbishops' Palace and Gothic cathedral, and the tiny, ivy-clad house of Charles Trenet. The *chanteur* wrote La Mer (Beyond the Sea) while on a train passing the lagoons of the nearby coastline.

Narbonne has its own beach, part of a swathe of Tramontane-swept sand which extends to the Cap d'Agde. Here families head to the amusement and water parks, swerving the naturist camp and padel-playing retirees who power-walk the coastal footpath to Sète, 19km (12 miles) away.

Sète is a marvel. Known as the 'Venice of the Languedoc' for its network of canals, the port town sits on a spindly isthmus between the sea and the saltwater Étang de Thau. Enjoy a *tielle*, the local octopus tart, with a glass of the Languedoc's Terret white wine in one of the fish restaurants; during summer's Fête de la Saint Louis, water-jousting is staged on the royal canal. **CONTINUED ON P54 »**

local angle
Wines of the Languedoc

'Domaine Sainte Cécile du Parc, the vineyard we bought in 2005, is located in Pézenas on the glorious terraces at the foot of the Cévennes Mountains, which my fellow winemakers and I call the "St-Émilion of the Languedoc". This reference to the prestigious Bordeaux appellation is ironic, given the local mistrust of Bordeaux wines, born from a historical animosity that dates back centuries.

'The Languedoc is increasingly regarded as home to some of the most exciting and imaginative wines in the world. The presence of basalt gives the terroir its unique character on a mosaic of soils composed of Villafranchian pebbles, clay, schist, limestone and sandstone. The vineyards thrive in the hot Mediterranean sunshine, soothed by the refreshing maritime breezes. Thanks to this exceptional climate and affordable land prices, the area has attracted producers from all regions of France and beyond, who continue to enhance its winemaking reputation.

'Pézenas is best known for its spicy reds, often made from one or more of the classic Syrah, Carignan, Cinsault, Grenache Noir and Mourvedre varieties. Wine is a remarkably sophisticated natural cocktail. It is extraordinary how something like a glass of wine can bring people together and, at the same time, have such personal significance to everyone. For me it means love, sweat and poetry.'

Christine Bertoli, winemaker and oenologist in Pézenas

THE MEDITERRANEAN

ALONG THE TARN VALLEY

A road trip taking in the best of the region's museums, wine and food

Distance 129km (81 miles)

Duration Two days

Start Castres

Finish Montauban

❶ Castres
Start the day in Castres at the former Bishop's Palace, where the Musée Goya is dedicated to Spanish art. The collection includes many of Francisco Goya's sketches; his *Self-portrait with Spectacles* (c 1800) gives him a strangely modern appearance. It will take a morning to wander through the galleries featuring works by Sorolla, Dalí, Velázques and Miró, as well as a substantial collection of early weaponry.

❷ Albi
The drive north towards Albi passes stone bastides and terraces of vineyards beside a village called Lautrec, but that's just a coincidence. The real Henri de Toulouse-Lautrec was instead born in Albi to an aristocratic family and spent his early life there, suffering from a series of especially unpleasant ailments before heading to Paris and a new life at the Moulin Rouge. His mother founded Albi's Musée Toulouse-Lautrec in 1922, donating a huge collection of his works, including childhood drawings along with his last painting, *Examination at the Faculty of Medicine* (1901), completed soon before he died at the age of just 36. With your head now filled with art, spend the night at the Hôtel Saint Antoine near Albi's magnificent, fortress-like cathedral. ***40 km (25 miles)***

❸ Gaillac
Motor on west among the vineyards (ideally bring a designated driver) to taste the wines at Gaillac's Maison des Vins, set in the Abbaye Saint-Michel on the banks of the Tarn. There are plenty of riverside restaurants to try the region's local dishes – *cassoulet* (a stew of sausage, pork and beans), *croustade* (flaky-pastry fruit tart) and *confit de canard* (salt-cured duck slow-cooked in its own fat). ***22 km (14 miles)***

❹ Montauban
Follow the Tarn River westward via Saint-Sulpice-la-Pointe to Montauban, where the Musée Ingres Bourdelle, in a former medieval chateau among the pink-brick houses, is dedicated to the painter Jean-Auguste-Dominique Ingres and sculptor Antoine Bourdelle, both born in Montauban. Ingres is the star of the show – the collection includes 4500 of his drawings, 45 paintings and his violin. ***67km (42 miles)***

FRANCE

↖ Renaissance frescoes adorn the interior of Sainte-Cécile cathedral in Albi.

↙ 13th-century Sainte-Cécile is the world's largest brick-built cathedral.

THE MEDITERRANEAN

MONTPELLIER GUIDE

A chic metropolis set back from the coast

taste
BRASUCADE DE MOULES

Traditionally prepared outdoors over a barbeque made with old vines, the *brasucade de moules* is one of Montpellier's favourite seafood dishes. Mussels from the nearby Étang de Thau are cooked in a flat pan with sliced onions, and drizzled with a sauce of pastis, white wine, olive oil, red chillies, rosemary and olive oil.

culture
MUSÉE FABRE

Masterpieces by Géricault, Courbet, Bazille and Delacroix line the main hall of the grand Musée Fabre, set in an 18th-century palace with colonnades and vaulted galleries. The museum has one of France's finest art collections outside Paris but its unique attraction is the 20 pitch-black oil paintings donated by local artist Pierre Soulages (1919–2022). His artistic *outrenoir* (beyond black) revelation in January 1979 caused him to paint almost exclusively in black. Organised visits with children to the Soulages room are entitled, 'Who's afraid of the dark?'

buy
GRISETTES DE MONTPELLIER

Grisettes de Montpellier are grey sweets the size of peas, handmade from honey and liquorice and sold in fancy hexagonal boxes all over the city. Originally manufactured as a cure-all by Montpellier's apothecaries as far back as the 13th century, they served a secondary purpose as currency between traders and pilgrims on their way to Santiago de Compostela.

> "A dramatic architectural foil to the mazy streets of the medieval Old Town"

explore
ANTIGONE

A stunning development running east from the Place de la Comedie to the Lez River, the Antigone district was finished in the year 2000. Designed by Catalan architect Ricardo Bofill, it's an epic-scale assembly of office and apartment blocks, government buildings, cafes and restaurants, all conceived as a neoclassical metropolis with oversized pilasters and pediments. Stone-paved plazas, triumphal arches, an Olympic-sized pool and soaring sculptured fountains form a dramatic architectural foil to the mazy, narrow streets of Montpellier's medieval Old Town.

nightlife
CAFÉS LITTÉRAIRES

Before the onslaught of the ubiquitous cafe-coworking space, Montpellier had a lively tradition of *cafés littéraires*, frequented by Bohemian poets and the city's huge student population. The Georges Café, Café BUN and Le Bookshop close a little early for a big night out; local intellectuals then head on to the Gazette Café, which hosts its own conferences, concerts and dance classes. Alternatively, explore the Old Town's assortment of small theatres and arts clubs.

THE MEDITERRANEAN

ACROSS THE SALTPANS OF THE CAMARGUE
During the 18th century, the towers on the ramparts surrounding Aigues-Mortes were used to house Huguenot prisoners. Today, they provide visitors with panoramic views of the pink and purple saltpans that surround the walled town – the French Kingdom's first port on the Mediterranean – and the distant vineyards set on sand at the Domaine Royal de Jarras, Europe's largest wine estate. Latin for 'dead waters', Aigues-Mortes' identity is defined by its grey-tinted rosé wine and salt, with giant grit-salt hills in the surrounding saltpans and shelves of crystallised *fleur de sel* on the town's boutique shelves.

Aigues-Mortes is also the western gateway to the Camargue Delta. A wild landscape of shallow lagoons, rice fields and meadows of bulrushes, the Camargue is dominated by trident-carrying *gardians* (cattle-herders) on horseback and hundreds of thousands of migrating birds. Running free are white horses, black bulls and, on the lagoons, pink flamingos. Each 24 May, Gypsies from all over Europe congregate at its seaside capital, Saintes-Maries-de-la-Mer, for a pilgrimage in the name of Saint Sara, whose statue they process into the sea. Caravans line the seafront for two days of horse races, bullfighting and religious processions with bonfires, flamenco and the sounds of *manouche* guitar drifting out to sea.

On the eastern, less-visited edge of the Camargue is the town of Salin-de-Giraud and its terraces of compact brick houses, built for salt-workers in the 1850s. Out towards the shimmering horizon, a single-track passes alongside giant pyramids of salt up to land's end, where the Plage de Piémanson is a long sweep of creamy sand, occupied by joyous dogs and kite-surfers. **CONTINUED ON P58 »**

↓ A *gardian* rounds up a semi-feral black bull. The Raço di Biòu breed of domestic cattle originates from the Camargue region.

know-how
Birdlife in the Camargue

↑ A hoopoe, crest raised, flies in to feed its chicks. The hoopoe's diet consists of insects, frogs, small lizards, seeds and berries.

↗ An adult greater flamingo, coloured pink by the carotenoid pigments in the algae and the shellfish it consumes.

Two-thirds of all bird species found in Europe can be observed in the Camargue Delta, making it a wonderland for ornithologists. Designated a Regional Nature Park and UNESCO Biosphere Reserve, and home to a bird sanctuary, the Camargue's fresh and saltwater marshes, reedbeds, groves and fields of bulrushes each attract different avian species – including vast flocks of migratory birds stopping over on their journey from Africa to northern Europe. Visitors can walk or cycle marshland trails with observation platforms to see pink flamingos, herons and plovers as well as scarcer species which stay year-round, such as kingfishers, white storks, glossy ibis and purple gallinules. Colourful and distinctive species to watch out for include:

Greater flamingo At their only nesting site in France, thousands of flamingos remain all year in the Camargue, feeding on the carotenoid algae and shrimps in the lagoons.

Black-throated loon With its distinctive pinstriped collar and wings, the loon is seen during the winter months at the Pointe de Beauduc, an area of gently sloping sand dunes.

Eurasian spoonbill Present during migrating periods in the delta's saltwater marshes, spoonbills feed on a variety of insects and crustacea using sideways sweeps of their bill.

Common snipe The camouflaged and hard-to-track snipe is a winter visitor to the reserve's saltwater lagoons and the Étang du Vaccarès.

Hoopoe A summer resident of the Parc Ornithologique du Pont de Gau, this solitary forager is easy to spot, with a fanned crown of feathers and distinctive wood-knock call.

THE MEDITERRANEAN

ROMAN OCCITANIE

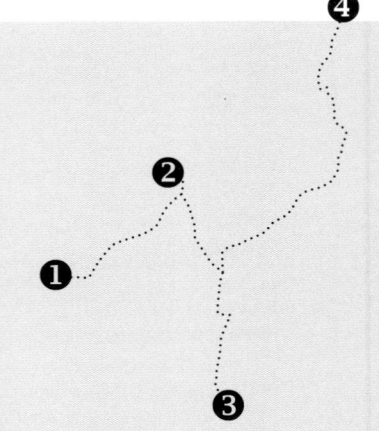

A drive back through millennia to explore the ancient sites of Provence

Distance 129km (80 miles)
Duration Two days
Start Nîmes
Finish Orange

❶ Nîmes
Survey this former Roman city from Mont Cavalier, the site of the long-beheaded Tour Magne. More than a dozen such towers once stood here, a power move by Emperor Augustus to symbolise the strength of Nîmes. Another of his masterpieces is the Maison Carrée, just to the south. Though abandoned after the Roman era, it has been in almost constant use since the 11th century and now hosts a movie about the history of Nîmes. Take a stroll south along tree-shaded blvd Victor Hugo for the big finish. Well-preserved Les Arènes was one of the largest amphitheatres in all the Roman Empire, today still in use as a performance venue.

❷ Pont du Gard
Nîmes would have been nothing without its water source, an aqueduct meandering some 50km (31 miles) from its own source in Uzès. Head northeast of the city to the formidable aqueduct bridge now known as the Pont du Gard. Its three tiers support 52 limestone arches, looping elegantly above the Gard River. *19km (12 miles)*

❸ Arles
Drive south along roads fringed by poplars towards Arles, whose star came into ascendance following the Great Roman Civil War (49–45 BCE). The ensuing era of prosperity left behind numerous fine monuments. Below ground in Arles' Place du Forum are the Cryptoportiques, vaulted tunnels thought to be a former barracks. Walk five minutes east to find the magnificent double-tiered Les Arènes amphitheatre, once capable of holding more than 21,000 people. Stop overnight at L'Hôtel Particulier, which retains all the luxurious style of its former life as a private townhouse. *40km (25 miles)*

❹ Orange
The quickest way to Orange is to bolt north and join the highway – but the majesty of your final destination demands a more leisurely route, following the bends of the Rhône River on the D2. Orange's Théâtre antique is one of only three intact Roman theatres in the world. Seats fan out from its 37m-high stage wall, where pulleys once raised and lowered a curtain. Presiding over this grand scene is a statue of Augustus. *70km (43 miles)*

↖ The Pont du Gard was constructed from limestone in the 1st century CE.

↙ The Théâtre antique in Orange, also 1st century CE, once seated over 7000.

THE MEDITERRANEAN

THE CÔTE-BLEUE WEST OF MARSEILLE

Like squabbling twins, the neighbouring ports of Sausset-les-Pins and Carry-le-Rouet vie to host the best *oursinades* each January and February. These sea-urchin festivals welcome thousands of visitors (and seagulls) on six consecutive Sundays to enjoy a plate of the sweet, orange-coloured 'coral' of the urchin with a glass of white Bandol wine.

Heading east, umbrella pines and rocky coves are replaced by heavy industry at L'Estaque as it nears Marseille's clanking docklands. Paul Cézanne painted L'Estaque between 1860 and 1884 when it was still a fishing village – a place that granted the artist his 'altered gaze' and where, according to art critic Véronique Serrano, Cézanne became Cézanne.

When factories began to arrive on the coast, Cézanne turned his obsession inland to paint the almighty Mont Sainte-Victoire, east of Aix-en-Provence. His atelier in Aix, intact as he left it, is a steep walk from the city centre where Cézanne went to school with his best friend Émile Zola. They used to recite Latin verses in the playground here before heading off for a smoke then a swim in the Arc River.

Aix was founded by the Romans as Aquae Sextiae thanks to its natural springs, and the city's warm water still bubbles up in the mossy fountains along the cours Mirabeau. Either side are mansions built in huge blocks of golden stone, with doorways held up by Atlantes (male figures), and plane trees inhabited by a phalanx of crows seeking protection from the Mistral wind. Beneath them mingles a sophisticated crowd – law students, visitors to the Musée Granet and, in the early evenings, opera lovers enjoying a pre-show *apéro*. **CONTINUED ON P62 »**

↖ Fishing boats moored in the harbour of Sausset-les-Pins on the Côte Bleue. A seafood market is held here most days of the week.

↑ Part of an irregular maze of streets in the old town of Aix-en-Provence, lined with 16th, 17th and 18th century mansions.

FRANCE

local angle
Festival d'Aix-en-Provence

'Founded in 1948, the festival has become an enduring cultural institution, a kind of "Mediterranean" Salzburg Festival, in the tradition of open-air theatre. At first focused on Mozart, it has now expanded to include lesser-known baroque and contemporary operas, featuring works by Rameau, Monteverdi, Purcell and Haydn. The innovative programming integrates opera with prestigious symphonic and chamber music concerts; sets created by renowned painters like [the late] André Derain and Suzanne Lalique have enhanced its artistic reputation. The festival continues to prioritise musical discovery, scenic audacity and diversity, embracing jazz, Mediterranean traditions and contemporary operas.

'The particular alchemy of the venues is of paramount importance to me. The Théâtre de l'Archevêché, which provides a magical setting for opera performances under the stars, and the Théâtre du Jeu de Paume, an 18th-century Italian-style hall, offer perfect conditions for enjoying our programme of baroque and chamber opera.

'For many years, the festival has been committed to making this all-encompassing art form accessible to all. Aix's vibrant cultural scene, supported by its rich history and local policies, ensures the festival remains a global leader in opera, commissioning new works and fostering artistic experimentation. Putting together a season is a fascinating job, one that keeps us busy all year round – even several years! Aix is a place where you can find the best orchestras, ensembles and singers on the international opera scene – which for us means planning their arrival years in advance.'

Pierre Audi, director of the Festival d'Aix-en-Provence

THE MEDITERRANEAN

MARSEILLE GUIDE

A city defined by its bond with the sea

explore
LE PANIER

buy
SAVON DE MARSEILLE

Blocks of soap from the Middle East were brought back to Marseille by Crusaders 700 years ago and copied here (using olive oil) to wash bodies and clothes, also to relieve cramps and rheumatism. Savon de Marseille is now used all over France, but make sure you buy the right stuff – the genuine article comes in only two colours, green (based on olive oil) or white (based on coconut oil).

Steep, uneven staircases lead past the crumbling, pastel-fronted houses of Le Panier (The Basket) to the Vieille-Charité (above), a former poorhouse now home to a cinema, a café, museums and smart offices. Here, at the top of Marseille's oldest neighbourhood, washing lines hang over improvised *boules* courts and locals tease each other on the steps of shops selling rustic pottery, bottles of *pastis* and the local *navettes* (orange-blossom-flavoured biscuits).

taste
BOUILLABAISSE

Marseille's emblematic fish stew started out as a fishers' soup, a mixture of bony rockfish boiled with what was left in the nets. Today, it is still sacred but is served in the city's top restaurants. *Bouillabaisse* means 'when it boils, turn it down' which is how the stew is prepared, using a saffron, shellfish and vegetable base. The broth is eaten first with crusty bread and a spicy *rouille* sauce.

> *"Enticing aromas of* bouillabaisse *drift through the air"*

culture
CITÉ RADIEUSE

The Cité Radieuse (Radiant City) was modernist architect Le Corbusier's concrete answer to Marseille's housing crisis after WWII. This dazzling block of thick-walled duplex apartments, with sea and mountain views, rises up from one of Marseille's widest boulevards. On the third floor are galleries, a bar, and a hotel offering access to the rooftop terrace and its panorama of the Phocaean (ancient Greek) city's tightly packed neighbourhoods.

nightlife
VALLON DES AUFFES

Beneath the Corniche Kennedy, as it heads south from Marseille's Vieux Port towards the city's best beaches, is the Vallon des Auffes (above). This 'secret' cove is the perfect spot for a sunset drink: darkness falls through an arched viaduct where fishing boats are tied up among coiled nets, and aromas of simmering *bouillabaisse* and Chez Jeannot's seafood pizza drift through the air.

THE MEDITERRANEAN

→ The harbour in Cassis shelters a traditional Provençal style of fishing vessel known as the *pointu*, after the shape of its prow.

↘ Peering down the limestone cliffs of the Calanque d'En-Vau, one of the longest of this array of inlets between Marseilles and Cassis.

EAST OF MARSEILLE

Writer Virginia Woolf used to stay in Cassis at her sister Vanessa Bell's rented cottage in the grounds of the Château de Fontcreuse vineyard. In fact, so many of their peers headed to the seaside port in the late 1920s that it took on the name 'Bloomsbury-sur-Mer'.

Houses in shades of saffron and peach line Cassis' port, where nets are stacked outside seafood restaurants. Up the hill is Hôtel Les Roches Blanches, where Winston Churchill practised his watercolours, painting Europe's highest cliffs and the limestone inlets of the calanques.

Some 10km (6 miles) further along the coast is the far less chichi La Ciotat, site of the colossal former shipyards where, from the late 19th century, everyone from emperors to marine engineers would flock to witness the launch of a gleaming ocean liner. The resultant swell sometimes overflowed the port, flooding restaurants.

At the Lumière family's summerhouse here, brothers Louis and Auguste showed *L'Arrivée d'un train en gare de La Ciotat* in 1895, one of the earliest cinematographic films. It would go on to cause a panicked audience to flee a Parisian theatre where the 50-second production was being shown, believing the train was about to crash into them.

While the Bloomsbury Set drifted towards Cassis in the late 1920s, Sanary-sur-Mer provided a refuge for writers fleeing the Nazi regime in Germany. Sanary's cafes hosted Thomas Mann, Bertold Brecht, Joseph Roth and Stefan Zweig, as well as British author Aldous Huxley, who lived in a villa overlooking the Bay of Bandol. **CONTINUED ON P66 »**

know-how
Pétanque

France's unofficial national sport was first played in La Ciotat in 1910, when local shopkeeper Jules Le Noir's rheumatism was so bad he could only throw his *boules* while sitting in a chair. Since *pétanque*'s predecessor in the south of France, Jeu provençal, involved a three-step runup, Le Noir's friends decided if he were playing, no one should move their feet. *Pétanque* – from the Provençal *pè tancat* (foot fixed) – was born. The rules are strict:

1 From inside a circle drawn at one end of a gravelly court, one player throws out a small wooden ball, known in La Ciotat as the *bouchon* (cork) and elsewhere as the *cochonnet* (little pig); it must land 6m to 10m away.

2 Their opponent throws a larger metal *boule* as close to the *bouchon* as they can. Players have three *boules* each (two if playing in a *triplette*); the nearest to the *bouchon* wins a point – but they can gain more points if they have other *boules* closer to the *bouchon* than their opponents.

3 The *boule* is held in a downturned palm and launched towards the *bouchon* or another *boule*, which can be knocked out of the way. The game continues, changing ends each time, until one team reaches 13 points.

THE MEDITERRANEAN

CORSICA GUIDE

Home to a distinct island culture

beach
PLAGE DE LA RONDINARA

Halfway between Porto-Vecchio and Bonifacio in the southeast of the island is Plage de la Rondinara, a perfect crescent of white sand protected at either end by beautifully symmetrical headlands. The clear turquoise water makes it ideal for swimming from one end to the other, or renting a kayak and exploring the sea beyond this clam-shaped bay.

activity
HIKING THE GR20

The Grande Randonnée 20 (GR20), one of France's (never mind Corsica's) toughest hiking trails, takes walkers across the island's elevated spine from Calenzana in the northwest to Conca in the southeast. It's a 12-day, 186km (115-mile) hike over the granite peaks and plunging gorges of the interior, but where better to find yourself than in a remote refuge near the Cirque de la Solitude or ascending the snowcapped Bocca Tumasginesca?

base
SAINT-FLORENT

Between the Désert des Agriates and the finger-shaped Cap Corse, Saint-Florent is a lively port, with excellent fish restaurants and cafes facing the marina and a long, sandy beach. This former Genoese stronghold has a hilltop citadel and is a great base for exploring the Nebbio Valley and visiting the vineyards of Patrimonio, or taking a day trip to Île Rousse and Calvi on the northern coast.

> "Performances in the Corsican language inspire a new generation"

explore
FILITOSA'S STATUES

Undiscovered until 1946, the stone statues of Filitosa, near Sollacaro, are estimated to have been carved over 3000 years ago. Lines of granite menhirs – some interpreted as phallic symbols, others as chiefs, warriors or enemies from the sea – gaze across the olive groves and wildflower meadows of the Taravo Valley. Experts believe the carved faces with swords, shields and helmets link Filitosa to the protohistoric cultures of the Eastern Mediterranean; for Corsicans, their chief significance is as part of the island's noble yet mysterious heritage.

secret
CANTU CORSU

Cantu Corsu, Corsica's enthralling polyphonic singing, can be heard in churches, chapels and late-night bars all over the island. Far from a disappearing art, the revolutionary-inspired lyrics, political content and performances in the Corsican language have inspired a new generation of singing groups. The *paghjella* is a hugely expressive form of the *cantu*, sung in three vocal registers in traditional form, and recognised by UNESCO as part of the island's intangible cultural heritage.

THE MEDITERRANEAN

→ An installation at the Villa Noailles in Hyères. The 1920s modernist villa included specially commissioned furniture and artworks.

HYÈRES AND THE ÎLES D'OR

Queen Victoria spent a month in Hyères in 1892, travelling in a donkey-drawn carriage. The town was one of the Côte d'Azur's first winter resorts, but with the advent of summer holidays, sea swimming, boating and sunbathing, Hyères' perched-above-the-coast location saw it drift down the Riviera's pecking order, turning instead to supplying cut flowers and palm trees to the rest of France. Today, it's a laid-back, uncrowded town, with aristocratic residences and a cobbled medieval heart.

In 1923, Parisian art patrons Marie-Laure and Charles de Noaille commissioned the architect Robert Mallet-Stevens to construct a modernist villa on the hill above Hyères. The resulting Villa Noailles was an astonishing Cubist palace in concrete and glass which included Europe's first indoor swimming pool, featured in Man Ray's short film *Les Mystères du Chateau du Dé*. From the terrace, you can see the town's sloping terracotta-tiled roofs, along with palms, pines and the nearby Îles d'Or.

The largest of those three 'golden islands', Porquerolles, is crisscrossed with walking trails and cycle tracks. It's also home to a fort and the Fondation Carmignac arts centre, where visitors are welcome to wander, barefoot, around a sculpture garden. Port Cros island is a national maritime park covered with dense forest, scented with eucalyptus and mimosa. Almost all of the most easterly island, Le Levant, is occupied by the French military; the exception is Heliopolis, a naturist colony created by the pioneering Durville brothers in 1931. **CONTINUED ON P70 »**

local angle
Domaine du Rayol

'The Domaine du Rayol Mediterranean Gardens were created by a businessman from Bormes-les-Mimosas, Alfred Courmes, who bought a promontory of land in the Var in 1910 and set about building a farm, manor house and gardens. We still have some of the original eucalyptus and agave he planted over a century ago.

'The property was bought in 1940 by aeronautical designer Henri Potez, who extended the gardens. The site was abandoned in the 1960s but eventually acquired by the Conservatoire du Littoral in 1989, which asked landscaper Gilles Clément (of Paris's Parc Citroën and Musée du quai Branly fame) to redesign the garden, then it was opened to the public.

'The area is divided into locations in the world that share the Mediterranean climate, such as California, southern Australia, Mexico, and parts of South Africa, Chile and the Canary Islands. There's also a marine garden full of Neptune grass, sponges and rare algae. Our nursery allows us to restock the gardens but also to supply rare Mediterranean species to other places.'
Sybille Bernard, director of Domaine du Rayol, in Rayol-Canadel-sur-Mer

THE MEDITERRANEAN

THE ALPES-MARITIMES

A thrilling drive into hill country alongside the Italian border

Distance 71km (44 miles)
Duration Two days
Start Menton
Finish Castérino

❶ Menton
Acquired by Monaco's Grimaldi family in the mid-14th century from the wealthy Genoese Vento dynasty, Menton only became part of France in 1860, by which time its mild winters were already attracting European aristocrats and a host of tuberculosis-suffering artists and writers in search of respite. The unyielding streets of the Old Town – some so steep they have handrails – lead up to the hilltop cemetery and a full panorama of the coast, the pebbled forecourt of the Basilique St-Michel Archange and the town's many botanical gardens.

❷ Sospel
Head north into the hills past Castellar and Castillon on the D2566, a twisting road of hairpin bends and plunging drop-offs. Just before Sospel, stop off at the Fort Saint-Roch; this network of corridors carved into the rock beneath concrete blocks formed part of the defences of the Alpine Maginot Line in the early 1930s. Sospel's lopsided Pont-Vieux was first constructed in the 13th century as a crossing point on the Routes du Sel, mule trails used by traders from the coast to transport salt to the mountain villages. Walk along the banks of the Bévera River to see the *trompe l'oeil* facades of the shuttered houses. *18km (11 miles)*

❸ La Brigue
Continue through Breil-sur-Roya and Saorge, gateway to a world of canyoning, hiking and icy river pools. Stop in La Brigue, famous for its beehives and the Chapelle Notre-Dame-des-Fontaines. Known as the 'Sistine Chapel of the Alpes-Maritimes', its walls are covered in frescoes from the 14th and 15th centuries, including a candid, colourful rendering of the birth of Mary, the Passion of Christ and the Last Judgement. *37km (23 miles)*

❹ Castérino
Follow the Torrent de Bieugme northwest to Castérino. At 1500m, the village is surrounded by pine forests and, in summer, meadows of wildflowers. In the warm months, hike in the Parc National de Mercantour and explore the prehistoric rock engravings of the Vallée des Merveilles; in the winter, there's dog-sledding and cross-country skiing. Stay the night at the Chamois d'Or hotel, a log chalet with a restaurant and open fire. *16km (10 miles)*

FRANCE

↖ A chamois looks out over the peaks of the Parc National de Mercantour.

↙ The 13th-century Pont-Vieux (Old Bridge) in Sospel crosses the Bévera River.

THE GOLFE DE SAINT-TROPEZ

Summer nights in St-Tropez are lit up from the sea by immense superyachts squeezed into the marina like portly drinkers at a beach bar. This is the Riviera set in full, hedonistic flow, where waiters can be seen balancing platters of gleaming seafood to the sound of after-dark dance shows and the growl of sports cars searching for a space along the port's periphery.

Daytime starts late and extremely gently. There's a fish market near the tourist office, a butterfly gallery and a museum solely dedicated to the cinema. Modern St-Tropez was transformed from an unpretentious coastal village into surely France's most glamorous tourist destination following Roger Vadim's *Et Dieu… créa la femme* (And God Created Woman), the 1956 film that helped project a young Brigitte Bardot to international stardom.

St-Tropez sits at the northern edge to a peninsula. On its southern flank is the Plage de Pampelonne, 5km (3 miles) of fine, white sand backed by low dunes, a pine forest and scores of fashionable beach clubs. Behind them on an undulating plane are vineyards and stands of parasol pines which lead up to the arty, medieval village of Ramatuelle.

In winter, everywhere goes quiet here. St-Tropez's peach-toned streets take on a greyish hue and the boutiques selling Roman sandals and straw hats shutter up for the season. Conspicuous life remains only in Sainte-Maxime, a family resort across the gulf with a cobbled Old Town. The rusty remains of an amphibious Sherman tank, buried here beside the Plage de la Nartelle, are a reminder of the Allied landings on 15 August 1944, which freed Provence from the Nazis. **CONTINUED ON P72 »**

↓ Turquoise waters contrast with terracotta roof tiles at the Port de Saint-Tropez, home to luxury yachts both small and super.

FRANCE

local angle
Musée de l'Annonciade

↑ Galleries of the Musée de l'Annonciade in St-Tropez; painter Paul Signac first 'discovered' the fishing port in his yacht *Olympia*.

'When visitors arrive, they are stunned by the quality of the collection we have at this tiny art museum in the chapel of L'Annonciade on the Vieux Port. The collection began with the artist Paul Signac, who fell in love with the sea and light of St-Tropez on a sailing trip in 1892 and encouraged his neo-impressionist friends to join him. Matisse, Bonnard, Derain and Marquet came to see this "marvel" – the Golfe de Saint-Tropez – with mountains behind, blue sky, the sea's reflections, and the Mistral wind, which gave this part of the coast a particular light.

'In 1922, Signac and his fellow artists offered paintings for a museum in the local town hall, but it wasn't until 1936 when aesthete and collector Georges Grammont donated his collection of their works that the idea of having a fine arts museum in St-Tropez took hold. The collection was transferred to a 16th-century chapel in 1951 which was being used as a small shipyard and performance hall – it included Grammont's expanded collection of pointillist, Nabi and Fauvist art, including works by Henri Manguin and Kees van Dongen.'
Séverine Berger, curator of the Musée de l'Annonciade, St-Tropez

THE MEDITERRANEAN

→ Rue des Bains in Antibes, near the Musée Picasso and the Port Vauban, the largest marina in Europe with over 2000 moorings.

↘ La Croisette in Cannes; the Carlton Hotel, to the fore, opened in 1911 and hosts stars attending the annual Film Festival.

THE FRENCH RIVIERA
Would-be starlets mingle with conference-goers and tourists on La Croisette, Cannes' seaside promenade. Opposite the beaches are the flagship stores of the world's big fashion houses and a handful of lavish hotels – the Martinez, the Carlton and the Barrière Le Majestic – all spruced up for the Film Festival in May. High above them is the town of Le Cannet, which separated from its coastal neighbour in 1774. The Cannettans are still said to be wary of the Cannois.

Heading east past the glorious sandy beaches of Cannes-la-Bocca and Juan-les-Pins is Antibes, the sailing hub of the Riviera. Its star-shaped Fort Carré was remodelled by the French military engineer Vauban in the 1680s, who planned to make Antibes – then the last town in France – a maritime base to rival the great Toulon. The town's chateau, which sits just inside the seafront ramparts, is now the Musée Picasso, a showcase for his playful ceramics; it provides cover for the Provençal market below, open in the mornings for olives and oranges, and in the evenings for jewellery and hand-spun dreamcatchers.

A few kilometres inland is the medieval village of Haut-de-Cagnes, where the streets are so steep, locals play *pétanque* with square *boules* that rattle along the cobbles like giant dice. Haut-de-Cagnes' crenelated chateau was built by the Grimaldis in 1309 but is now a museum whose top floor is dedicated to portraits of Suzy Solidor. The jazz-age cabaret performer used to wear a mother-of-pearl swimsuit which would still shock the crowds on Cannes' beaches. **CONTINUED ON P76 »**

know-how
The Cannes Film Festival

The world's most prestigious film festival takes place over two weeks in May, a fortnight of glamour, controversial prizes and all-night parties with the paparazzi snapping stars on the steps of the Palais des Festivals. Movie industry players gather as films are shown in the Palais as well as at selected cinemas around the town and, nightly, on a giant screen set up on the beach. Historic Cannes moments include:

1 At the first festival in 1939 only one film was screened, William Dieterle's *The Hunchback of Notre Dame*. Germany invaded Poland on the day the festival was to be inaugurated, and the event was cancelled.

2 France was in social turmoil in May 1968 and at the festival, jury members resigned and directors withdrew their films in protest, culminating in François Truffaut, Jean-Luc Godard, Miloš Forman and Roman Polanski clinging to the red curtain on the stage to prevent the screening of Carlos Saura's *Peppermint Frappé*.

3 At the closing ceremony in 1987, director Maurice Pialat raised his fist at the jeering public as he collected the Palme d'Or for *Under the Sun of Satan,* declaring, 'You don't like me? Let me tell you that I don't like you either!'

THE MEDITERRANEAN

NICE GUIDE

A hub of old-world Provençal glamour

taste
PAN BAGNAT

A lunchtime staple, the *pan bagnat* (literal translation, 'bathed bread'), is essentially a *salade niçoise* in a roll. Its exact composition is hotly disputed at every bakery and snack-bar counter across Nice, but *les essentiels* are tuna fish, black olives, tomato, anchovies and slices of boiled egg in a powdery roll which has been drenched in olive oil and rubbed in garlic.

culture
PALAIS LASCARIS

Hidden among the bars and boutiques of Nice's Old Town is the gloriously lavish Palais Lascaris, a baroque palace with a collection of gilded furniture from the 17th and 18th centuries alongside rare musical instruments. Walk up the twisting grand staircase between Atlantes and Caryatids, where the walls are mesmeric *trompe-l'oeil,* and the frescoed ceiling includes a depiction of Mercury carrying Psyche to Olympus.

explore
QUARTIER DES MUSICIENS

Lined with elegant belle-époque buildings, art deco apartments and art nouveau *palais*, the Quartier des Musiciens is an open-air gallery of Nice's finest winter-resort architecture. North is rue Beethoven; to the south, rue Verdi and rue Rossini cross rue Berlioz and rue Gounod; Lenin and Chekhov stayed in the Hotel Oasis on the latter. In between is where French tennis star Suzanne Lenglen learnt to play the game on a court that is now Place Mozart, a park with a raised lawn and exotic palms which provide shade for the neighbourhood's miniature dogs.

buy
PERFUME

Nice is the showcase for the region's perfumes – distilled essence of Provençal lavender, scents of mimosa, jasmine, and rosewater from Grasse. The Molinard perfumery on rue Saint-François de Paul runs workshops where you can create your own bespoke fragrance; at Fragonard on the cours Saleya, bottles of perfume and matching beauty creams are surrounded by silk scarves, dressing gowns, washbags and monogrammed slippers.

"Distilled essence of lavender, with scents of mimosa and jasmine"

nightlife
RUE BONAPARTE

Rue Bonaparte comes alive after dark. Three blocks north of the port, this blue-painted street has a jazzy assortment of restaurants and rainbow-flagged bars, a meeting place for Nice's in-crowd, antique dealers from the rue Ségurane, and crew from the nearby superyachts. Napoleon stayed there in 1794, preparing his troops for their assault into Italy while he seduced the teenage daughter of his host, Count Laurenti, in what is now the courtyard of L'Abeille hotel.

THE MEDITERRANEAN

→ The old port in Menton, the last stop on the Côte d'Azur before Italy and home to a Fête du Citron (Lemon Festival) each winter.

↘ A view 430m down towards Saint-Jean-Cap-Ferrat from the Jardin Exotique d'Èze, established in the ruins of a medieval fortress.

THE CORNICHES TOWARDS MENTON

Three roads head east from Nice towards Menton and the Italian border. The Grande Corniche is a twisting route high above the coast which rises to La Trophée des Alpes, a broken circle of white Doric columns that celebrated Emperor Augustus' victory over 45 of the local Alpine tribes. Plundered for stones when the Roman Empire fell in 476 CE, the site lost its magnificence but is high enough to give views of Monaco, the Alps and far-off Liguria.

Halfway down to the sea is the Moyenne Corniche; its midpoint is Èze, a village built on a spiral of cobbles and crags – philosopher Friedrich Nietzsche appeared here in 1883 after scrambling up the steep slope from the waterfront. His eponymous path is now semi-paved as visitors with daypacks climb between Èze and the Basse Corniche coast road below. The Riviera wouldn't hit its golden age for another few decades, but by the late 19th century there were already belle-époque villas along the waterfront, hosting winter parties for the British and European upper classes.

The Basse Corniche is for poseurs in open-topped sports cars and day-trippers heading to Villefranche-sur-Mer for a seafood lunch, or afternoon tea at the Villa Ephrussi de Rothschild in Saint-Jean-Cap-Ferrat, a sumptuous palace in ivory and pinks where rows of musical fountains soar to the sound of classical music.

Just before Menton, the three corniches become one, swallowed up in Monaco's tunnels as the coast road crosses into Italy above the Balzi Rossi caves.

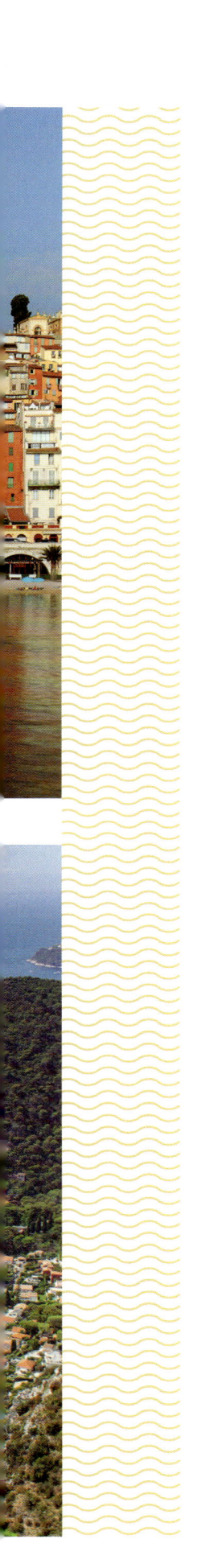

FRANCE

local angle
Musée Matisse

'Born in Le Cateau-Cambrésis in the northeast of France in 1869, Henri Matisse discovered the Mediterranean at the turn of the 20th century. He wasn't initially meant to become an artist but, in his twenties, he took art classes and attended academies. It was after the Salon d'Automne in 1905, when he'd become one of the Fauves, that people began to collect his art. During the 1930s, he was still considered a radical artist.

'After WWII, a period during which he remained in Nice, Matisse was portrayed as something of a hero in the press, becoming an important cultural figure in the city.

'He believed Nice was a collage of everything typical of the Mediterranean, a prosperous place where there was cinema, art, entertaining things to do and the Riviera, a huge draw to collectors and fellow artists like Renoir, Picasso and Bonnard. He loved the constancy of the light in Nice and would often drive into the city's Arrière-pays (back country) in a car.

'Matisse first came to Nice in 1917, staying in hotels on the seafront before moving to an apartment on the cours Saleya in 1921, and then to the Régina in Cimiez on the hill above the city, where he had his studio. Matisse's heirs planned to donate this to Nice, to make it accessible to students, but it wasn't to be, so the City of Nice acquired a hilltop mansion, the Villa des Arènes, and converted it into the Matisse museum (above) which opened in 1963. The collection includes paintings, cut-out papers, drawings, engravings, photographs and sculptures, as well as numerous objects of Matisse's personal collection.'
Aymeric Jeudy, director of the Musée Matisse, Nice

THE MEDITERRANEAN

MONACO GUIDE

Surprises beyond the principality's glitz

buy
F1 MEMORABILIA

Tickets for the Monaco Grand Prix can be astronomically expensive, but Formula One memorabilia is the perfect souvenir from this car-obsessed place. Ferrari caps, polo shirts, autographed helmets and model racing cars fill racks and shelves at the Prince's Automobile Collection museum on the Port Hércule, a few metres from where the F1 cars speed past every May.

explore
LE ROCHER

The streets are spotless on Le Rocher, site of the Palais Princier de Monaco, a Genoese fort turned into royal apartments, with mounds of polished cannonballs outside and a changing of the guard every lunchtime. Visitors can watch jellyfish revolving in a giant tank at the Principality's magnificent Musée Océanographique (above), while Hibernophiles can pore over a pea-green first edition of James Joyce's *Ulysses* (1922) in the equally spotless Princess Grace Irish Library situated close by.

nightlife
SASS CAFÉ

Drift down the slope to the east of the Place du Casino, past the high rollers' lounge, Buddha Bar and Fairmont Hotel, on past the family Italian restaurants on the rue du Portier, to the avenue Princesse Grace and along to the SASS Café. This alluring piano bar and late-night venue is smothered in burgundy leather and leopard-print, and hosts A-list celebrities, their presence eternalised by the owner's private photographer. Take the lift to Twiga Monte Carlo nightclub before dancing till dawn at Jimmy'z.

culture
FRANCIS BACON

In tune with the discrete flamboyance of the British artist, the Francis Bacon MB Art Foundation opens only by appointment made well in advance but possesses the world's largest collection of his early paintings, furniture, letters and photographs. Bacon lived in Monaco from 1946 until the early '50s but returned regularly until 1990, just two years before his death. He loved the Mediterranean sea air and visiting the casino, believing gambling's element of chance was equally crucial to his artistic creation.

taste
L'ORANGERIE

Monaco's crop of bitter oranges used to be traded with passing ships to stave off scurvy; today, they're hand-picked in January and February, washed, peeled and infused in alcohol to produce L'Orangerie, the tangy orange liqueur made by La Distillerie de Monaco. The distillery, located down a back street in la Condamine, offers tastings and cocktail counsel.

"Gambling's element of chance was crucial to his artistic creation"

TRIESTE
Veneto
VENICE
Liguria
Emilia-Romagna
GENOA
RAVENNA
CINQUE TERRE
ADRIATIC SEA
VENTIMIGLIA
San Marino
PISA
ANCONA
Tuscany
Le Marche
LIGURIAN SEA
PARCO NAZIONALE DEL GARGANO
Abruzzo
Lazio
ROME
Campania
NAPLES
MT VESUVIUS
AMALFI
Sardinia
BARBAGIA
CAGLIARI
TYRRHENIAN SEA
PALERMO
MT ETNA
Sicily

CHAPTER THREE

ITALY

NOBLE PALACES OF GENOA ～ **WALKING THE CINQUE TERRE**
LIGURIAN WINE ～ **SARDINIA'S BEACHES** ～ **ROMAN TUSCANY**
SFOGLIATELLA IN NAPLES ～ **AMALFI COAST ROAD TRIP**
PUGLIESE OLIVES ～ **SICILY BY RAIL** ～ **VENETIAN CICCHETTI**

BARI
Puglia
LECCE

Calabria

IONIAN SEA

THE MEDITERRANEAN

→ Vieste is a clifftop town in the Gargano National Park of southeast Italy, overlooking the Adriatic.

The landmass of Italy and the Mediterranean Sea are deeply linked, covering some 7900km (4910 miles) of coastline. The ancient Romans named that sea the Mare Nostrum (Our Sea), and the great maritime republics of Genoa and Venice proved them right: in varied ways, navigators who left from these shores can be said to have created so much of the modern world. And what a world they left behind them.

The dramatic Alpine cliffs in the northwest morph into technicolour towns that never lose their allure, no matter how often we see them – on paper, on screen or in person. Go south and myths of Greek gods, goddesses and sirens mix with abundant meals served at tables that miraculously always seem to have room for more. Across the Strait of Messina, Sicily is a living monument to so many emigrants, so many navigators who lost and found their way. And in the distance, Sardinia is less an island than a world unto itself, where giants are said to have once roamed.

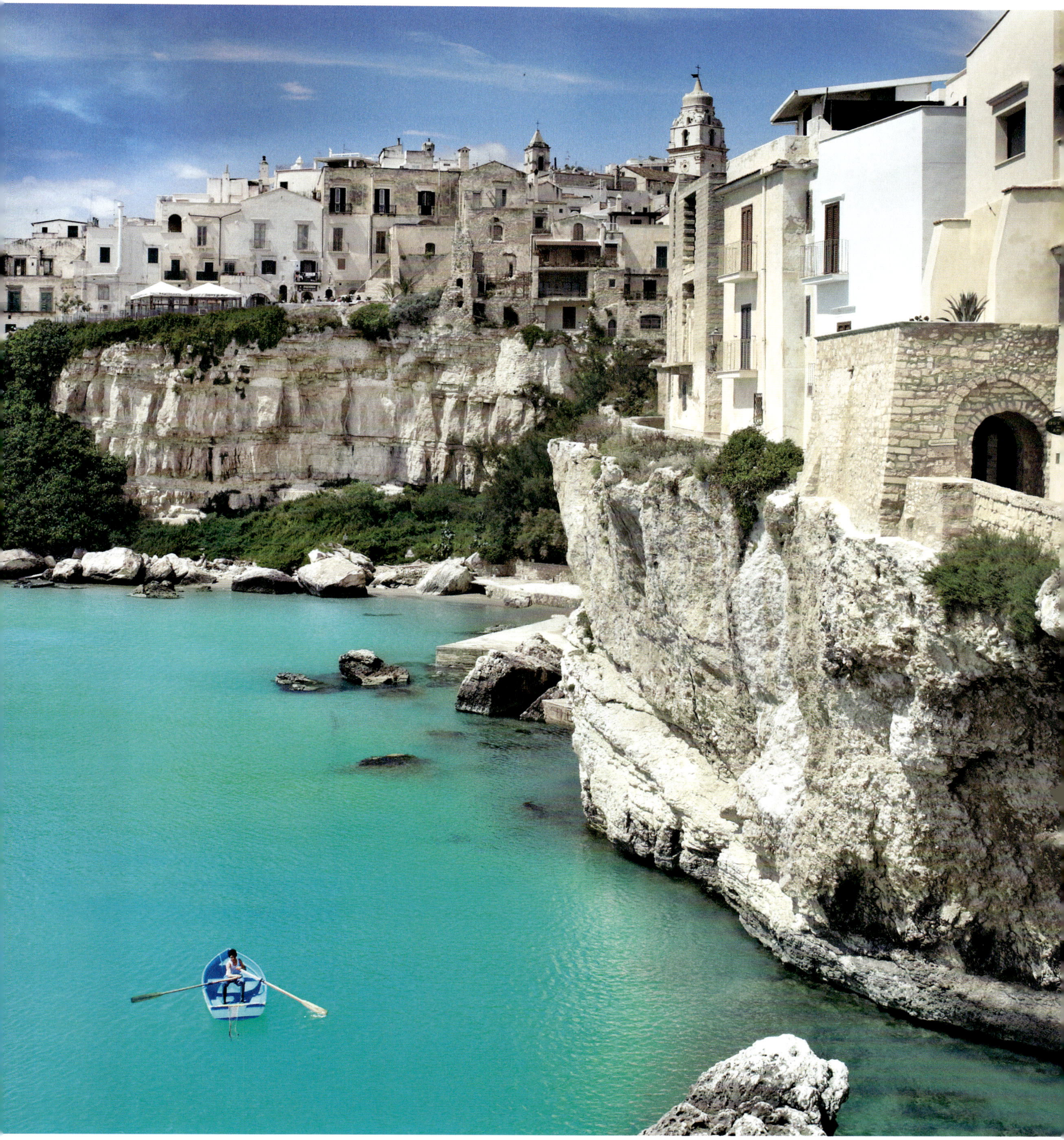

THE MEDITERRANEAN

↓ The SS1 passes Capo Noli, by the vivid waters of the Ligurian Sea. This 697km (433-mile) road connects the French border with Rome.

THE NORTHERN COAST TO GENOA

The town of Ventimiglia was originally known as Album Intimilium, the ancient capital of the Ligurian Intimilii tribe. Today, it's the gateway between France and Italy, just 7km (4 miles) shy of the border and with a distinct sense of sitting between two worlds. Its Friday market once traded cattle but is now known for Italian perfumes, shoes, clothes and bags at suspiciously low prices. Like all liminal spaces, Ventimiglia feels slightly outside of jurisdiction, as if answerable only to the great blue expanse in front of it.

This is perhaps because the act of driving the coastal SS1 highway is as close as one can expect to get to walking on water. The ancient Via Aurelia cleaves in and out of the mountains here, mirroring the road at many points along its sinuous 160km (99 mile) journey between Ventimiglia and Genoa.

This four-hour stretch is definitely not for faint-of-heart drivers, but the rewards include hiking stops at the Passeggiata degli Innamorati and particularly memorable views of the Saraceni Bay, both of which seem designed to make you feel small but not insignificant.

Alternatively, the option of taking a Genoa-bound train along the Ligurian Riviera from Ventimiglia allows you to sit back and watch the beautiful seaside scenes unfold through the window, a book left untouched on your lap as those transfixing views glide by. Be sure to step off at the halfway point in Savona, a port city that specialises in *panissa* and *farinata*, both moreish chickpea-based snacks. Compare those and pair them with a glass of Colline Savonesi, a local white wine with plenty of bite. Just the thing for toasting the sea ahead. **CONTINUED ON P88 »**

know-how

The Caruggi of Genoa

Caruggi (alleyways) meander down to the port of Genoa. Here ambushes were once set to help defend the city's maritime wealth.

Getting lost in the maze of suffocatingly narrow streets within the oldest part of Genoa is practically de rigueur, given the city was designed in the 9th century with precisely this intention. Known as *caruggi*, the ancient system of alleys were defensive fortifications against pirate invasions, a frequent concern during Genoa's rise to a maritime republic. The *sestieri* (neighbourhoods) closest to the sea were built to enclose and bewilder anyone who did not belong there, making it impossible to penetrate the city above.

But built environments are not benign, and the *caruggi* began to take on sinister qualities that loomed large under the cover of night. Dark corners meant shady dealings, and the allure of conquest became just as attractive for many *genovesi* as it did for those arriving from foreign lands. Before long the *caruggi* became a universe apart, where pirates could come for a night with one of the *maddalena*, the women who worked in the shadows.

Genova's maritime prowess faded in the 19th century, the *caruggi* lost their strategic significance, and degradation crept in. However, the city has begun to breathe life into the narrow airways of these streets, and today people are far more welcoming than wary. But in the stillness of a sultry summer night, the *caruggi* still have a sense of the forbidden, and it is thrilling to bask in this hazy glow. Listen closely and you can almost hear the cacophony of voices coming into port, bringing the world to ground.

THE MEDITERRANEAN

GENOA GUIDE

A port city built on medieval riches

taste
PESTO

Originally invented as a means for sailors to transport herbs with them on board ship and so stave off malnourishment, pesto has become the signature dish in Genovese cuisine. But its influences mirror the world in which it was created: basil from India, pecorino from Sardinia, garlic from ancient Rome.

buy
A PAIR OF JEANS

If there were a fabric with which to weave together the Mediterranean, it would be the rough-hewn cotton-and-linen blend that gave the world jeans, christened for the city that invented them (Gênes being the French name for Genoa). For centuries we have sailed the seas, conquered the Earth and buttoned our flies clad in strong and durable denim: carry on the tradition by picking up a pair from source on the so-called Via del Jeans in Genoa's centre.

explore
STRADE NUOVE

In its medieval heyday, Genoa was effectively the first World Bank, and the glorious architecture of the Strade Nuove ('New Streets', which include Via Garibaldi) just north of the port was a testament to this power. Now a UNESCO World Heritage site, the Palazzi dei Rolli here are a collection of noble palaces, many of which have been transformed into public museums. Some of the *palazzi* are privately owned, but do occasionally open their doors to visitors (you can arrange access via appointments booked through the museums).

> *"It has always been a city built to look outwards, on towards the sea"*

culture
GALATA MUSEO DEL MARE

Throughout its complicated life cycle, Genoa has been both the seat of untold riches and a den of global iniquity. But it has always been a city built to look outwards: far beyond the confines of the jagged mountains that separate it from the rest of Italy, and on towards the sea. This maritime history may not be quite so palpable these days, but the high-tech exhibits of Galata Museo del Mare at the Porto Antico manage to bring to life a compelling story of Genoa's seafaring past.

nightlife
PIAZZA DEL ERBE

No matter the starting point, nights out in Genoa tend to finish in Piazza delle Erbe (below), a spectral square in the heart of the medieval centre. Once the hectic vegetable market, the *piazza* is now a multigenerational spot for *movida*, the particularly Italian term for nightlife with a touch of ruckus that never goes too far. Sit with a spritz or dance under the Putto fountain – and don't worry about keeping the beat. In this town, they've seen it all.

THE MEDITERRANEAN

→ The town of Portofino has been a draw for Europe's aristocracy (and associated people-watchers) since the 19th century.

↘ The Gothic-style Chiesa di San Pietro in Porto Venere was built in 1198 on the site of a 5th-century-CE Christian church.

THE LIGURIAN COAST TO LA SPEZIA
Though the Ligurian Riviera is 350km (217 miles) long, the 80km (50-mile) stretch from Genoa to La Spezia is concentrated mystique. At tiny Boccadasse, just 5km (3 miles) from the centre, the shift in mood is palpable. The steep lanes that connect land to sea, described by singer Fabrizio de Andrè as *Crêuza de mä* (sea alleys) in his famous song of the same name, create haunting tunnels where the wind whistles sharply.

The Via Aurelia continues south but travel around here is by sea. This coast enjoys an unfair distribution of beauty, as if divine breath blew too hard and forgot how much more of the world needed to be covered. Vivid emerald waters around Portofino seem almost to tug at the tumbling town, pulling it into the deep, inspired perhaps by the Med-submerged statue of Jesus at the nearby Abbazia di San Fruttuoso.

Heading south, the towns of the Cinque Terre are slung along a 40km (25-mile) stretch of coast: though they have become well-trodden steps on the tourist circuit, they remain radiant from the sea. The playfulness of pastel houses perched on vertiginous cliffs creates a cognitive dissonance only poets could unravel in their verse.

And so they did. Some 20km (12 miles) on south, the Castello Doria at Porto Venere feels haunted by the ghost of Lord Byron, one of many literary giants – including Percy Bysshe Shelley – who lived in the area. The Gulf of Poets, lying before La Spezia's industrial harbour, still manages to evoke those romantic verses of Grand-Tour yearning as it winds into the wild Tuscan coast. **CONTINUED ON P90 »**

know-how
Ruling the Seas
~~~

The maritime republics of Venice, Pisa, Amalfi and Genoa each excelled in conquering the seas during the Middle Ages, but it was in Genoa where Mediterranean trade flourished. Nicknamed both La Superba (The Superb) and La Dominante (The Dominant), Genoa's power was displayed through brilliance, whether in the shine of its coin or the glimmer of its sword. One of the earliest colonial powers in the world, the Republic of Genoa made the innovative decision to switch to banking and finance as its main source of overseas revenue, a move that allowed it to prosper for centuries.

But Genoa was much more than a medieval coin purse, and its legacy reaches far beyond its shores. The Galata Tower in İstanbul, now an icon of the city, was a Genovese watchtower. Once the emblem of the Republic, the St George's Cross was adopted by the English, who have used it since the Crusades. And none have forgotten the Genovese explorer and navigator Christopher Columbus (depicted below), who sailed the ocean until he stumbled upon a New World.

There is a word that Genovese people evoke to describe themselves: *mugugno*, a grumbler, followed by the observation that, 'It's not a coincidence that Liguria is shaped like a frown.' Perhaps that not inconsiderable quantity of vinegar coursing through the Genovese bloodstream is fed by a sense of innate restlessness.

THE MEDITERRANEAN

→ The smallest of the villages of the Cinque Terre, Corniglia is reached by walkers via the 383 brick steps of the Lardarina.

↘ A sign on the trail between Volastra and Corniglia; the route takes in compact vineyards and views 100m down to the sea.

WALKING THE CINQUE TERRE
Though you could (and should) see the Ligurian coastline from the sea, the cluster of five small towns known as the Cinque Terre are best experienced on foot. It will take longer and you'll need to pack lighter, but nothing allows you to feel more immersed in this extraordinary setting than to feel the earth beneath your feet.

The Parco Nazionale delle Cinque Terre is crossed by more than 120km (74 miles) of trails but, by patching together some of the routes, it's possible to visit all five towns in a full-day hike. Starting from Monterosso, the largest of the towns, it's a 4km (2.5-mile) walk to colourful yet rugged Vernazza, the footpath traversing one of the ancient stone bridges that shepherds used centuries ago, and threading through an unforgiving landscape that gives a sense of how difficult life once was here. Head south and slightly inland for 3.5km (2 miles) towards Corniglia, a rocky outcrop at the halfway point in the Cinque Terre. From here, there's a steep climb up to Volastra (a shuttle bus provides a less strenuous alternative) before the route descends through vineyards and olive groves towards Manarola, a perfect patchwork of colour perched 70m above the sea.

The final stretch is the famed Via dell'Amore, a 1km (0.6 mile) trail that has opened again after decades of restoration and ends in Riomaggiore, the southernmost town of the Cinque Terre. There you'll find a cluster of candy-coloured buildings set into the hills, where sailboats bob in the port and the restaurants lining Via Colombo wait for the catch of the day to come in. **CONTINUED ON P94 »**

local angle
Liguria's Underwater Wines

'We talk about the importance of terroir for wines, and how the earth gives them a particular character. Well, what about the sea? I think of it as *mareoir*, the character that the sea imparts through the gentle process of underwater maturation.

'I only age sparkling wines underwater, because they are the only wines that truly benefit from being placed in this environment. Indeed, this idea started because I wanted to begin making sparkling wine, but I needed a place to do it. Due to my background as an art history professor, I began to think of the discoveries of amphorae in the sea, how they retained liquid and indeed how it was still intact. The idea began to form: to let the wine rest in the depths of the sea.

'This part of the Ligurian coast, near Portofino, is uniquely suited to an idea like this because it's very deep right off the shore. We lower the wine into a perfectly controlled environment, 60m under the sea. The temperature is a steady 15°C, there's very little light, and the currents lull the bottles, allowing the sediment to move just enough. Those things, coupled with the absence of oxygen and a depth-pressure that creates a perfect balance between what's inside and out of the bottle, means the wine matures almost in harmony with itself. It's as if wine was meant to be joined with the sea.'
Pierluigi Lugano, winemaker and founder of Bisson Winery, Sestri Levante

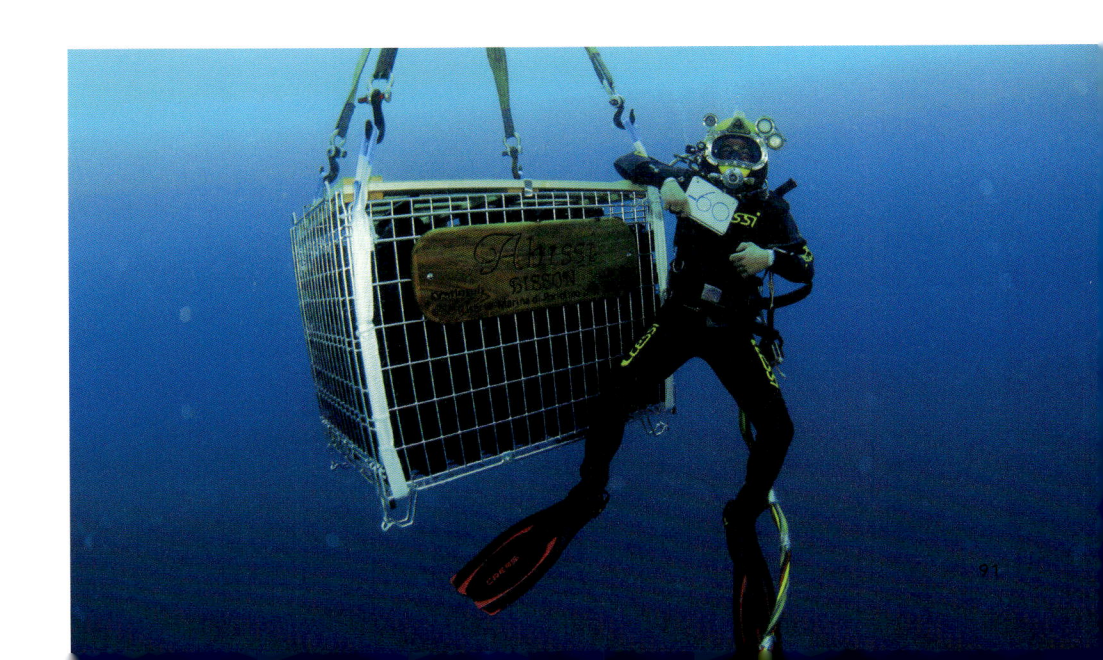

THE MEDITERRANEAN

SARDINIA GUIDE

From azure shallows to mountain heritage

beach
LA PELOSA

The term 'paradise' gets overused – which is a shame, because La Pelosa is simply one of the finest beaches in the world and few other words do it justice. Lapping the shoreline near the northwestern tip of Sardinia, the turquoise water is so shallow and placid that you can walk to the squat 15th-century tower that sits 150m offshore.

base
CAGLIARI

Cities that seem to grow out of the sea itself possess – and are possessed – by an energy so unique that it is almost intoxicating. Cagliari (above) is one of these cities, and the ideal place to ground yourself on the island. From the quaint Castello district lying above to the sultry Marina quarter below, and to the pristine beaches within walking distance of the city centre, Cagliari represents the soul of Sardinia.

activity
SPOTTING NURAGHI

As you travel through Sardinia, you'll see strange recurring structures that look like they could have been part of a Stonehenge tribute band. These are *nuraghi*, round Bronze Age constructions built from slabs of stone that are unique to the island. The greatest remaining assemblage of them is at Su Nuraxi di Barumini, roughly 60km (37 miles) north of Cagliari, where a central tower dating to 1500 BCE is surrounded by circular interlocking buildings tumbling down a hillside.

explore
BARBAGIA

Every year, the Autumn in Barbagia festival invites the world to dive into some of Sardinia's most deeply held artisanal, gastronomic and cultural traditions. From September to December, the cluster of 31 towns that belong to this extraordinary region in the central, mountainous Nuoro are alive with musical performances, displays of arts and crafts, and feasts of roast suckling pig.

"One of the finest beaches in the world – few words can do it justice"

secret
ISOLA DI SAN PIETRO

Sardinia has many faces but its Isola di San Pietro (St Peter's Island), just off the coast of Sant'Antioco in the southwest, is the one that stares wide-eyed into the rest of the Mediterranean. The town of Carloforte here was founded by shipping scions from just outside Genoa, who shared permission to settle the island with fishing families from Tabarka in Tunisia. Carloforte maintains strong links to Liguria, evident in its unique language and dishes like lasagne made with local red tuna and pesto. The narrow streets end in gentle slopes, hinting at the world beyond.

THE MEDITERRANEAN

ANCIENT SITES ON THE TUSCAN COAST

The Tuscan coastline bears little resemblance to the rolling hills and neatly manicured vineyards that spring to mind when visualising central Italy. Instead, the 230km (143 miles) that run from Carrara to Capalbio are a tangle of twisted curves, soggy marshland and craggy cliffside bungalows that cling to the mountains like Mediterranean scrub. Napoleon's Elba sits just off the coast of Punta Ala, 100km (62 miles) south of Livorno and close enough to imagine his longing. As you wind your way south, swimming coves peek out from under giant pine trees; pause for some *spaghetti alla bottarga* at the I Pescatori di Orbetello co-operative, where mullet roe is cured and turned into this local delicacy.

The Tuscany shore is also one of Italy's oldest inhabited coastlines. The Etruscan civilisation that pre-dated the Romans lorded over the centre from Tarquinia, named for one of its greatest rulers and now a quaintly pastoral town 100km (62 miles) from Rome, just north of the massive necropolis at Cerveteri.

Not to be outdone, the Romans then established one of their most important ports at Ostia, today a sprawling archaeological site and absolutely worth a stop on any trip. You might even catch a concert at the ancient amphitheatre, set against the backdrop of pines.

But once you pass Rome, expect the land and sea to begin to dance together to a different tune. Where the northern coast is defiant, the south becomes supple. Somewhere around Terracina, you'll spot that the sand starts to soften and the turquoise waters brighten, together hinting at what lies ahead. **CONTINUED ON P98 »**

↓ The ruins of Ostia Antica (Ancient Ostia), once the sea port of Rome at the mouth of the Tiber. The site now lies inland due to silting.

know-how
The Myth of Parthenope

During his epic journey home after the Trojan War, the mythical hero Odysseus and his men were caught by a trio of sirens who attempted to enchant the sailors with an intoxicating song that would compel them to walk overboard and drown. Odysseus, no stranger to strange events, blocked his men's ears with wax and tied himself to his ship's mast so that he could hear the song but resist being coaxed into the deep. His gambit worked. Upon failing to seduce the men, the siren Parthenope drowned in despair. When her body was brought to shore it was absorbed into the earth, giving life to the city that would bear her name until the Greeks called it Neapolis (now Naples), the new city, in the 6th century BCE. How's that for an origin story?

Though the details of the story are hazy, the myth of Parthenope belies the intimate connection that Neapolitans have to the sea. The Mediterranean exerts a mystic, almost supernatural presence in daily life along the coast here. After all, even though Odysseus resisted Parthenope, legend has it he built monuments in her honour on the coast she created. Later on, the ancient Romans would evoke her name to explain the anger of the god Jupiter, who created Vesuvius when the mermaid did not return his love. Perhaps it's no coincidence that so many still dream of coming here: the siren's song retains its bewitching potency today.

THE MEDITERRANEAN

NAPLES GUIDE

Explore an ancient, revitalising city

taste
SFOGLIATELLA

Although the *sfogliatella* was technically invented in a monastery on the Amalfi Coast, this delectable treat has become a perfect symbol of Naples. The delicate layers of pastry form a clamshell shape that covers a rich, dense creamy middle with touches of citrus throughout. Grab one as soon as you arrive at the Central Station or sample a few throughout the day.

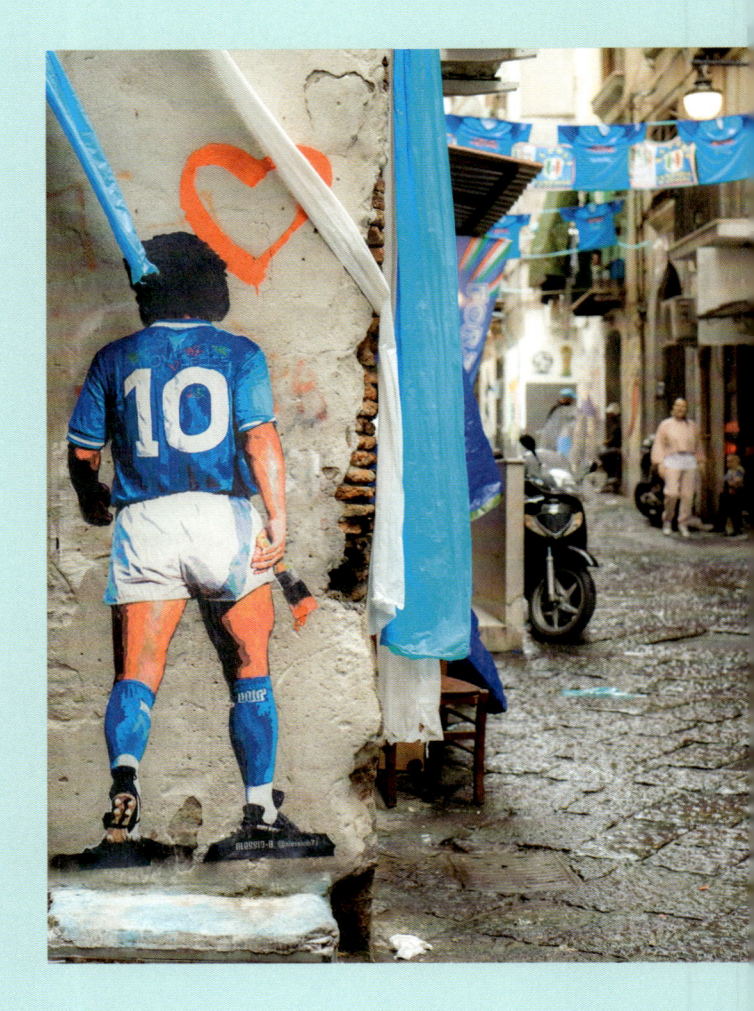

explore
QUARTIERI SPAGNOLI

For decades the Quartieri Spagnoli was known as a densely populated grid of impassable alleys cloaked in the spectre of malfeasance. But the neighbourhood has risen and is now home to some of the finest street art in Naples, centred around near-sacred murals of the city's SSC Napoli football hero (above) on so-called Piazza Maradona, along Via Emanuele de Deo. Pause to listen to the buzz of life here.

culture
FEAST OF SAN GENNARO

The blood of Naples' patron saint, San Gennaro, is said to have been saved by a devotee after his death in 305 CE; today, it's the focus of the city's Feast of San Gennaro, which takes place three times a year. On the first Saturday in May, 19 September, and 16 December, thousands of faithful flock to Naples' ancient centre, crowding into the Duomo for a glimpse of the miraculous liquefaction of this precious relic, known here as the 'treasure'.

> *"This delectable treat has become a perfect symbol of Naples. Sample a few throughout the day"*

nightlife
MERGELLINA

The Mergellina neighbourhood stretches along the coastline and evokes a nostalgia for a bygone era when fishers would bring in their daily catch here as the sun went down. Take a seat at one of the chalets that have been feeding revellers for decades – whether with crispy, spiced *taralli* biscuits and a beer, or the legendary *graffa*, sweet doughnuts whose aroma mingles with the salt air.

buy
NATIVITY MINIATURES

Wander along Via San Gregorio Armeno (below), one of Naples' Roman-era *decumani* (east–west roads) and famous for the handmade nativity scenes that have been crafted in workshops here for centuries. These days you can also expect to see bobbleheads of public figures alongside miniatures of baby Jesus, giving it the unmistakable atmosphere of something akin to a seaside fever dream.

CIRCLING VESUVIUS

At the time of writing, Mt Vesuvius hasn't erupted in 80 years and the last major event was in 1631, but as you navigate the Gulf of Naples it will loom large. Industrial centres like Torre del Greco or Torre Annunziata are palimpsests on an ancient canvas, dividing the foot of Vesuvius from the Gulf of Naples. A maritime hub that rose from the ashes of a town destroyed alongside Pompeii, sprawling Castellammare di Stabia now delineates the beginning of the Sorrento Coast. Climb Monte Faito, 18km (11 miles) to the south, or hike through the Monti Lattari range, 22km (14 miles) further, and you need only look down to see the pumice pebbles that flew through the air to land here in 79 CE.

The Gulf of Naples was formed around Vesuvius, and travel here is measured by how well you can see the volcano and from what side it appears in your view. From Ercolano, plan to climb (or drive) to the summit, where vineyards cling to the rocky soil, then you can peer into the peacefully sleeping crater. Arrive here in September to witness the harvest of Lacryma Christi grapes, or tour the famous unearthed Roman ruins at the volcano's feet, from Herculaneum (buried under an immense pyroclastic flow during that cataclysmic eruption of 79 CE) to Pompeii (which fell to a similar fate at the same time).

But to feel Vesuvius, and understand the visceral power it holds over those that live around it, you must look into the eyes of a Neapolitan the first time they spot it after a trip abroad. They may seem to calculate the distance through invisible maths, fractions of time when they did not see its towering peak. Though it slumbers, Vesuvius is alive. **CONTINUED ON P100 »**

↑ Mt Vesuvius viewed at sunrise, with Naples lying 9km (6 miles) beyond and the Valle del Gigante (Giant's Valley) to the fore.

know-how

Campi Flegrei Caldera

↑ A Roman statue and a mosaic of wrestlers at the Villa a Protiro appear at the Baiae Sommersa underwater archaeological site.

Just west of Naples, Campi Flegrei is one of the oldest settlements in Italy and also one of the most seismically active places in the world. This is a massive crater – really a sinkhole – that includes eight towns and the islands of Ischia and Procida. Here the Parco Archeologico di Cuma preserves the first ancient Greek settlement outside of Greece: founded in the 8th century BCE, it was where much of Virgil's *Aeneid* is thought to have been written. But it's even more impressive below the waves: the Baiae Sommersa is an underwater archaeological site with immaculately preserved ruins of Roman villas that once stood on shore.

How those villas got there is what makes Campi Flegrei so special, and so fascinating. The seismic activity here is known as bradyseism (from the Greek for 'slow movement'), whereby the Earth's surface lifts and sinks as magma flows empty and fill subterranean chambers. This movement creates a ripple along the ground, at times dramatic: the tremors that sunk the town of Baiae in 1538 lasted a week and resulted in the birth of Monte Nuovo, the youngest volcano in mainland Europe.

THE MEDITERRANEAN

→ The harbour of Vico Equense; the town itself rises 1000m up on cliffs of tuff rock, formed from compacted volcanic ash.

↘ By the Gulf of Salerno, Punta Campanella is a marine nature reserve with beds of seagrass and around 50 submerged caves.

TOWARDS THE AMALFI COAST

Naples is separated from the tip of the Sorrento Peninsula by less than 70km (43 miles), but that distance feels considerably greater. Perhaps this is because you could spend eternity inching your way around the Gulf of Naples and never tire of the history, the food or the scenery that you'll encounter.

Just 10km (6 miles) south of Naples, the archaeological ruins at Herculaneum are a smaller snapshot of the 79-CE eruption of Mt Vesuvius that consumed Roman cities including Pompeii. Herculaneum was a wealthier enclave at the time, and many residents sought refuge on the beach below the city; this recently restored area allows you to walk in their ancient footsteps.

Whether you travel by car or the famed Circumvesuviana train, Vico Equense lies another 30km (19 miles) south and is what many consider to be Italy's best city for food. That's saying quite a lot, but when you've got Michelin-starred chefs and the L'Università della Pizza restaurant and cooking school in the same town, there's reason to brag.

But whatever you might have seen along the way will pale in comparison to Punta Campanella, 25km (15 miles) south of Vico Equense and accessible only by footpath. This southernmost point of the Sorrento Peninsula is arguably its most dramatic: the island of Capri rises grandly in front of you, separated only by the shimmering waters of that mythical sea. There is a temple of the goddess Athena here, and legend has it that Odysseus built it with his own hand. Soaking up the views, it's easy to understand why this spot was chosen. **CONTINUED ON P106 »**

local angle
The Last Master Builder

'My father didn't want me to be a boatbuilder, even though it was his work and that of his father before him. Meta was once a place where half the people who lived here worked at sea, and the most prestigious thing one could become was a captain. He wanted that for me, but what can you do? Building boats was in me.

'The frame, the skeleton of the *gozzo* (a traditional wooden boat), must be made from mulberry wood, which was planted around Sorrento to feed silkworms. Today it's much harder to find, but we still use it because this is the only suitable wood.

'The ships that were built at the Alimuri beach in the 19th century were not huge. Where people now go to swim, there were seven or eight at any time being worked on. This was where they would load goods and crew before heading to Naples to take passengers emigrating to America. Today people come here for an *aperitivo* or to lay under an umbrella in the summer but back then, this was a place that worked day and night. Wood is a living thing, and the work of building a boat from wood is never done.'
Michele Cafiero, *maestro d'ascia* (master builder) of *gozzi* in Meta di Sorrento

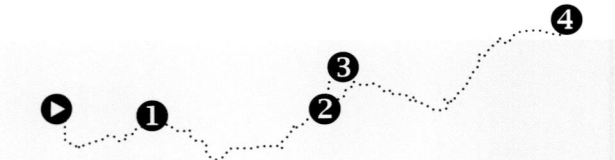

THE AMALFI COAST

A drive along one of Italy's most celebrated coastal stretches

Distance 59km (37 miles)
Duration Three days
Start Piano di Sorrento
Finish Salerno

❶ Positano
The Strada Statale 145 (or SS145) is sometimes known as the 'Road of a Thousand Curves', and it won't take long to work out why: you'll lose count of the switchbacks. As you set off from Piano di Sorrento (avoid Sorrento itself, as the traffic is incessant) and climb the curves toward San Pietro, you're welcomed with glimpses of the sapphire Gulf of Salerno. Take your time getting used to the road on this stretch but do enjoy it, because these are spectacular views. Positano itself is like a dream come to life, clinging to cliffs in pastel relief. Park for the night at Positano's Parcheggio di Gennaro and perhaps reward yourself with a stay at the swish Hotel Murat. *11km (7 miles)*

❷ Amalfi
The stretch of road southeast of Positano might feel ripped from every daydream you've had of making this drive. As you leave Li Galli islands in the distance, head straight (ish) for the indomitable Fiordi di Furore, a natural cove crested by the road and a popular photograph stop. If you've snagged a car as glamorous as an Alfa Romeo Spider, now's the time to let the top down and go for lunch in tiny Marina di Praia. Roll into Amalfi by late afternoon when the tour buses clear out and the alleyways feel like just the place where secrets would have been shared. Watch the sunset from the main Marina Grande beach and gaze at the terraces framing this ancient maritime republic. *17km (11 miles)*

❸ Ravello
Heading out from Amalfi, plan to take a slight detour from the Statale and ride up to Ravello, the city of music that overlooks the coast from magnificent heights. From there, descend via the road that takes you to Sal de Riso *pasticceria* in Maiori; around here, pastries are a major food group. *6km (4 miles)*

❹ Salerno
En route to Salerno, grab a table with a view of the boats coming in at Cetara, a fishing village famous for its Roman-origin *colatura di alici* fish sauce. Past the ceramic-crafting streets of Vietri sul Mare, where time is measured by the baking of terracotta, historic Salerno is a genteel breeze of a city, where baroque churches and tiny trattorias envelop a bay that echoes with the addictive bustle of southern Italy. *25km (15 miles)*

ITALY

↖ A classic convertible Alfa Romeo Spider is ideal for this Amalfi Coast drive.

↙ Amalfi town, once the capital of the Duchy of Amalfi, a trading power in medieval times.

THE MEDITERRANEAN

SICILY GUIDE

An island blend of ancient cultures

activity
TRENO DEI VINI DELL'ETNA

What better way to multitask than to take the Treno dei Vini dell'Etna (above), stopping at wineries on the slopes of the volcano for tastings and meals? Board the train at the retro Piedimonte Etneo station, from where it inches past tangles of vines and remnants of the volcano's bursts. Fear not, for there is white (wine) at the end of the tunnel.

secret
ISOLA DI SAN PANTALEO

Just a short ferry hop across briny waters from Marsala, where mountains of salt gather like foam, is San Pantaleo Island. Covered in native scrub and vineyards, this tiny outcrop was once the site of Phoenician Motya, dating from the 8th century BCE and rivalling the great port-cities of Carthage. Of the ancient artefacts displayed at the island's Museo Giuseppe Whitaker, the greatest treasure is *Il Giovinetto di Mozia* (above), a 5th-century-BCE Carthaginian-influenced marble statue of a young man.

beach
VENDICARI

Vendicari, near Noto, is an experience that goes beyond the candy-striped parasols of most Sicilian beaches. Part of a sprawling natural reserve, Vendicari is actually five beaches: take your pick from the turquoise waters of crescent-shaped Eloro or the wild isolation of Marianelli. As you travel between the two, visit flamingo reserves and ancient fisheries.

explore
VALLEY OF THE TEMPLES

The Valley of the Temples in Agrigento is more of a hill, but it's nonetheless home to some of the best-preserved ancient Greek ruins in the world. Wandering among the seven temples and various scattered relics, it's easy to feel as though you've been transported back to a time when gods roamed the Earth and all of them met here. A short way west, a dip in the sea at the famed Scala dei Turchi (Stair of the Turks) is unmissable.

"Palermo is the sum of so much that humanity has managed to fit into our brief history – an extraordinary pastiche"

base
PALERMO

If aliens were to make an official appearance on Earth, we would do well to schedule the meeting in Palermo (the Piazza Bellini is below), for it is the sum of so much that humanity has managed to fit into our brief history. First Phoenician, then in turn Greek, Roman and Arab, Palermo is an extraordinary pastiche of flavour, sound and sensuality. Everything is abundant and will leave you breathless.

THE AMALFI COAST TO PUGLIA

After Salerno, the real adventure of the south begins. After you pass through the cheesemaking capital of Battipaglia (where you can stop just about anywhere for exemplary *mozzarella di bufala*), visit the archaeological ruins of Paestum, 40km (25 miles) south of Salerno and once one of the largest cities in the Magna Graecia. Expect to find three majestic Doric temples, dating from 550 to 450 BCE. Paestum is at the doorstep of the massive Parco Nazionale del Cilento, which encompasses the most pristine stretches of coastline in the country. You could spend days discovering waterfalls in the middle of forests and caves at the mouth of the sea here, but if you bask on one beach make it postcard-pretty Palinuro, 47km (29 miles) south of Paestum.

Turning eastward, the heel of the Italian boot may only be 60km (37 miles) at its widest but the wild country roads here will take considerably longer to navigate, allowing you time to appreciate the otherworldly landscape of Basilicata.

Once you reach the Gulf of Taranto you'll receive the first glimpse of the limpid waters that stream in from the Ionian Sea, setting the region of Puglia apart from the rest of Italy. Indeed, the whole area starts to feel a little Greek: as you cut across land once again, silvery olive trees blanket the landscape and whitewashed towns bake in the fierce southern sun.

You'll start to notice traditional farmhouses known as *masserie* dotting the hills, many converted into characterful places to stop over. These hearken back to a time when agriculture was the lifeblood of Puglia. In many parts, it remains so: once you reach the Adriatic coast, the table is set and waiting. **CONTINUED ON P112 »**

↓ The peaceful Spiaggia Marinella, Palinuro, facing the appropriately named Baia del Buondormire (Good Sleep Bay).

ITALY

↑ Chef Celso Laforgia prepares a dish of cheese-topped, fiery *spaghetti all'assassina* at his L'Assassineria Urbana restaurant.

know-how

Bari's Spaghetti all'Assassina

Like those of all great heroes, the origin story of *spaghetti all'assassina* is a little hazy. Most people agree that it was invented sometime in the 1960s or 1970s, and the consensus is that it was created in Bari by a chef from Foggia who put so much red pepper in this dish that he was branded an assassin by his northern Italian visitors.

What makes *spaghetti all'assassina* so special is not the spice level but the method: instead of being boiled in salted water, the pasta is cooked directly in a cast-iron pan. A thin tomato sauce is slowly added, allowing the pasta to soften by absorbing the liquid, risotto-style. Unlike a traditional pasta dish where the sauce imparts the flavour, it's the spaghetti itself that transforms. Imagine a meal made from the delicious burnt bits on lasagne: crispy, browned, and that you can't stop eating.

Chef Celso Laforgia may not have invented *spaghetti all'assassina*, but in a way he embodies it. His boundless enthusiasm and broad smile remind every person who comes to his L'Assassineria Urbana restaurant in central Bari that food is fun, and the only rule is to make people feel like they belong where they eat.

THE MEDITERRANEAN

BARI GUIDE

The flavours of Puglia's capital

explore
BARI VECCHIA

Though it's recently become more open to tourism, there is something about Bari Vecchia that still feels preserved in time. The alabaster slabs on which this small medieval centre is built reflect light from the Adriatic, and trap the briny smell of the sea in alleyways that all seem to connect with one another. In no time you'll have your favourite bar, and they'll know your usual order.

culture
ORECCHIETTE

In the narrow streets of Bari's medieval centre, the women who sit outdoors making traditional *orecchiette* pasta keep their community alive, trading gossip and watching children as they work. *Orecchiette* are named for their resemblance to tiny ears, with perfect examples only emerging from years of practice and just the right flick of the thumb.

nightlife
PIAZZA MERCANTILE

Some cities dance, others vibrate, and still others quietly glow. Although Piazza Mercantile is one of the most animated squares in Bari and is full of fantastic restaurants, there's an almost gentle hum here as voices bounce off the medieval walls and paving stones. Families circulate on summer nights, greeting each other over the course of a *passeggiata*, and young love shyly glances across crowded lanes.

taste
FOCACCIA BARESE

Every Italian town has its own version but none are quite like *focaccia barese*, which takes the pillowy, crunchy bread you'll find in Genoa and supercharges it with ripe tomatoes, olives and oregano. There's no escaping it wherever you go in the city: every restaurant will have it on the menu and sometimes it will come to the table before you even ask. But then again, weren't you going to order it anyway?

> "Families greet each other over the course of a *passeggiata, and young love shyly glances across crowded lanes*"

buy
PUGLIESE OLIVE OIL

The blood of every Pugliese must be at least half composed of olive oil because more than in any other region in Italy, the population here lives and breathes according to the harvest. Get anyone talking about what kind of olive produces the best oil and you'll be in for hours of animated conversation. Farms all over Puglia sell their own stocks, and stores throughout Bari have a selection of local oils; at Frantoio Vurro, the last remaining oil mill in central Bari, you can watch the production process for yourself.

THROUGH SALENTO

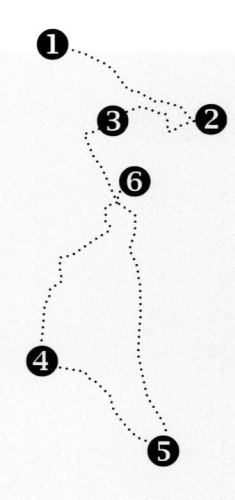

Follow the rhythm of *taranta* music on a drive across southern Puglia

Distance 162km (101 miles)
Duration Five days
Start Lecce
Finish Melpignano

❶ Lecce
The baroque elegance of Lecce is but a cloak for the frenzy that erupts here in summer months, when *taranta* performances and *pizzica* dance take over the central Piazza Libertini. *Taranta* is a traditional folk music from Salento, but it's also catharsis, freedom and community, uniting every town in southern Puglia.

❷ Torre Sant'Andrea
Follow the music to the whitewashed town of Torre Sant'Andrea, where emerald seas vibrate in unison with thumping feet at concerts or spontaneous jams. **30km (19 miles)**

❸ Calimera
Head back inland towards the heart of Grecìa Salentina, a cluster of nine towns that have preserved the Greek-derived Griko dialect for millennia. *Taranta* originated here, where legend has it that the bite of the *Lycosa* tarantula spider could render people (especially unmarried women) hysterical. Many believe that the *pizzica* (spider bite) could only be cured with a choreographic therapy that would incite a trance-like state of frenzy. These traditions are alive in tiny Calimera, where Italian is hardly spoken but every night the music plays and the *pizzica* is danced. **27km (17 miles)**

❹ Ugento
Leave the lush fields around Galatina and head to coastal Ugento, where Crusader shields stand guard at the ancient Cripta del Crocifisso. **34km (21 miles)**

❺ Santa Maria di Leuca
Priestesses are said to have conjured cures for the *Lycosa* tarantula bite at this town on the southeasternmost tip of Italy. Stand at the confluence of the Adriatic and Ionian Seas, where the water runs deep-blue and the faithful dance at the Basilica Santuario di Santa Maria de Finibus Terrae, literally at the 'End of the Land'. **25km (15 miles)**

❻ Melpignano
The region's most famous Griko-speaking community, small-town Melpignano is a magical place all year, but it's most renowned for hosting the August finale of the Notte della Taranta festival, a summer-long series of free performances. Nothing can prepare you for the Concertone, which sees *taranta* groups and global musicians whip a huge crowd into a collective trance. **46km (29 miles)**

ITALY

↖ The baroque-style Basilica di Santa Croce in Lecce; it took 200 years to build.

↙ The Arco degli Innamorati (Lovers' Bow) and sea stacks of Torre Sant'Andrea.

THE MEDITERRANEAN

→ The limestone-perched resort town of Vieste lies at the tip of the Gargano Peninsula, in the Parco Nazionale del Gargano.

↘ The 18th-century Duomo di Ravenna. In 407 CE a cathedral was consecrated here when Ravenna became capital of the Roman Empire.

PUGLIA TO VENICE ALONG THE ADRIATIC

The sandy outcrops of Italy's Adriatic coastline sit in stark contrast to the jagged ridges along the Tyrrhenian, but it's only when you start travelling its length that this all starts fitting together. There's more drama in store: just over 100km (62 miles) north of Bari, the Parco Nazionale del Gargano manages to awaken each sense simultaneously in a thrilling sort of symphony. The greens are so vivid here that you can taste them, lapping at the shore and cresting overhead in the ancient Foresta Umbra.

Almost at the halfway point of Italy's Adriatic shore, Ancona might seem like an industrial port city best worth skirting around. But this is the beating heart of the Italian Adriatic, and indeed is well worth a stop. In any case, it's hard not to be seduced by the surrounding Riviera del Conero, with its moulded ridges and hidden azure coves; or by generous plates of *moscioli*, a wild native mussel.

Just over 120km (75 miles) south of Venice, the Byzantine grandeur of Ravenna is an open secret in these parts, but no less a revelation. And though you're likely covering ground by car, it's two wheels only on the AdriaBike cycle path from Ravenna to Venice; this slow, flat meander is the best way to hug the coast and watch it turn yet again into something new. The bracing salt air of Chioggia is all the more delicious when you're gliding through it, and La Serenissima awaits, a pot of gold at the end of the Adriatic rainbow. **CONTINUED ON P116 »**

know-how

In Cod We Trust

Baccalà (salted cod) for sale at the Mercato di Ortigia in Syracuse, Sicily. It is traditionally eaten at Lent and on Christmas Eve.

It's a curious fact that, in a country lapped by a sea full of fish, the one that's become universally consumed isn't even from these parts. You'll find dishes made with cod all over Italy, which locals will often consider the local 'signature' – whether it's the dried *stoccafisso* that stars in stews from Genoa and Ancona, or the salted *baccalà* that's a central feature of Roman, Neapolitan and Venetian cuisine. However, cod does not swim in the Mediterranean: its corpulent flesh develops in the frigid North Sea. So how did it get here? The accepted legend is a combination of opportunity, creativity and the Catholic Church. In 1431, the Venetian entrepreneur Pietro Querini found himself adrift in the North Sea and was rescued by Nordic fishermen. His convalescence was aided by a diet of dried white fish which, in his zeal, he brought back to Venice with him. Chefs were initially unimpressed. At the same time, the church was in the midst of some soul-searching of its own, and decided to pivot to a more humble lifestyle; a dried, foetid fish was the perfect way to end (or continue) a fast. Dried cod was portable, cheap – and now part of divine rule.

VENICE GUIDE

Local discoveries in La Serenissima

taste
CICCHETTI

Why settle on one dish when you can have a bite of everything? *Cicchetti* (Venetian 'tapas') are served in *bacari*, compact bars around Venice where a glass of wine or spritz is but a pretext: small slices of bread are topped with local specialities like *baccalà mantecato* (a whipped salt-cod spread) or *sarde in saor* (sweet-and-sour fried sardines with pine nuts, raisins and onions).

explore
CASTELLO

Castello, Venice's largest *sestiere* (district) is also its least-known and most worthy of a visit. The area where most Venetians actually live is full of parks and public spaces, including the Giardini della Biennale and Parco della Rimembranze. The Arsenale (above), a former naval yard turned event space, is one of the many reasons to make your way over here.

culture
FESTA DEL REDENTORE

Carnevale may be the best known party in Venice, but the Festa del Redentore is its most significant. It commenced in 1577 to mark the end of one of the most terrible plagues in Venice's history, which killed 50,000 people, including the famed painter Tiziano Vecellio (Titian). Every year, always on the third Sunday in July – timed to align with the Catholic Church's Feast of the Most Holy Redeemer – the city is illuminated with candles and glorious fireworks. A focal point for the Festa del Redentore is the area surrounding the island of Giudecca.

"The eerie glow of street lamps on the placid canals is the perfect background for an extended aperitivo"

nightlife
ACCADEMIA

Once the sun sets, the eerie glow of street lamps on the placid canals is the perfect background for an extended *aperitivo*. Take a cue from the students around Accademia who enjoy *cicchetti* and drinks sitting on the low walls that line the waterways, watching the gondolas glide their way home under the light of the moon.

buy
MURANO GLASS

Get on the *vaporetto* (water bus) and head to Murano, an island in the Venetian Lagoon renowned for its glass-making factories. Watch the masters at work (below) in one of the workshops still in operation and visit the Museo del Vetro, which traces the centuries-long history of Murano glass. Then, pick out a piece to take home: it's sure to be one of a kind.

AROUND THE CITY BUILT ON STICKS

Travelling through the six *sestieri* of Venice – Cannaregio, Santa Croce, San Polo, Dorsoduro, Castello and San Marco – feels like a funhouse, with buildings crookedly sagging into the limpid lagoon. You'll hear that 'Venice is sinking' when the *acqua alta* tide rises in Piazza San Marco; and as you weave your way onto the Ponte Rialto over the Grand Canal, you'll inevitably notice the lopsided – though lovely – skyline. Visit the outer islands of Burano, Torcello and Sant'Erasmo, all within 5km (3 miles) of the main Venetian archipelago, and they too will give the sense of walking home after a night of too much Prosecco.

But despite reports of its demise, Venice isn't exactly sinking. You could say instead that it's breathing. This is a sleight-of-hand city, willed into being by visionary medieval engineers and still today almost fully balanced on wood. Venice is built on giant logs, in essence a forest in reverse.

How do you build a city in the middle of a lagoon formed entirely from mud, without rock or even soil to carry the weight of houses and churches and palaces scattered over 118 islands? The piling system dates back to ancient Rome, but the extreme conditions in Venice presented a completely new challenge to those medieval civil engineers. Ock, larch and pine trees transported by boat from the Veneto highlands were hand-driven into the sea floor, where they petrified after being trapped in mud and deprived of oxygen. Wooden lattices known as *zattere* were laid on top, all supporting the weight of a Most Serene Republic. The wooden piles are still maintained, and the system is essentially the same. Because it may be bowed, but Venice is never broken. **CONTINUED ON P118 »**

↓ Venice's Grand Canal and the Basilica di Santa Maria della Salute, a scene captured by artists including Canaletto and JMW Turner.

local angle

Preserving Maritime History

'Everything started [with] two guys, Enrico and Tommaso, who met in Venice. Enrico worked as a *squerariòlo*, someone who builds and repairs small boats, particularly gondolas; Tommaso had a different background but was passionate about local history. As they started to hang out more, an idea began to take shape over spritzes at the bar: what if we buy an old boat and restore it to use for some kind of activity?

'After that, they found out that the *Freccia Azzura*, a 21m 1950s-era wooden barge, was for sale. The guys had no money but talked to the owner for ages about the idea until finally, the boat was given to them. About a year after that, just when the association began to get off the ground, a horrible storm capsized the *Freccia*, and we lost everything. But we rebuilt, and we're slowly bringing this bit of Venetian history back to life.

'People, even Venetians, forget that boats like these used to travel inland on the Adige, the Brenta and the Piave Rivers. Our boat transported sand as well as the wooden piles that Venice is built on, and we need to make sure that people remember this story. There's so much to learn from the people who live here.'
Alessandra Varotto, president of the Batipai Cultural Association

THE MEDITERRANEAN

→ 19th-century neoclassical facades in Trieste's Piazza della Borsa; the cafes below have long fueled the city's love of coffee.

VENICE TO TRIESTE

The curves of La Serenissima melt into the paludal coastline of the Venice Gulf as you round the last shoulder of the Italian Mediterranean; the high reeds outside of Caorle, 70km (43 miles) to the northeast, make for a moody scene worthy of a film noir. Marshlands frame the route toward the ancient city of Grado, whose imposing seawall is often slapped by fiercely foaming spray, all the while keeping its Roman centre blissfully unaware.

Beyond Grado, the land begins to lift and the hills perch over the silver Gulf of Trieste, a shallow bay bordered by Italy, Slovenia and Croatia. Make a stop at the Cooperativa Fra Pescatori di Monfalcone for a delightful plate of fried sardines in front of the northernmost point in the Mediterranean – when you've made it this far, celebration is in order.

Trieste is a Gordian knot in urban form, belonging to nowhere. It's been called 'Vienna by the Sea' and there's something to that; this former Imperial Free City of the Habsburgs feels like a central European capital caught in a cyclone and carried southward, settling in without a hair out of place. Trieste's Canal Grande is angular and precise, lined with mansions built during its 18th-century heyday as a tax-free port where the world converged. You'll still see Serbian churches and Orthodox synagogues, and everyone meets at Caffè degli Specchi for a potent espresso served alongside steaming drinking chocolate. In its way, Trieste is the most Mediterranean city of them all: defiant, melancholy and free.

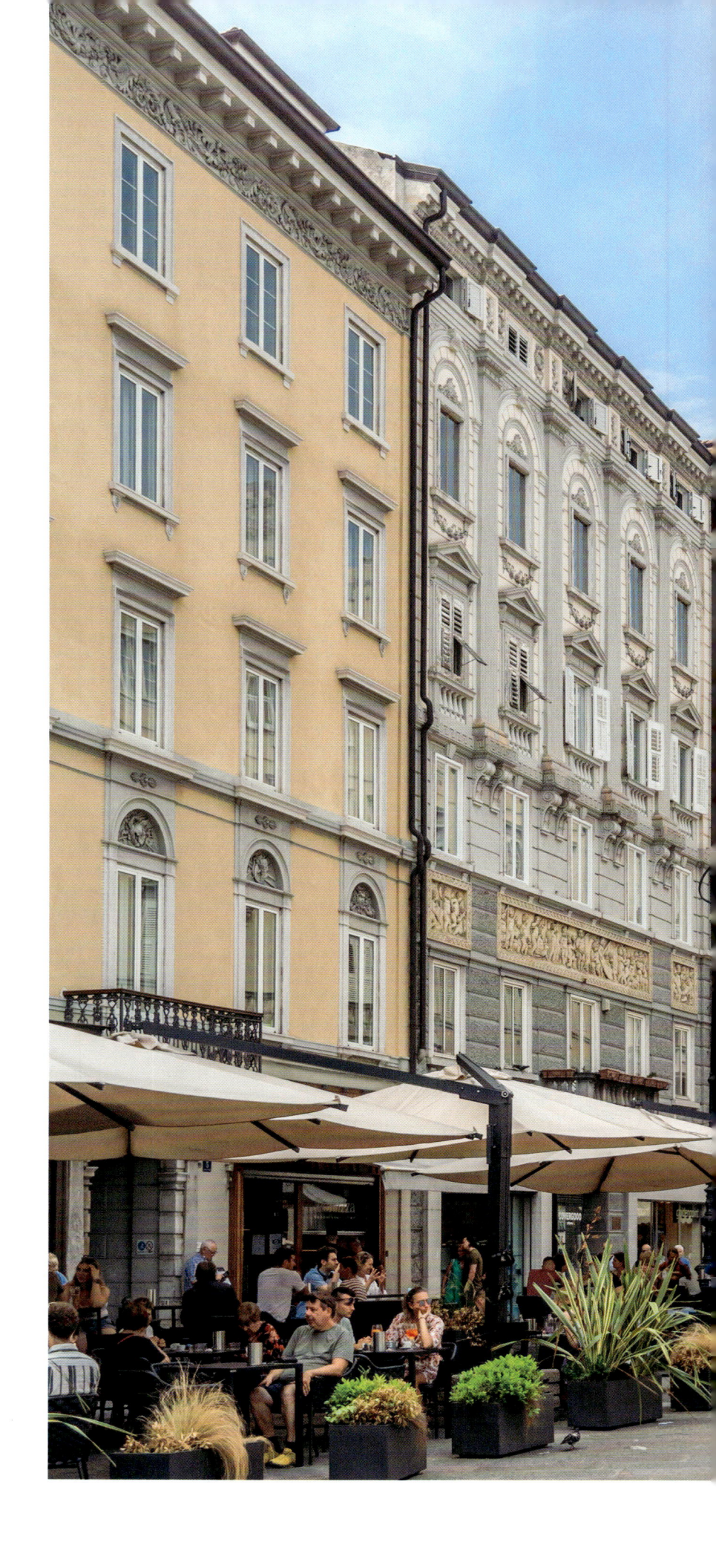

ITALY

know-how

The Bora Wind

If you've never believed in ghosts, you might have difficulty accepting that something invisible can shape, and indeed transform, the course of daily life. But then, if you've ever been to Trieste when the Bora is blowing, you'll find the existence of apparitions to be the least of your problems. From the Greek *boreas*, the Bora is a powerful, cold wind that blows from northern Europe onto the Adriatic regions of Italy, Slovenia and Croatia. It usually arrives in the winter and can take two forms: *bora chiara* indicates clear skies with wild gusts, while *bora scura* means the dark churning of cyclone clouds overhead.

Whether on land or sea, people around Trieste know that when the Bora comes it's time to take cover. Sailing is nearly impossible: choppy, high waves with white crests ripple violently over the surface of the water and small drops formed by the wind create an effect known as 'sea smoke', which reduces visibility to near zero. On land, chains and ropes have long been fastened to buildings for people to hold onto as they walk (or try), as gusts can reach anywhere from 120km/h to 200km/h (75mph to 124mph). It's the sort of wind that can drive people mad, and it has: French novelist Stendhal wrote about the effect that the rattling of windows had on his sanity; James Joyce exalted in its fury. Like Trieste itself, the Bora is a meeting point, where Nordic frost and Mediterranean ferocity collide.

119

THE MEDITERRANEAN

Primorska

PIRAN •

Istria

ROVINJ •

PULA •

CHAPTER FOUR

THE ADRIATIC

**SALTMAKING IN PIRAN, SLOVENIA ～ ISTRIAN GASTRONOMY
CROATIA'S BRIJUNI ISLANDS ～ TASTING LIQUEURS IN ROVINJ
RIJEKA CARNIVAL ～ ROMAN SPLIT ～ SCULPTOR IVAN MEŠTROVIĆ
MONTENEGRO'S MARITIME HERITAGE ～ VJOSA RIVER RAFTING IN ALBANIA**

SLOVENIA

RIJEKA

KVARNER
GULF

ZADAR

CROATIA

Dalmatia

SPLIT
BRAČ
HVAR TOWN

**BOSNIA &
HERCEGOVINA**

NEUM

DUBROVNIK

ADRIATIC SEA

KOTOR
BUDVAR

Lake Skadar

MONTENEGRO

DURRES
TIRANA

ALBANIA

DIVJAKË-
KARAVASTA
NATIONAL
PARK

VLORË

Vjosa

KSAMIL

THE MEDITERRANEAN

→ The Pakleni islands off Hvar, in Croatia's Adriatic archipelago, are a haven for yacht sailors and sunseekers.

Embarking on a trip through five countries along the eastern shore of the Adriatic Sea, from the Gulf of Trieste to the Strait of Otranto, means experiencing the most diverse stretch of the Mediterranean. With over 1000 islands in the Croatian archipelago alone, there are seemingly infinite spots for dips in the cerulean sea or sailing off to a hidden cove. Through much of the region, the Dinaric Alps' jagged peaks provide sensational vistas and a sense of awe, and there are still places along the coast where glimpses of wading flamingos or playful dolphins don't come as a surprise. The head-spinning legacy of civilisations that have come and gone throughout history – Greeks, Romans, Byzantines, Venetians, Ottomans, Habsburgs – is palpable in the ancient ruins, grand walled towns and treasure-packed churches and museums. And with boundless fruits of both land and sea, plus centuries-old olive-growing and winemaking traditions, even a modest meal becomes a memorable affair.

THE ADRIATIC

THE MEDITERRANEAN

NORTH OF PIRAN

The cloak of La Serenissima looms over Slovenia's Primorska ('by the sea') region. From Ankaran, once an outpost for Venice's Benedictine monks, road signs are in both Slovene and Italian along a 47km (29-mile) stretch of Adriatic coastline. The Venetian Gothic facades of seaside towns' medieval cores hint at centuries past, when *fleur de sel* from Piran's saltpans was coveted by the maritime republic. Diverge slightly inland to stone-walled Istrian villages overlooking olive groves and truffle-endowed woods, and you could be in Croatia.

Both formerly islands, just 7km (4 miles) apart, Koper and Izola may have a shabbier feel than Piran down south, but there's more to each than their workaday port-city personas. Behind Koper's sprawling cargo harbour, the Old Town retains baroque and Renaissance *palazzos* festooned with reliefs and medallions. The fishing skiffs lolling in Izola's marina signal you'll dine on superb seafood here – perhaps mussels *alla busara* (simmered in wine).

You can almost see the coast from hinterland villages perched atop rolling hills that supply Istria's gastronomic riches, with vineyards cultivating Malvazija and Refošk grapes, and mills producing fancy orange- or chilli-flavoured olive oils. In summer, truffle-hunters' dogs sniff their way through oak and chestnut forests searching for the prized aromatic tubers.

Further along, to the west of Izola, the Strunjan Landscape Park brings the promise of exhilarating walks. The wild beach of Moon Bay – a sliver of pebbles beneath a towering cliff – can only be reached on foot. A path takes you past the saltpans to the edge of the 80m-high crag for memorable views of the Adriatic. **CONTINUED ON P126 »**

↓ The old town and marina of Izola face the Bay of San Simon, once used by the Romans to access trade with the colony of Aquileia.

know-how

Piran's Saltmaking Heritage

↑ At Piran's Sečovlje saltpans, traditional wooden rakes are still used to harvest coarse flakes of salt from crystalisation bays.

Dubbed the 'Town Built on Salt', Piran cherishes the 700-year-old tradition of harvesting the gift of its nearby saltpans: *fleur de sel*. Shaped by the Istrian soil, sea, sun and wind, and hand-harvested using ancient tools and procedures, mineral-rich Piranska *sol* (salt) has been prized for its distinctive briny taste since Venetian times. Once the main source of wealth and now considered cultural heritage, saltmaking still infuses the region's lifestyle.

The Saltworks Festival enlivens Piran on 23 April, the day of St George (the town's patron saint) with a salt-themed journey into the past. A fair on Tartinijev trg celebrates all things salt, along with other gourmet goodies – fishing competitions, boat shows, artisan crafts, folk dances and recreations of olden-days salter-family life round out the festivities.

Two of the northernmost saltworks in the Mediterranean lie in the vicinity of Piran. Just south of town, the birdlife-rich Sečovlje Salina Nature Park is a patchwork of working saltpans, levees and channels that can be traversed on foot or by bike. Its hands-on Museum of Saltmaking presents revamped salter-family living quarters and a warehouse for the storage of salt. In summer, the *Solinarka* sails to the heart of the salt fields, landing at the pier in the Grand Channel.

Snuggled in the middle of the saltpans is the stylish, open-air Lepa Vida Thalasso Spa. With a saltwater swimming pool, a choice of mud and brine wellness treatments including soaks, wraps and massages, and a range of sea-mineral-based cosmetics, this represents true Mediterranean-style unwinding.

THE MEDITERRANEAN

→ The Old Town of Piran juts out into the Gulf of Piran and was part of the Republic of Venice between 1283 and 1797.

SOUTH OF PIRAN

In late August, the subtle chords of chamber music performed on baroque string instruments echo through the vaulted cloister of Piran's Minorite Monastery during the Tartini Festival. But even outside those enchanting summer evenings, it's easy to imagine how the Venetian Gothic Old Town inspired its native son, composer and violinist Giuseppe Tartini (1692–1770).

At the tip of a finger-shaped peninsula, the winding alleyways of Piran's historic core converge on the marble-paved oval plaza that was formerly an inner harbour. Mansions with tracery windows huddle within the 300m-long section of medieval town walls.

A shop on Tartinijev trg offers pretty soaps, candles, bath salts and body scrubs made from Piran salt. But it's not only *fleur de sel* that's long been the town's trademark – the delectable Piran sea bass, or *brancin*, draws seafood aficionados to local restaurants. Salt-crusted and baked in the oven, it's often filleted at your table.

A 10-minute drive southwest, there's a holiday-riviera vibe to the resort of Portorož. In summer, kayaks, windsurfs and sailboats glide across the bay past packed beaches. Only 5km (3 miles) away, pygmy cormorants, little egrets and many other bird species flock within the expanse of Sečovlje saltpans.

Join cyclists who pass the traffic along the Parenzana Trail, sea breeze on their shoulders. Tracing a former narrow-gauge railway, Slovenia's 30km (19-mile) stretch swoops along the Adriatic shore, foraying through old stone tunnels into the neatly-kept farms and vineyards of Istria's hills. **CONTINUED ON P128 »**

local angle

Istrian Gastronomy

~~~~~~

'Living in Istria has deeply influenced how I approach cooking. The food in Slovenia's coastal region is all about seasonal and local ingredients – including olive oil and renowned white truffles. Thanks to our sunny weather and fertile soil, we can grow amazing produce that's mostly organic. I'm particularly fond of artichokes, capers, persimmons, wild garlic, Istrian young corn, chard, figs, mussels and Adriatic hake. They not only taste great but also support sustainable farming practices.

'Recently, Slovenia's fine-dining scene has been growing, and I opened COB to be a part of that, aiming to showcase authentic Istrian flavours in a fun and interactive way. One of my favourite Istrian dishes is *bobiči*, a minestrone made with very young corn. Another is a traditional cod-fish spread served with polenta, which we've transformed into a savoury polenta macaron with the cod-fish spread in the centre. *Žgvacet* is similar to a stew, made with rooster and seasonal vegetables, and always featuring sun-dried tomatoes and onions.

'We also focus on local wines, as Slovenia has many great boutique wine producers. In Istria, Malvazija and Refošk are popular, but there are also unique blends and lesser-known grape varieties. For example, Maločrn produces an excellent, slightly fruity sparkling rosé; I particularly enjoy the one from Ražman Winery. Another notable local red grape is Cipro, and Mahnič Winery makes a great rosé from it, with subtle floral notes that pair wonderfully with our rabbit pâté. A red blend from Steras Winery, combining six different local grapes, pairs beautifully with Istrian beef.'

Filip Matjaž (pictured), owner/chef at Cooking Outside the Box, Portorož

THE MEDITERRANEAN

→ A Byzantine mosaic above the ciborium in the Euphrasian Basilica, Poreč. To the left, St Euphrasia is holding a model of the church.

↘ In Vrsar, a traditional wooden vessel waits to carry visitors on a cruise towards the Brijuni Islands, in a region known for boatbuilding.

AROUND THE ISTRIAN PENINSULA
Shaped like a bunch of grapes hanging over the Adriatic in Croatia's north, Istria is strewn with vestiges of its ancient Roman past. Yet it's the Byzantine 6th-century Euphrasian Basilica in Poreč that has earned UNESCO World Heritage status. Its belfry soars over the Old Town, a jumble of faded-crimson rooftops on a spit of land protruding into the sea.

Some 10km (6 miles) further along, on a sea-facing hillside, tiny Vrsar is where Casanova stopped by in the 1740s. You can take a tour following in his footsteps, along stone alleys draped in bougainvillea and redolent with romance. South of town, shellfish is farmed at the deep end of the 12km-long (7.5-mile) fjord-like Lim Channel; oyster shacks serve freshly harvested delicacies.

Skirting fashionable Rovinj, the route around the peninsula leads to Pula. Behind its shipbuilding grit, the remarkably preserved 1st-century Roman amphitheatre dominates the cityscape. Locals snap up fresh fish at the nearby market before sipping their morning coffee in the shade of chestnut trees. On summer evenings, watch the skyline explode with colour as the Uljanik Shipyard's huge cranes are illuminated in a contemporary-art light show.

On Istria's southernmost tip, kayakers and windsurfers are drawn to the rocky coves and translucent waters of Cape Kamenjak, where seagulls rest, wildflowers sprout and dinosaur footprints are etched in the stone. Up on the east coast, hike the 3km (2 mile) path through pinewoods from the fishing village of Rabac to Labin for art galleries and pottery workshops behind medieval facades. **CONTINUED ON P134 »**

know-how
Brijuni's Historic Glamour

A dash of mid-century glamour lingers over the small archipelago floating off the southwestern coast of Istria. With swathes of oak and laurel forests roamed by deer and mouflon, the Brijuni Islands were proclaimed a national park in 1983. They have an intriguing history, evidenced by the dinosaur footprints on the rocky southern coves, the remnants of Roman villas and, more recently, the vestiges of the Yugoslav era when Brijuni served as President Tito's private summer retreat.

The 1902 Secession-style boathouse in the port of the largest island, Veli Brijun, is the legacy of Paul Kupelwieser, an Austrian industrialist who turned these once malaria-ridden islands into a fashionable destination for European high society. Interactive exhibitions shed light on everything from Brijuni's submarine world to their illustrious past.

Tito's White Villa on Veli Brijun hosted monarchs, revolutionaries and global movie stars. This eminent lineup – immortalised in black-and-white photographs – ranges from Queen Elizabeth II and Fidel Castro to Richard Burton and Elizabeth Taylor. The gallery commemorates the 1956 signing of the Brioni Declaration, which ushered in the Non-Aligned Movement; parked outside, the dark-green 1953 Cadillac Eldorado used by Tito to show off the island to visiting celebrities is available for a spin (at a price).

→ Three of the 14 islands in the Brijuni archipelago. In 1815 they became part of the Austrian Empire, when quarries here began supplying stone to Vienna.

ROVINJ GUIDE

Exploring Istria's highlight city

taste
TRUFFLES

Rovinj's restaurant menus are bursting with excellent seafood, olive oil and wines, but it's the local *tartufi* (truffles) that steal the show. The pungent black or white fungi growing in the depths of Istria's forests are served every which way – from seafood or game in truffle sauce to risotto or *fuži* (Istrian hand-rolled tubular pasta) topped with shaved-at-the-table truffles.

explore
THE OLD TOWN

The allure of Rovinj is best appreciated by making the Old Town (above) your base. Treat yourself with a stay in a boutique hotel – perhaps one set in a restored Venetian *palazzo*. Occupying a hilly, egg-shaped islet turned peninsula, the fully pedestrianised old Rovinj is a joy to explore. This swirl of pastel-hued, tightly packed tall houses punctuated by *fumaioli* (exterior chimneys) is overseen by the winged lion of Venice, recalling its maritime past. Along the slippery cobblestone lanes, artists' studios showcase contemporary creatives.

culture
BATANA BOATS

Bobbing in the marina (below), a group of fishing skiffs attest to Rovinj's enduring maritime heritage. The traditional flat-bottomed wooden boat, or *batana*, is celebrated just a skip away at the Batana Ecomuseum. From seafaring artefacts donated by the locals to audiovisual projections explaining boat construction and fishing techniques, and recordings of *bitinada* sea shanties in a regional dialect, it's a glimpse into the city's soul.

buy
LIQUEURS

Some of the top treats to take home from this stronghold of Istrian gastronomy include delicious liqueurs. Among the popular local tipples are Teranino and Pelinkovac. The former, made from *teran* (red wine), has a sweet and fruity flavour; the latter, characterised by its bitter aroma, is made with *pelin* (wormwood) and other herbs. Those produced by Rovinj's own Darna liqueur factory are based on century-old recipes.

"A swirl of pastel-hued tall houses is overseen by the winged lion of Venice"

nightlife
THE WATERFRONT

Sunset calls for a long, slow stroll along the waterfront promenade south of the Old Town, towards the Zlatni Rt Forest Park. The golden-hour views across Rovinj's marina – a rainbow of weather-beaten facades culminating in the elongated silhouette of St Euphemia Church's bell tower – are pure romance. Pick an outdoor terrace to enjoy this glorious vision of Rovinj over a glass of crisp Malvazija white wine as the sun meets the sea.

THE MEDITERRANEAN

→ Opatija's neo-Romanesque Church of our Lady of the Annunciation, built from 1906 and known locally as 'the German Church'.

↘ Sveti Petar and Ilovik islands, in the Kvarner Gulf; the natural harbour between the two has been used since ancient times.

ALONG THE KVARNER GULF
When a railway linking Rijeka to Vienna was built in 1873 under Austro-Hungarian rule, it brought the first tourists to the Kvarner Gulf. There's still a touch of Habsburg chic to Opatija, 13km (8 miles) west of Rijeka, where spa hotels with chandeliered ballrooms and gardens of exotic plants provide an indulgent getaway. A slab-paved promenade hugs the coastline past rocky inlets and belle époque villas sheltered by fragrant oaks and laurels.

Between shipyard cranes and elaborate Secession-style buildings, Rijeka thrives at night. Ballet and opera are staged in the neo-baroque theatre, which has ceiling canvases painted by a young Gustav Klimt. Minutes away, a ruin bar in a tunnel beneath the railway tracks thumps with jazz, dance and alternative beats. Visit in February, and you'll witness the port city turn into a riot of creativity for the annual Carnival.

Rijeka is also a launchpad for the islands. Steeped-in-history Krk was a stronghold for the medieval Glagolitic script, its wiggly letters carved into tombstones and the doors and altars of the island's squat old churches. To the southwest, linked by a swing bridge across a narrow channel, Cres and Lošinj have an end-of-the-road feel. Griffon vultures cruise above Cres, feasting on the free-roaming sheep of its karst pastures, while bottlenose dolphins and sea turtles frequent Lošinj's quiet bays. Pag's barren landscape, with salty herbs whipped by the Bura wind, is said to enhance the tanginess of the island's renowned sheep's-milk cheese. In the Old Town, local artisans sit stitching on sun-bleached porches, selling dainty lacework. **CONTINUED ON P136 »**

know-how
Rijeka Carnival

It may not have the romantic allure of Venice, but the Carnival in Rijeka – Croatia's gritty port and a major naval hub since Austro-Hungarian times – gives its counterpart across the Adriatic a run for its money. Stemming from medieval pre-Lenten processions to ward off winter, Croatia's biggest Mardi Gras has its own historical flavour: in local lore, it was men masked with animal heads who scared off the Ottoman invaders. The Habsburg authorities outlawed mask-wearing in 1449, but the Carnival was revived during the Yugoslav era to become the raucous 'fifth season', as it's known today.

With 100,000 visitors descending on Rijeka every winter, the festivities last from mid-January to Ash Wednesday. They kick off with the ceremonial presentation of the city keys to the honorary 'mayor' and the election of the Carnival queen. The Governor's Palace hosts a charity ball attended by local celebrities, and the children's parade gathers youngsters posing as fairy-tale characters. Under the official motto of 'Be whatever you want to be', the main spectacle on the last Sunday before Lent is a burst of colour, music and imagination as 10,000 costumed revellers stroll and dance along the Korzo promenade. Hailing from Rijeka's hinterland, the *zvončari* (bell ringers), clad in sheepskin and freakish animal heads, provide the parade's noisy soundtrack of bells and rattles to scare away evil spirits.

→ According to folk custom, during the time of Rijeka Carnival, *zvončari* would march from village to village scaring away evil spirits.

THE MEDITERRANEAN

SPLIT GUIDE

The Dalmatian city with a Roman core

taste
DALMATIAN SEAFOOD

Seafood is the star in Split. Veli Varoš, the old fisherfolk's quarter, has some excellent seafood *konobe* (taverns). Sample Dalmatian specialities like *brudet* (flavour-packed seafood stew, with onions and tomatoes), *crni rižoto* (black risotto, which gets its colour and flavour from cuttlefish or squid ink), or octopus slow-cooked with potatoes under a *peka* (domed lid).

explore
DIOCLETIAN'S PALACE

A heritage hotel squeezed within the ancient walls of the thoroughly lived-in Diocletian's Palace makes for a memorable stay. This vast fortified town by the harbour, built for the Roman emperor Diocletian in the 4th century CE, is the heartbeat of Split. Once trodden by Roman soldiers and servants, the chiselled-in-stone maze of arcaded courtyards (below), plazas and passageways of the 200-building former imperial residence now teem with cutting-edge bistros, wine bars and boutiques, while Splićani haggle at the fish market and awestruck tourists wander.

culture
EMANUEL VIDOVIĆ

The Emanuel Vidović Gallery honours the Split native whose paintings are considered as the establishment of Croatia's modern art in the early 20th century. Famed for his landscapes and cityscapes, many featuring his hometown, Vidović fused Impressionism, Expressionism and Symbolism into his own unique style. His lyrical harbour motifs, the interplay of light and colour in his church interiors and skilful black-and-white drawings of Split are a wonderful homage to this historic city.

"This vast fortified town by the harbour is the heartbeat of Split"

nightlife
THE RIVA

Evening is the perfect time to join the locals on the Riva, Split's beloved promenade, hugging the seafront westwards from the harbour to Marjan Hill. Along the palm-fringed, white-stone pathway, families saunter up and down, stalls offer artisan crafts and cafes make prime spots for people-watching. Clamber the 300-odd steps up to Teraca Vidilica, set on the edge of Marjan Hill, for a panorama of Split at cocktail-glass level.

buy
GOURMET CHOCOLATES

Split's popular artisanal-chocolate producer, Nadalina, was established by former punk band lead singer Marinko Biškić and serves up a unique taste of Dalmatia to take home with you. The locally crafted bean-to-bar gourmet chocolates come in a range of intriguing flavours, most of which hail from the region's signature produce. Expect to find figs, carob, sage, lavender, Prošek (sweet dessert wine) and even olive oil in the chocolates you can buy here.

THE MEDITERRANEAN

→ Dwellings and shops sit tightly packed in the medieval Old Town of Dubrovnik, encircled by vast walls completed in the 16th century.

THROUGH DALMATIA

Two 21st-century sound-and-light installations on Zadar's waterfront have come to personify this Illyrian-founded city. The *Sea Organ*, set within the stone steps descending into the sea, emits soulful tunes when the lapping waves push air through the pipes beneath. Nearby, the glass panels of the *Sun Salutation* circle embedded in the promenade absorb solar energy, generating a hypnotic light show from dusk till dawn. It's a perfect entrance to Dalmatia.

En route to Split, stop to appreciate the view of islands floating on the horizon along the shore-hugging Adriatic Hwy, blasted through limestone mountains during the Yugoslav era to link ancient walled towns, fishing ports and countless sparkling bays.

Croatia's sunniest island is a two-hour ferry ride from Split. Hvar Town steals the limelight with glamorous yachts anchored in the marina, all-night-party beach clubs and swanky restaurant terraces. Further out are isolated coves of white pebbles and rocks, scented lavender fields and centuries-old plots of olive groves and vineyards.

Back on the mainland, the cable-stayed Pelješac Bridge bypasses the 20km (12-mile) stretch of Bosnia & Hercegovina's Adriatic coast (centred around the resort of Neum), with Dubrovnik beckoning to the south. This fortified city's gleaming lanes reverberate with the multilingual chatter of visitors marvelling at Renaissance-Gothic palaces, baroque churches and ornate columns and fountains. Tear your eyes away from the ancient splendour, and modern-day life unfolds here too. **CONTINUED ON P140 »**

local angle
The Art of Ivan Meštrović

'The famous Croatian sculptor Ivan Meštrović (1883–1962) chose Split to build a monumental summer villa amidst a Mediterranean park (above), overlooking the bay of Ježinac and middle Dalmatian islands. The world-renowned artist, whose works adorn public spaces from Split (*Monument to Gregory of Nin*) to Chicago (*Indians – The Bowman and the Spearman*), returned to Croatia from abroad in the 1920s. He bought a plot of land in the Split Meje area, drawn here by the bayside location, the mild climate and the company of friends and acquaintances.

'The Meštrović Gallery was originally conceived as a summer residence. With time, the original idea grew into something bigger and the central part took on an exhibition character. The gallery now exhibits some of the artist's masterpieces executed in marble, bronze and wood, covering all the periods of his rich creative career. Some of the most famous statues in marble and stone, such as *Psyche*, *Contemplation* and *Reverie*, reflect his drawing from classical sources – antiquity and Renaissance – and the Mediterranean tradition.'
Zorana Jurić Šabić, museum advisor of the Meštrović Gallery, Split

THE MEDITERRANEAN

BRAČ GUIDE

An island famed for its vivid shores

explore
BLACA HERMITAGE

Etched into a cliff face high over the island's southern coast is a 16th-century hermitage (above), founded by monks escaping the Ottomans on the mainland. Having grown from a cave refuge, by the 18th century it functioned as a school, printing house and astronomical observatory. Sadly, the last resident monk here passed away in 1963. A tour of this extraordinary site provides historical insight and a peek at antique furnishings and rare manuscripts still homed here.

secret
BRAČ STONE

High-quality white limestone has been quarried on Brač since Roman times. It was hauled to build many Croatian architectural showpieces including Diocletian's Palace in Split (and a local rumour even claims the White House in Washington). The Stone Masonry School in Pučišća preserves this esteemed tradition, training students in ancient stone-carving techniques.

base
BOL AND SUPETAR

Brač Island's two main settlements both make a fine base. Bol has resort-style complexes along the pine-scented seashore and guesthouses scattered around the terracotta-roofed Old Town – ideal for those drawn to its showstopper beach or looking for some windsurfing action. With its small harbour, shallow bays, handful of swimmable beaches nearby and plenty of private digs to choose between, the more low-key Supetar is a haven for families.

> "A limestone relief blanketed with pine forests and olive groves"

activity
HIKING TO VIDOVA GORA

For a different perspective on Brač, embark on a two-hour hike up to Vidova Gora (778m). As the highest point in the Adriatic islands, it offers stupendous views: a limestone relief blanketed with pine forests and olive groves, the 'Golden Cape' jutting out into the cobalt-blue sea and neighbouring Hvar in all its glory, with Pelješac Peninsula and Biokovo mountain range on the horizon. From Bol, the signposted 102 hiking path winds uphill through fragrant woods.

beach
ZLATNI RAT

A gorgeous spit of soft, tiny white pebbles backed by a swathe of black pines, Zlatni Rat (Golden Cape, below) lives up to the hype – this must be the most photographed beach in Croatia. Protruding into the glistening waters at Bol for about 400m, the beach's tongue-like shape is known to change at the whim of the currents and the Maestral – the strong westerly wind that also makes Zlatni Rat such a popular destination for kite- and windsurfers. Blowing from April to October, the Maestral can usually be expected to build to its peak in the early afternoon.

THE MEDITERRANEAN

AROUND THE BAY OF KOTOR

Legend has it that the narrowest part of the Bay of Kotor, the Verige Strait, was named after the iron chains (*verige*) that spanned the passage in medieval times to prevent enemy galleons from reaching the inner folds of the bay. Ferries now run back-and-forth across the 250m-wide inlet, but taking a full jaunt around its green-blue depths, hemmed in by vertiginous cliffs, is a Montenegro highlight.

Guarding the gulf's entrance, Herceg Novi's formidable bastions and sunny plazas tumble down to the sea alongside countless stairways, enveloped in sweet-smelling acacia blossoms in late winter. A breezy promenade wiggles along the shore, dipping in and out of tunnels. In summer, watch local boys playing water polo by the harbour as taxi boats set off to coves and grottos across the bay.

Some 30km (19 miles) further, there's a sense of nostalgia about diminutive Perast. Time-worn *palazzos* set at the water's edge evoke its famed seafaring past; offshore, a pair of islets in the glassy bay – one holding a blue-domed chapel, the other a cypress-shaded monastery – add to the serenity.

Wedged in the deepest, moodiest recess of the bay lies Kotor. The medieval fortifications here seem to defy gravity, arcing up the foothills of Mt Lovćen to form a protective loop that's halo-like when lit up at night. Below, Kotor's Venetian-flavoured triangular core hums with life, much as it has for centuries. Small piazzas bear evocative names after the produce once traded here – for instance Trg od Mlijeka (milk) or Trg od Brašna (flour) – while market stalls set in the bulwarks offer delicacies including *Lovćen pršut* (prosciutto) and smoked carp from Lake Skadar. **CONTINUED ON P144 »**

↓ Montenegro's Bay of Kotor twists 28km (17 miles) inland from the Adriatic Sea, flanked by the Orjen and the Lovćen mountains.

know-how

Boka Kotorska's Maritime Heritage

The Bay of Kotor (Boka Kotorska) is home to a naval tradition that stretches back centuries. Shipbuilding and maritime trade – as well as fighting off pirates and invaders from the sea throughout history – are intertwined with the story of the Boka Navy; established in 809 CE, it's believed to be the oldest seafarers' fraternity in the world. This proud heritage lives on in colourful festivals and sights around the bay.

Occupying a baroque *palazzo* in Kotor, the Maritime Museum of Montenegro celebrates the city's role as a naval power – particularly during its four centuries under Venetian rule. This romantic age is brought to life through photos, paintings, sea captains' uniforms, exquisitely decorated weaponry, scale models of ships and all manner of sea-navigating contraptions.

Dating back to 1463, Boka Navy Day on 26 June sees its sailors – clad in traditional velvet-and-silk garments embroidered in gold – perform the *kolo* (circle dance) after receiving the national flag and Kotor city keys.

The festive atmosphere goes up a notch during the Boka Night jamboree in mid-August, with a fleet of decorated and lantern-studded boats parading through the bay like dancers in a masquerade ball, and fireworks lighting up the sky.

The glamorous Porto Montenegro is a makeover of Tivat's Yugoslav-era naval base and shipyard into the country's swankiest neighbourhood, complete with superyacht marina. Housed in a restored sawmill, its Naval Heritage Collection reimagines the Arsenal shipyard (founded by Austria-Hungary in 1889). Dry-docked outside is the P-821 *Heroj* submarine, once the pride of the Yugoslav navy.

↑ The town of Tivat borders the Bay of Kotor; its naval base has been redeveloped as a marina for luxury yachts and more.

THE MEDITERRANEAN

MOUNTAIN TO LAKE

Trace the soul of Old Montenegro on this drive through a compact nation

Distance 126km (78 miles)
Duration Two days
Start Kotor
Finish Budva

❶ Kotor
Set out from atmospheric Kotor, Montenegro's historic heart.

❷ Lovćen National Park
Brace yourself for a white-knuckle ride on the serpentine road that snakes up Mt Lovćen (1749m) to the west of Kotor. Its 25 switchbacks reveal panoramas of the bay, dazzling in the Black Mountain's embrace. Atop Jezerski Vrh (1657m) is the Njegoš Mausoleum; this final resting place of Montenegro's favourite son – poet and *vladika* (prince-bishop) Petar II Petrović Njegoš (1813–51) – is graced with Ivan Meštrović's black-granite sculpture of Njegoš, shielded by the wings of an eagle. A rotunda gives incredible views across much of Montenegro. Continue to Njeguši on Lovćen's northern edge. The Petrović dynasty's ancestral village is renowned for its *pršut* (smoke-dried ham) and cheese. Sample both at Konoba kod Radonjića, a family-run tavern. *50km (31 miles)*

❸ Cetinje
The P1 route skirts the park southeast towards Cetinje, shadowed by craggy peaks. This old royal capital's 19th-century heyday is reflected in its elegant mansions. Big-hitter museums – including King Nikola's palace – speak of the past through relics such as the bishop's cross of Njegoš or the first book printed in Cetinje (in 1493). The 15th-century Cetinje Monastery and the art gallery showcasing Montenegrin greats like the Modernist painter Petar Lubarda, add to the town's cultural weight. Soak up the olden-days ambience by overnighting at La Vecchia Casa guesthouse. *15km (9 miles)*

❹ Rijeka Crnojevića
Head on southeast to Rijeka Crnojevića, a village slumbering on the banks of the Crnojevića River that feeds Lake Skadar. Once a peaceful winter escape for the Petrović royals, its simple stone dwellings are centred around the triple-arched limestone bridge built in 1853 by Prince Danilo. Roam the lake by boat in the warmer months, and tuck into flavourful *riblja čorba* (fish soup) at Stari Most restaurant on the riverside promenade. *17km (11 miles)*

❺ Budva
Take the M2.3 southwest to end this historical sojourn back on the coast at Budva. *44km (27 miles)*

THE ADRIATIC

↖ At a cafe near Lake Skadar, which straddles the borders of Albania and Montenegro.

↙ The Mausoleum of Njegoš was built in the early 1970s and is accessed by 461 stairs.

143

THE MEDITERRANEAN

→ Ulcinj is one of the oldest settlements in the Adriatic, founded in the 5th century BCE; it was captured by the Romans in 163 BCE.

SOUTH OF THE BAY OF KOTOR
From the myth of Budva's origin (involving ancient Greek gods and lovers turned into snakes) to the true story of medieval Ulcinj as a notorious pirates' lair, this expanse of the Adriatic serves charm and intrigue behind the terracotta roofs of coastal settlements.

Budva's split personality makes it all the more fascinating. The walled Old Town rising from the sea becomes a moonlit podium for thespians and wordsmiths during the Grad Teatar summer festival, competing with the riviera beaches and city nightclubs that throng with the sun-and-fun crowd.

Along the highway, medieval Orthodox monasteries are endowments of the Paštrović clan, who commanded here for centuries. Step inside a faintly lit church, and serene faces of sainted Serbian royalty gaze down at you from earth-toned frescoes – a biblical storybook plastered on the ancient walls.

The most famed Paštrović foothold, though, was Sveti Stefan. Just 10km south of Budva, past cypress- and pine-forested headlands, the fortified island village hangs off a narrow isthmus leading to a pink-hued beach. You'll feel like lingering by this fishing hamlet turned luxury resort just for the views.

Down south, the mood keeps shifting. Behind Bar's industrial port, the overgrown hillside ruins of Old Bar poke out amid groves of gnarled olive trees, many over a millennium old. Lanky minarets piercing Ulcinj's skyline recall the ramshackle Old Town's three centuries of Ottoman rule. And kitesurfers flock to kilometres of shallow, sandy beach backed by birdlife-rich saltpans towards the Albanian border. **CONTINUED ON P146 »**

local angle
The Birdlife of Lake Skadar

'As the largest freshwater reservoir in the Balkans, Lake Skadar shelters a diverse array of bird species as well as other fauna. Birds with a large wingspan attract the most attention here: pelicans, herons, egrets, eagles, vultures.

'Early mornings are the best time for spotting the birds and hearing their song, but the hours before nightfall, when they are most active, are also good. I like to visit hidden places by kayak and sunbathe a little in order to get as close as possible and photograph them.

'What a falcon is in the air, a cormorant is in the water. Pelicans like to follow them around, because cormorants dive deep underwater to catch fish, forcing the other fish to scatter and emerge closer to the surface, where pelicans can snap them up. What do the cormorants get out of this? Maybe they feel protected, or they just like the company.

'The fisherfolk of Lake Skadar dislike the cormorants – perhaps they are jealous of their hunting skills. According to them, these birds are why there aren't enough fish in the lake. That's a misconception and a justification for overhunting, which systematically threatens both the birdlife and fish of Lake Skadar.'
Mihailo Jovićević, ecologist, Montenegro

THE MEDITERRANEAN

NORTH OF THE ALBANIAN RIVIERA
The only clue that Albania's largest port was once the springboard for the Via Egnatia – the Roman road that carried traders, armies and missionaries from the Adriatic all the way to Byzantium – lies in the stone road-markers exhibited at its archaeological museum. These days, angular high-rises dwarf the remnants of Durrës' ancient Roman amphitheatre; come summertime, brightly coloured elbow-to-elbow beach parasols dot the sandy shore.

Just over an hour's drive south, tranquillity reigns over the Divjakë-Karavasta National Park. Cyclists and kayakers navigate through swamps, meadows, sand dunes and pine forests for a glimpse of graceful pelicans and herons nesting in the lagoon.

Further along the coast, more ancient ruins and coastal wetlands await. The forlorn Greco-Roman city of Apollonia – another Via Egnatia gateway – lies on a hilly plateau north of the Vjosa River delta, gazing out to the Adriatic. Traces of the ancient temples, theatres, porticos and arches conjure up bygone glory once rivalling that of Durrës.

The drive south skirts the Nartë Lagoon to reach the port of Vlorë. In the warmer months, you can take a boat tour to shrouded-in-secrecy Sazan Island, a Cold War–era submarine base strategically guarding the bay. Derelict abandoned buildings of the former naval base and bunker shells popping out from the shrubland like huge concrete mushrooms exude a ghost-island feel. Pointing towards Sazan is the lonesome Karaburun Peninsula, with white-pebble coves along its crumpled western shore, sea caves that are a magnet for speedboats and snorkellers, and enigmatic centuries-old inscriptions carved by seafarers into limestone cliffs. **CONTINUED ON P148 »**

↓ A monument in Vlorë marks the declaration of independence of Albania from the Ottoman Empire on 28 November 1912.

THE ADRIATIC

know-how
Vjosa Wild River National Park

↑ Rafts set out on the undammed Vjosa River, which winds for 272km (169 miles) in total, with the first 80km (50 miles) being in Greece.

Named Europe's first wild-river national park in 2023, the Vjosa River traverses southern Albania for 192km (119 miles) from the border with Greece to join the Adriatic Sea at Vlorë. This untamed waterway, dappled with small islands of white gravel, cuts its course through narrow gorges and fertile valleys latticed by fir and oak forests, olive groves and vineyards. Centuries of history unravel in ancient settlements set in the river basin. After years of campaigning, efforts of environmental NGOs and the Albanian government have reached a milestone in safeguarding the Vjosa's wilderness and biodiversity while embracing eco-tourism.

The Vjosa-Nartë Protected Landscape, just north of Vlorë, encompasses the river delta and a coastal lagoon. A melange of sand dunes and wetlands sheltering migratory birds, it's one of the best places in the region to spot pink flamingos or Dalmatian curly pelicans taking flight. Loggerhead turtles and monk seals count among the endangered creatures splashing about the estuary.

Albania's challenging UNESCO Cycling Route loops around the country, taking in parts of the coastline as well as stretches of the Vjosa. One of the stops is historic Tepelenë, straddling the river as the perfect finish line for a thrilling ride from Vlorë with plenty of climbs, descents and panoramic vistas along the way.

Further upstream, Përmet is a base for rafting, kayaking and horse riding. Such escapades run along the Lengarica Canyon, carved by the river over millions of years and home to caves with traces of Neolithic settlement, spring-fed waterfalls, and Ottoman-era stone bridges flanked by sulphuric thermal baths.

THE MEDITERRANEAN

→ The 19th-century Ottoman Porto Palermo Castle served as a Soviet submarine base during Albania's communist regime.

↘ Defensive bunkers overlooking the Ionian Sea; more than 750,000 of these were built in Albania between the 1960s and '80s.

ALONG THE ALBANIAN RIVIERA

Jutting out into the Strait of Otranto like a thumb, the Karaburun Peninsula stamps the invisible line where the Adriatic and Ionian Seas meet. From here, a ribbon of breezy beach resorts extending towards Greece defines the once-rustic stretch of coastline now known as the Albanian Riviera.

Heading south from Vlorë, a narrow coastal road curves up and down the cloud-sheathed Llogara Pass, past windswept cliffs, alpine meadows and dense old-growth forests still roamed by wolves and deer. Roadside restaurants serving succulent roast lamb allow a welcome stop on this heart-pounding drive.

The riviera's two main resorts, Himarë and Sarandë, may be swarming with beachgoers throughout summer, but quiet coves with green-tinged waters are only a short drive away. For more solitude, head to a tiny promontory tucked within Porto Palermo Bay, just beyond Himarë. Once the stronghold of ruthless Ali Pasha, its Ottoman-era fortress spurs contemplation with eerily dark vaults and shimmering sea views from the battlements.

South of Sarandë, backed by a vast lagoon where shellfish is farmed, Ksamil is the most charming of the riviera's villages, with four verdant islets within swimming distance of its sandy beach. In summer, you can tour the lagoon by fishing boat to harvest mussels; back on the shore, the haul is cooked and served alfresco with local wine.

The riviera's finale is just as remarkable as its beginning. Enveloped in greenery, the ruins of Butrint whisper of civilisations that waxed and waned along this coast over some 2500 years.

local angle

Butrint's Multilayered History

'Strategically positioned at the tip of the Ksamil Peninsula in today's Albania, Butrint controlled vital maritime routes from antiquity through modern times, linking Venice with Spain and the Ionian Islands. These influences are layered into the urban topography of the site, with imposing monuments and exquisite structures bearing witness to centuries of cultural exchange.

'The theatre of Butrint is a testament to the ambitions of King Pyrrhus from the 3rd century BCE. Hewn into the hillside in classic Greek style, it's supported by robust analemma (retaining) walls; seats for dignitaries were fashioned with lion-footed terminals. In the 2nd century CE, the Romans transformed the stage into a two-storeyed structure with splendid marble statues.

'Renowned for its size and intricacy, the 6th-century Baptistery is one of the grandest of its kind in the Mediterranean. Its striking mosaic pavement is composed of seven concentric bands, connecting themes of protection, paradise and spiritual cleansing.

'The Triangular Fortress was built by the Venetians after 1572 to defend its fishing grounds once the town of Butrint had been abandoned. It passed into Ottoman hands in the early 19th century and served as a military stronghold. Today, the fortress stands as a silent witness to a time when the great powers shaped the fate of Europe in the Corfu Channel.'

Ilir Parangoni PhD, expert in heritage and tourism, Albania

GREECE

- Thessaloniki
- Alexandroupoli
- Halkidiki
- Mt Athos
- Mt Olympus
- Meteora
- Corfu
- Parga
- Mt Pelion
- Volos
- Aegean Sea
- Ionian Islands
- Lamia
- Mt Parnassus
- Delphi
- Messolonghi
- Patras
- Athens
- Saronic Gulf
- Pyrgos
- Nafplio
- Hydra
- Peloponnese
- Myrtoan Sea
- Cyclades
- Kalamata
- Naxos
- Gythio
- Samaria Gorge
- Crete

CHAPTER FIVE

GREECE

**HIKING THE CORFU TRAIL ~ ANCIENT PELOPONNESE DRIVE
KALAMATA OLIVES ~ OLYMPICS IN ATHENS ~ ART OF HYDRA
WINDSURFING IN NAXOS ~ VOLOS' MEZEDES ~ PELION MYTHS
THESSALONIKI NIGHTLIFE ~ CRETE'S PALACE OF KNOSSOS**

Dodecanese Islands
Rhodes
•LINDOS

THE MEDITERRANEAN

→ The Temple of Poseidon in Sounion in the south of Greece dates from around 440 BCE. There's also a Temple of Athena here.

The fabled coastline of Mediterranean Greece stretches over 13,000km (8078 miles), taking in the flanks of the Peloponnese, the Saronic Gulf and the Pelion Peninsula. You're unlikely to be able to cover it all – just look to the story of Odysseus for proof – so instead, revel in the interplay of rugged cliffs, sun-drenched beaches and turquoise waters. Pause frequently to dine at shade-dappled tables in seafront tavernas, the fresh sea scent wafting onshore. Head, too, to the islands – diverse beauties, each with their own character, culinary traditions and ways of life. Your journey will be further torn between the pleasures of the seafront and the ruins of ancient civilisations – Greek, Byzantine, Ottoman and Venetian – each of which set up grand outposts along this coast. Most of all, enjoy the Greeks' rich tradition of *filoxenia*, the warm welcoming of visitors, which dates back to Odysseus' travels and remains a feature of everyday life along these hallowed shores.

GREECE

THE MEDITERRANEAN

CORFU GUIDE

An island still echoing its past

activity
HIKE THE CORFU TRAIL

Hiking a section of the Corfu Trail is an exhilarating way to experience the island's varied landscapes. Waymarked and suitable for all skill levels, the 220km (137-mile) north–south trail traverses the length of Corfu, weaving through ancient olive groves, along rugged coastal paths and into charming villages. Route highlights include soaring views from Mt Pantokrator in the northeast, and the southwest's peaceful Korission coastal lagoon.

explore
CORFIOT CUISINE

With influences stemming from periods of Venetian, French and British rule, Corfu's standout gastronomy differs from that of the rest of Greece. In seaside tavernas and upscale gastro-temples, the emphasis is on quality seafood, local olives and fragrant herbs. Look for dishes like *sofrito* (tender veal in garlic and white wine) and *pastitsada* (spicy beef stew with pasta).

base
CORFU TOWN

Corfu Town's central location allows easy access to beaches, countryside and villages, and its UNESCO-listed fortified Old Town blends Venetian, British and Greek influences in its architecture and celebrated cuisine. Scramble across the impressive 14th-century Palaio Frourio (Old Fortress), taking in panoramic views of city and harbour, then stroll the charming Liston arcade to a terrace cafe. The pilgrim-thronged Church of Agios Spyridon nearby, dedicated to Corfu's patron saint, reveals the city's deep spiritual roots. From here, get happily lost in the labyrinth of narrow alleyways – *kantounia* – before emerging into animated squares.

secret
AKOLI

Seek out the little-known hike to Akoli Beach in rural northeastern Corfu. You'll need to follow a rocky path as it winds through olive groves and dense forest before emerging on a wonderful remote beach where soft, cream-coloured sands blend with sparkling pebbles and clear waters shushing at the shore. In the winter you might be fortunate enough to spot clusters of dolphins playing and feeding off the coast here.

beach
PALEOKASTRITSA

Recline between cliffs and forested slopes on Paleokastritsa's beaches (below), where shores of smooth grey pebbles, lapped by limpid waters, make picture-perfect settings for swimming and snorkelling – especially blissful when crowds diminish outside of high season. Explore the unique rock formations here and discover shimmering marine life from above and below the sea's surface.

"Get happily lost in narrow alleyways before emerging into animated squares"

THE MEDITERRANEAN

→ Krioneri Beach in Parga; the small islet of Virgin Mary just offshore is reachable by strong swimmers or on a rented pedalo.

↘ The Ionian resort town of Parga was a centre of resistance first to the Ottomans in the 18th century and then Axis forces in WWII.

THE IONIAN COAST

The Greek coast near the Albanian frontier hugs the Ionian Sea and is part of the mountainous Epirus region. Seaside villages alternate with sheer cliffs and serene bays as far south as rough-and-tumble Igoumenitsa. The port here is the gateway to beautiful Corfu, and is a major hub for ferries serving Italy. Beyond, the Ionian Sea laps at sandy beaches for some 45km (28 miles) until you reach Parga, an amphitheatre of a village.

Some 20km (12 miles) beyond Parga, the 4th-century-BCE ruins of the Nekromanteion of Acheron – a mystical site once used for speaking with the dead – mirror the massive Roman ruins of Nikopolis, sprawling casually by the road 36km (22 miles) further south. Nikopolis was built in 28 BCE by Octavian (later Augustus), after he defeated Mark Antony and Cleopatra in the naval Battle of Actium (Aktion).

Immediately south, and perched over the entrance to the Ambracian Gulf, the town of Preveza has a low-key international scene at its yacht harbour, set amid Venetian fortifications. Linger here, enjoying tranquil beaches and local seafood. The unsung but glorious island of Lefkada beckons just offshore, connected by a narrow causeway.

Messolonghi sits on the strategic northern edge of the Gulf of Patra, a beguiling blend of salt flats and rich wetlands that supports some 290 resident and migratory bird species, including flamingos and curlews. Fisherfolk practising traditional aquacultural techniques have long worked Messolonghi's twin lagoons, still overlooked by wooden fishing huts today. **CONTINUED ON P158 »**

GREECE

local angle
Sustainable Tourism in Messolonghi

↑ The Garden of Heroes in Messolonghi. Poet Lord Byron died in the town in 1824 and some claim either his heart or lungs are buried here.

'Our hope is to develop a model of responsible tourism in Messolonghi where visitors can enjoy exploring smaller destinations and having authentic experiences with local people. Tourism here can take place throughout the year, not just in the summer.

'Sustainable tourism in our case means connecting with the local community. We began our project by mapping the cultural identity of Messolonghi with the involvement of locals: its history, antiquity, traditions, arts, products, activities, architecture and environment.

'We want tourism to enhance the quality of life of the community here, exchanging knowledge and experiences. For instance, we recommend a ride on one of the traditional boats in the lagoon. Or we take people to visit our cultural sights while explaining their importance, like our Xenokrateion Archaeological Museum, art gallery, Garden of Heroes, Salt Museum and more.

'We have developed cultural routes and activities that allow people to experience the area through the eyes of locals. Our activities don't distinguish between locals and visitors; they bring everyone together with a common goal of seeking knowledge and experiencing something beautiful. Another example: our region is known for its delicious fish, so visitors who seek fish made using our local recipes will encourage businesses to continue featuring such traditional dishes.

'Our objective is to stimulate the local economy, to encourage young people to return to their home town and to protect the environment. For us, showcasing our region is such a wonderful way to achieve this.'
Alexandros Panagiotopoulos, co-head of Messolonghi by Locals

THE MEDITERRANEAN

→ Kalamitsi Beach, near the village of Kardamyli on the Western Mani – or the Outer Mani as it's known locally – and by the Messinian Gulf.

THE WESTERN PELOPONNESE

Journey south to Greece's third-largest city, Patra. Though there's a gritty side to this busy port, it has attractive squares and a great bar and restaurant scene fuelled by 20,000 university students. The annual Patra Carnival is one of the country's best, with costume parades and colourful floats rolling for seven weeks before Orthodox Easter.

The port of Kyllini, 71km (44 miles) south, serves Zakynthos and Kefallonia; beyond, the coastline skims Ancient Olympia, along vast beaches like those at glitzy Costa Navarino resort. Hugging the Peloponnese's southwest peninsula for 108km (67 miles), you reach Kalamata, famous worldwide for its olives. Most travellers blitz through but give it a chance and you'll find a small, attractive Old Town below its *kastro* (fort).

To the southeast, the Mani covers the Peloponnese's central peninsula, a wild region still wonderfully under-explored. It's easy to see why Kardamyli, scenically set between the blue waters of the Messinian Gulf and the Taÿgetos Mountains, was one of the seven cities offered to Achilles by Agamemnon. The Vyros Gorge – perfect for hiking – emerges just north of town, running to the foot of Mt Profitis Ilias (2407m), the highest peak of the Taÿgetos. British writer Patrick Leigh Fermor lived his last decades in Kalamitsi Bay, just south of town, and wrote *Mani* here, considered by many to be the definitive book on the region.

Leaving the snow-tipped Taÿgetos behind you, continue south to the arid tip of the peninsula, speckled with abandoned stone towers. **CONTINUED ON P162 »**

know-how
Greek Olive and Olive-Oil Heritage

Olive production is a cornerstone of Greece's cultural and culinary identity, deeply rooted in its ancient history. The cultivation of olives here dates back over 3000 years, making Greece one of the oldest olive-growing regions in the world. Olive oil played a part in religious rituals and was slathered on the bodies of ancient Greek athletes, and it remains a key ingredient in the Mediterranean diet, celebrated for its health benefits.

Greek olive oil is renowned for its quality, with extra virgin oil being the most prized due to its low acidity and high content of monounsaturated fats and antioxidants. The production process involves careful harvesting, typically by hand, and cold-pressing of the olives to preserve their delicate flavours and nutrients.

Kalamata gives its name to the esteemed Kalamata olive, a plump, purple-black variety found in delicatessens around the world. The region's typically reliable winter rains and hot summers make for perfect olive-growing conditions.

The Kalamata tree (below) is distinguished from the common olive by the size of its leaves. Like its fruit, the leaves are twice the size of many varieties' and a darker shade of green. Unlike other varieties, Kalamata olives can't be picked green. They ripen in late November and must be hand-picked to avoid bruising. Buy and sample these olives, fresh, at the markets in Kalamata.

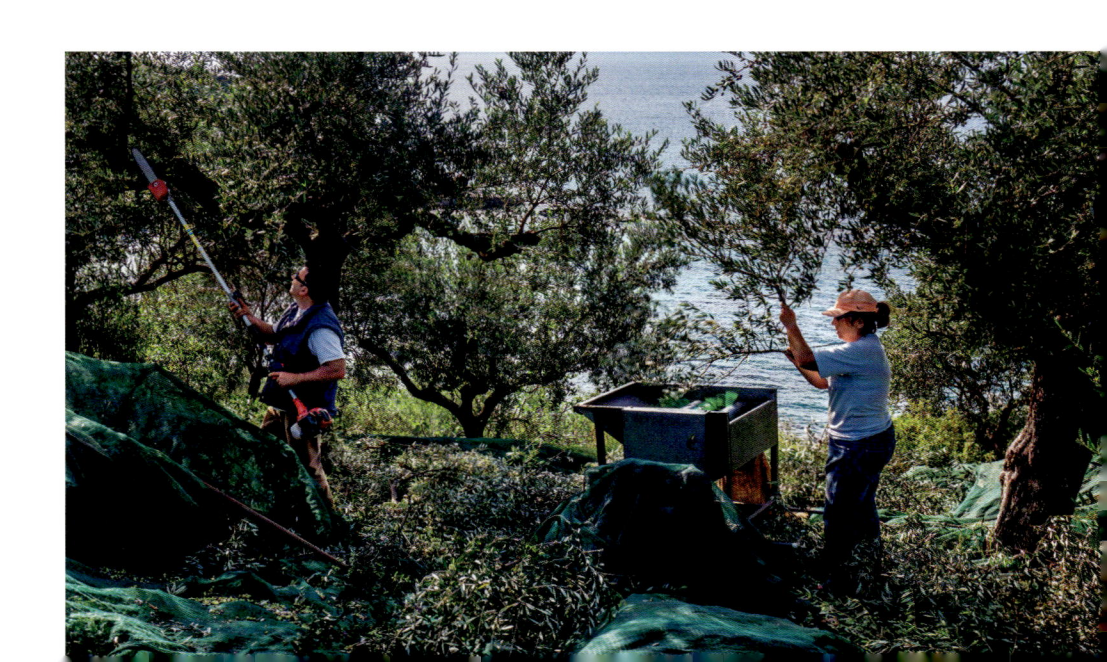

WESTERN PELOPONNESE

Plot a road trip between charismatic ancient sights and dramatic scenery

Distance 203km (126 miles)
Duration Two days
Start Pyrgos
Finish Mystras

❶ Ancient Olympia
Start at Pyrgos and drive east through rolling fields to Ancient Olympia, where you can stand in the stadium that hosted the first Olympic Games and imagine the roar of the crowd. The Games took place here every four years for over 1100 years, until their abolition by Emperor Theodosius I in 393 BCE. The Olympic flame is still lit here for the modern Games. Wandering between the tree-shaded ruins you can picture the blood and smoke of oxen sacrificed to Zeus and Hera, the jostling crowds and the oiled-up athletes waiting inside the original stadium. *20km (12 miles)*

❷ Ancient Messini
Driving south, you can choose between the coastal road or the longer 145km (90-mile) route inland via the mountain village, Andritsena. It overlooks the valley of the Alfios River and leads to the Temple of Epicurean Apollo, a UNESCO World Heritage site 14km (9 miles) south. Vast Ancient Messini was founded in 371 BCE after the Theban general Epaminondas defeated Sparta, freeing the Messinians from almost 350 years of Spartan rule. These ruins are as extensive as those of Olympia, yet receive only a fraction of the visitors. Picturesquely situated on a hillside below the village of Mavromati, the site comprises a large theatre, an *agora* (marketplace), a Sanctuary of Asclepius and an impressive ancient stadium. Break your journey at Mavromati's Messana Hotel, which blends traditional stone and wood construction with contemporary touches. *87km (54 miles)*

❸ Mystras
Finish at the captivating World Heritage–listed remains of Mystras, the most compelling set of medieval ruins in Greece. This massive ancient fortress town was the last stronghold of the Byzantine Empire and home to the court of the Byzantine imperial family for two centuries. Tread cobblestones worn smooth by centuries of footsteps, ducking into the ruins of palaces, monasteries and churches, most dating from between 1271 and 1460. The site spreads out over a steep mountainside and is surrounded by olive and orange trees. Rest for the night at nearby Mazaraki Guesthouse, which gives extraordinary views to Sparta and Mystras. *96km (60 miles)*

GREECE

↖ The ruins of Mystras, occupied successively by the Byzantines, Turks and Venetians.

↙ The Temple of Zeus, built 470–457 BCE, is a centrepiece of the site of Ancient Olympia.

→ Nafplio Old Town, first referred to in the 14th century BCE Mortuary Temple of Amenhotep III near Luxor, Egypt.

↘ The Lion's Gate, Mycenae; in the 9th century BCE, the poet Homer wrote about 'well-built Mycenae, rich in gold'.

THE EASTERN PELOPONNESE

Overlooking the Laconian Gulf, Gythio has well-preserved 19th-century architecture and a harbour busy with ferries to nearby Kythira. Visible from the shore, Marathonisi Islet is thought to be ancient Cranae, where Paris of Troy and Helen consummated the affair that sparked the Trojan War.

A short way east of town, pass the evocative shipwreck of the *Dimitrios* en route to the third of the southern Peloponnesian peninsulas, the Malea. Here the Kastania Cave is home to some of Europe's finest stalactites and stalagmites.

Travelling northeast for 39km (24 miles), with the Myrtoan Sea twinkling off to your right, Monemvasia rises from teal waters, a slab of rock and sheer cliffs topped by a medieval village. Plan for a few hours wandering its lanes, Byzantine churches and sea-view Ottoman-era buildings.

Leonidio is set at the mouth of the Badron Gorge, 92km (57 miles) north along a mountainous road. Now a magnet for climbers, it's also known for its Tsakonian aubergines, celebrated at the summer Melitzazz Festival.

At the apex of the Argolic Gulf, 80km (50 miles) north, romantic Nafplio occupies a knockout waterside location. The Old Town has attractive narrow streets, Venetian houses, neoclassical mansions and intriguing galleries. But the main draw lies inland: the ruins of Ancient Mycenae. For four centuries in the second millennium BCE, the Mycenaean kingdom was the most powerful in Greece, evidenced by the site's Lion's Gate, tombs and Agamemnon's Palace. **CONTINUED ON P166 »**

local angle
Athletic Traditions Reimagined

↑ The Panathenaic Stadium, built from Attic marble; the 329 BCE site was restored for the 1896 rebirth of the Olympic Games.

'Sports have held profound significance in Greek culture from antiquity to now, reflecting a deep appreciation for physical prowess and communal spirit. In ancient Greece, athletics were not merely recreational but integral to religious and societal practices. The most famed example is, of course, the Olympic Games, held in honour of Zeus. They were a vital aspect of Greek unity, transcending individual city-states and fostering a sense of shared Hellenic culture. Athletes embodied ideals of strength, discipline and excellence. The games also included musical and poetic competitions, emphasising our holistic view of human development.

'I was a competitive swimmer and introduced the teaching of baby-swimming to Greece, which has now become wildly popular. As an extension of my belief that athletic training develops both body and mind, I have opened a fitness-centred hotel called Alkima. Inspired by the ancient Greek word *alkimi*, meaning physical and mental strength and resilience, it's my goal to help visitors tap into the health and well-being aspects of Greek life.

'As part of our offering we give guests recommendations for great runs in Athens. We love the Apostolou Pavlou promenade, where you can jog from the Ancient Agora to paths on Filopappou Hill and along the Dionysiou Areopagitou walkway at the foot of the Acropolis.

'Also, in addition to getting a permit to run inside the Panathenaic Stadium, home of the first modern-day Olympic Games, you can run the 500m racetrack on its rim. The path is accessible from the rear, through a green gate on Arhimidous St, and it's very much open and free to use.'

Margarita Kontzia, swimming champion and owner of Alkima hotel, Athens

THE MEDITERRANEAN

ATHENS GUIDE

The Greek capital, ancient and modern

taste
SOUVLAKI

The capital's restaurants run from Michelin-starred fine-dining to traditional Greek tavernas like Diporto Agoras, in an unmarked basement. Athens also has many street-food options, *souvlaki* (skewers of grilled meat or vegetables, often served in a pitta) being the king among them. Every neighbourhood has its own *souvlatzidiko* – try central Athens' Elvis or Kosta.

culture
THE ACROPOLIS

The historic citadel of Athens' Acropolis (above) is a living symbol of ancient Greek achievement. Crisscross the famed archaeological site, perched on a craggy hill overlooking the entire city, to marvel at how the classical beauty and harmony of the Parthenon, Erechtheion and Temple of Athena Nike have endured through the ages. Democracy, science, art, drama and philosophy flourished centuries ago in these surroundings, and the likes of Socrates, Plato, Aristotle, Pericles and Thucydides once trod here.

buy
MASTIC-BASED PRODUCTS

People come from far and wide for chic neighbourhood Kolonaki's outstanding selection of shops and boutiques. Stop by Mastihashop to browse through a range of products made with mastic – a medicinal resin from rare trees only found on the island of Chios. Mastiha liqueur is a treat served as a digestive right across Greece, while the mastic-based body-care range runs from mouthwash to face packs.

"Countless cafe-bars rub shoulders with craftspeople's workshops"

explore
MONASTIRAKI AND PSYRRI

Start at Monastiraki's busy main square, one of Athens' key hubs, where people meet before hitting nearby bars and *souvlaki* joints. To the south, visit the Ancient Agora, the city's original civic meeting place, and the Roman Agora. Walk north through creative Psyrri, one of the liveliest quarters, plastered with street art and where countless cafe-bars rub shoulders with craftspeople's workshops. Set out early to sample the buzz of Athens Central Market and the streets around it.

nightlife
BOUZOUKIA

At Athens' *bouzoukia* (live-music clubs), traditional Greek music blends with contemporary genres. The largest are impressively glamorous venues that host the hottest names on the Greek *laïka* (folk music) and pop scenes, both based on the sounds of the *bouzouki*, a stringed instrument central to Greek music. *Bouzoukia* party till the wee hours; during the winter, the venues line Iera Odos and Pireos streets, while through the summer they migrate to open-air spaces along the coast.

THE MEDITERRANEAN

THE SARONIC GULF
The coastline of the Saronic Gulf, starting from Nafplio, winds through cliffs and secluded beaches around the Argolid Peninsula. It encompasses fashionable resorts like Costa (a jumping-off point for lovely Spetses) and fishing towns like Ermione, gateway to the car-free island of Hydra.

Continuing around the peninsula on narrow, curving roads for 89km (55 miles), you reach the astounding ancient theatre of Epidavros, set in pine-clad hills and famed for its acoustics. In its day, Epidavros was revered across the Mediterranean as a place of miraculous healing, and people travelled great distances to its tranquil Sanctuary of Asclepius to seek cures. Today the UNESCO World Heritage site's well-preserved theatre, in use for over 2300 years, is a fabulous venue during the summertime Athens Epidaurus Festival of performing arts.

Where the Peloponnese meets the rest of the mainland, you'll cross the Corinth Canal, 6km (4 miles) long and 23m wide, cut through solid rock. As you approach Athens, the coastline becomes more industrial. At Elefsina, some of the warehouses set by its ancient ruins have been converted into performance centres and galleries. Beyond, a series of lively communities, upscale marinas and resorts dubbed the 'Athens Riviera' extend from Piraeus (the massive port of Athens) to Cape Sounion. Sandy beaches surround the suburbs of Glyfada and laid-back Vouliagmeni, where a thermal lake is famed for waters that never fall below 21°C, ideal for all-year swimming.

The Saronic Gulf coastline concludes at Cape Sounion, known for its Temple of Poseidon – a vision of gleaming white-marble Doric columns topping a craggy spur from where the Aegean Sea seems especially wondrous at sunset. **CONTINUED ON P170 »**

↓ Spetses Museum, set in the 18th-century mansion of Hatzigiannis Mexis, a lead figure in the fight for Greek independence.

local angle
The Art of Hydra

'Hydra started to become a cultural focal point after WWII, especially during the '50s and '60s. Its tranquillity and distinctive light attracted creative people who sought an ideal retreat to be inspired and to express, plus there's the unique absence of vehicles here.

'During my workshops, I hope to share a sense of the inner expansion and profound innate realisation of empowerment that Hydra seems to instil in artists. I suggest hiking to naturally inspiring locations on the island, and I also like to direct visitors to places like the Lazaros Koundouriotis Historical Mansion. This ochre-coloured *arhontiko* (stone mansion) belonged to a Greek war hero and hosts an annual art exhibition. Then they can visit the home and atelier of Panayiotis Tetsis, one of Greece's best painters and a native of Hydra. His paints and paintings are intact, as is his family's grocery shop.

'On the waterfront, the Historical Archives Museum of Hydra hosts art and cultural exhibitions. You can walk down the coast to the Deste Foundation, where top-name international artists create a summer installation.'
Dimitris Fousekis (above), painter, illustrator and workshop leader in Hydra

THE MEDITERRANEAN

NAXOS GUIDE

A stepping stone into the Cyclades

beach
WESTERN COAST

Magnificent beaches known for their smooth sands and aquamarine waters unfurl along Naxos' western edge. South of Agios Georgios (Hora's town beach), blue-flag Agios Prokopios lies in a sheltered bay, and has a buzzy feel courtesy of the tavernas lining its shore. Beyond the turquoise shallows of Plaka Beach (above), the white sands of Glyfada continue as far as Agiasos.

activity
KITESURFING

Naxos is a top kite- and windsurfing destination, known for its reliable Meltemi winds and varied conditions. Beginners will enjoy calm, shallow waters at Laguna Beach Park, south of Hora, while the more advanced can tackle stronger winds and waves at Mikri Vigla, further along the west coast. Local surf schools rent out equipment and give lessons for all skill levels.

secret
FLERIO

Naxian marble has long been coveted, and in the ancient marble-working area of Flerio, two massive, unfinished *kouroi* (giant statues of young men) lie where they fell in what was once a quarry. The *kouroi* here were made here around the 6th or 7th century BCE, and were likely abandoned due to cracks or imperfections.

> "Naxos has undeniable charisma from the moment you see the Temple of Apollo at the mouth of its harbour"

explore
INLAND

Away from the coast, the 6th-century-BCE Temple of Demeter is a marble sanctuary dedicated to the goddess of agriculture. Head on through fertile plains and vineyards, up to mountain villages crowned with Byzantine churches and crumbling Venetian towers. Apiranthos, on the stony flanks of Mt Fanari, is known for its crafts, best seen at the Women's Association of Traditional Art, where they also sell homemade sweets. Farms here produce cheeses, olives and potatoes, offering a taste of the island's rich rural life.

base
HORA

The biggest and among the most magnificent of the Cyclades, Naxos has undeniable charisma from the moment you see the remains of its Temple of Apollo at the mouth of its harbour. In Hora (Naxos Town, below), a thrumming waterfront merges with a web of steep cobbled alleys climbing to a 13th-century Venetian *kastro*, the heart of the Duchy of the Aegean. Have sunset cocktails at Avaton 1739, with sweeping views of the town and sea. The summertime Naxos Festival delivers concerts, exhibitions and celebrations of food.

ALONG EASTERN ATTIKI

Following the eastern coast of Attiki, the region including Athens, you'll pass the small port towns of Lavrio and Rafina, both departure points for ferries to the Cyclades. Between them, and beside the estuary of the Erasinos River, Vravrona is home to a temple dedicated to Artemis, the goddess of the hunt.

31km (19 miles) north, Marathon needs little introduction for history buffs or runners. As related in the nearby museum, this was the location of the 490-BCE victory over a 25,000-strong Persian force by a vastly outnumbered army of Greeks and Plataeans.

Slide on east of Marathon to diminutive Schinias-Marathon National Park, where a sandy beach is backed by umbrella-pine forest and the shallow, calm waters make for wonderful swimming. The park encompasses the Kinosura Peninsula and the Gulf of Schinias, and its important coastal ecosystem blends together wetlands, Mediterranean scrub and olive groves.

Follow the coast around Nea Makri, lined with pebbly beaches and small fishing harbours, to reach the Euripus Strait, where a bridge connects the large island of Evia at Chalkida. Continuing north along the Euboean Gulf, you'll reach Thermopylae, where one of the greatest military feats of antiquity – still legendary 2500 years on – took place. In this narrow pass, Leonidas and 300 brave Spartans sacrificed their lives to halt Xerxes' vast Persian army long enough to secure an ultimate Greek victory.

Approaching the city of Lamia, the terrain becomes more mountainous, the hinterland peppered with thermal springs. Follow the E75 around Mt Othrys along the Pagasitikos Gulf to Volos, a university town on a natural harbour sheltered by the Pelion Peninsula, curving to the east. **CONTINUED ON P174 »**

↑ A bronze statue of the Spartan king Leonidas in Thermopylae, where he died in 480 BCE fighting the army of Persian king Xerxes.

local angle
Volos *Tsipouradiko*

'Volos is famous throughout Greece for the quality and quantity (over 500) of its *ouzeris* and *tsipouradika*, both varieties of small tavern. Established starting in the early 1920s by Greek refugees forced to leave Asia Minor, the *tsipouradika* serve the fiery spirit *tsipouro* (also called *tsikoudia*) made from grape pomace or must, together with *mezedes* (varied small dishes, also called *tsipouromeze*) of fish and seafood from the Pagasitikos Gulf and the Aegean. This revered sociocultural gastronomic tradition lives on at Volos' vintage joints and neo-*tsipouradika*.'

Andreas' 10 Commandments of Tsipouradika
1 Do not peruse the menu. Let your server decide.
2 Do not covet meat. Fish and seafood are king.
3 Honour the holy spirit *tsipouro* (or *ouzo*).
4 Only decide on *tsipouro* made with or without anise.
5 Do not take a sip without a bite of food.
6 Do not snub dishes, no matter how peculiar.
7 Do not eat, drink and run. Take it slow!
8 Do not monopolise *mezedhes*. It's meant to be shared.
9 Only drink beer if it's your final round.
10 Never refuse a complimentary *tsipouromeze*.

Andreas Diakodimitris, co-owner (with Grigoris Helmis) of new-wave *tsipouradiko* Mezen, Volos

THE MEDITERRANEAN

DELPHI AND METEORA

Drive between verdant foothills and pinnacle-topping monasteries

Distance 391km (243 miles)
Duration Two days
Start Athens
Finish Meteora

❶ Delphi
From Athens, drive northwest on the E65 across the rolling hills and vineyards of the Boeotian Plain. Approaching Delphi village, the road narrows and winds as it ascends the dramatic mountains of the Parnassus range. Of all Greece's archaeological sites, Ancient Delphi has the most potent spirit of place. Centring on the mountainside Sanctuary of Apollo, home to the ancient world's most renowned oracle, this sacred spot looks out over an unbroken expanse of olive trees, sloping down to the Gulf of Corinth. *165km (103 miles)*

❷ Iti National Park
Driving from Delphi to Mt Iti National Park, head northwest on the E65, passing through the Phocis region and the charming town of Amfissa, then winding through the forested foothills between Mt Parnassus and Mt Giona. You'll pass small villages like Gravia until, approaching the park, the road becomes more mountainous, bringing you into its hiking-trail-laced heart. Stretching across the upper slopes of Mt Iti (2151m), the park holds dense forests of fir and black pine, deep gorges and rock formations, as well as butterfly-filled upland meadows and snowmelt pools fringed by marsh orchids – habitats that support deer, boar and birdlife, from eagles to woodpeckers. According to mythology, Hercules built his own funeral pyre on Mt Iti, near the village of Pavliani, before joining his divine peers on Mt Olympus. After a day of hiking, indulge in a steam and massage at Alexakis Hotel & Spa in the village of Loutra, known for its thermal waters. *67km (41 miles)*

❸ Meteora
Back on the E65, leave the lushness of the park behind as you press on north. The road winds through the picturesque, agricultural Phthiotis region near Lamia, and as you approach the plains of Thessaly, the terrain flattens out to deliver expansive vistas. Near the town of Kalambaka, the charismatic rock formations of Meteora begin to emerge on the horizon. These towering monolithic pillars, topped by Byzantine monasteries, are set against the mountain backdrop of the Pindus range, and present another wonderful opportunity for walkers and climbers. *159km (99 miles)*

GREECE

↖ The Athenian Treasury at Delphi, built around the 6th century BCE to house votive offerings.

↙ Moni Agias Varvaras Rousanou, built in 1529 CE, one of Meteora's six active monasteries.

173

VOLOS TO THESSALONIKI

Loop east around the coast from Volos, along the foot of Mt Pelion, on to the western fringe of the glorious Pelion Peninsula, where forests of chestnut, pine and plane trees meet the Aegean Sea. Beaches like Kala Nera and Afissos are set against this green backdrop, all crisscrossed by walking trails.

When you eventually turn north again, take the E75 inland from Volos, skirting Mt Ossa just east of Larissa then swerving back to the coast near the Byzantine castle at Platamon, from where low-key beaches line the Thermaic Gulf. You are now at the foot of Mt Olympus (2918m, 9573ft), a looming backdrop to the shore. The cloud-covered lair of the ancient Greek pantheon, awe-inspiring Mt Olympus fires the imagination today just as it did for the ancients who venerated it. Greece's highest mountain, Olympus hosts more than 1700 plant species, some rare and endemic, as well as wolves, jackals, deer and more than 100 bird species. Its slopes are thickly forested and its peaks often shrouded in fog. Although you can drive up Olympus, many people hike, overnighting in mountain refuges. It's a tough climb, however; consult Litochoro-based hiking associations for maps and current conditions before setting out.

As you approach Thessaloniki, Greece's second-largest city, 100km (62 miles) north, the coastline transforms into an urbanised waterfront promenade. Old and new cohabit here wonderfully: the Arch of Galerius, an intricate 4th-century-CE monument, overlooks the busy shopping drag of Egnatia; Thessaloniki's most renowned sight, the White Tower, anchors a waterfront packed with cocktail bars. This is a city to get lost in. **CONTINUED ON P180 »**

↖ The clear waters of the Aegean Sea lap against the shores of Chondri Ammos in the south of the Pelion Peninsula.

↑ Oleander flowers bloom near the town of Litochoro, with the slopes of holy Mt Olympus rising in the backdrop.

know-how

Mythology of the Pelion Peninsula

The Pelion Peninsula is steeped in rich mythology, particularly linked to its densely forested slopes, dominated by Mt Pelion. The peninsula is known as the home of the *kentavri* (centaurs, above), mythical creatures with the upper body of a human and the lower body of a horse. The centaurs took delight in drinking wine, deflowering virgins and generally carousing around the countryside.

Not all centaurs were merely revellers. Considered the wisest of the group, Chiron was legendary for his skill in medicine. He's said to have lived in a cave on Mt Pelion, and it was hereabouts that he mentored many of Greece's greatest heroes, including Achilles, Asclepius and Hercules. Chiron's teachings and his tragic fate – wounded by an incurable arrow and unable to die due to his immortality – are central themes in Greek mythology.

Another important myth involves the Argonauts and their quest for the Golden Fleece. According to legend, *Argo* – the ship of Jason and the Argonauts – was built by the shipwright Argus in the forests of Pelion, using wood that's said to have come from these sacred trees. The subsequent adventures of Jason and his crew are crucial episodes in Greek mythology, symbolising heroism and the pursuit of glory.

Pelion is also linked to the wedding of Peleus and Thetis, the sea nymph. Their marriage, celebrated on Mt Pelion, was attended by many gods and goddesses, and led to the infamous Apple of Discord, which Paris awarded (as a token of beauty) to Aphrodite in exchange for marriage to the beautiful mortal Helen, and which ultimately resulted in the outbreak of the Trojan War.

THE MEDITERRANEAN

THESSALONIKI GUIDE

From barhopping to Byzantine churches

culture
BYZANTINE RELICS

A pivotal Byzantine city, Thessaloniki has a rich heritage memorialised at the Museum of Byzantine Culture and in resplendent churches like its 7th-century-CE Church of Agios Dimitrios (above), a significant pilgrimage site. The Rotunda of Galerius, originally a Roman mausoleum, was transformed into a grand church, the city's first, and later a mosque. The serene little 5th-century Church of Osios David, one of the most important early Christian sites in Thessaloniki, contains rare 12th-century frescoes and a 5th-century mosaic of Christ and the prophets Ezekiel and Habakkuk.

buy
KOMBOLOI

Thessaloniki is known for its high-quality *komboloi* – traditional Greek worry beads – which are meticulously crafted by artisans here. The beads are often made from local amber, wood or semiprecious stones, and each set has a distinct design reflecting an aspect of the city's cultural heritage.

taste
REVANI AND TRIGONA

This is Greece's gastronomic capital. Food here takes the bounty of the Thermaic Gulf and its fertile hinterland, preparing it using Greek, Turkish, Jewish and Slavic culinary traditions absorbed down the centuries. Look for Ottoman treats such as *baklava* and *basbousa* (syrup-drenched semolina cakes known locally as *revani*) at sweet shops like Chatzis. Buy the local classic, a custard-filled pastry triangle known as *trigona,* from its place-of-origin, Trigona Elenidis.

> *"Food here takes the bounty of the Thermaic Gulf and its hinterland"*

nightlife
LADADIKA

Ladadika, once a neighbourhood of olive-oil warehouses, thrums with Thessaloniki's most concentrated dining and social scene: a lively blend of traditional Greek tavernas and modern cocktail and music bars. The area buzzes with energy, music filtering out into the streets. Plan to barhop from Gorilla, a standout spot well known for its creative cocktails and eclectic ambiance, on through to the hard-partying Stones Rock Bar.

explore
ANO POLI

The steep, labyrinthine streets of Ano Poli (the view from it is below), Thessaloniki's upper town, have magnificent ruins, lesser-visited churches and much atmosphere. Only Ano Poli (then, the Turkish Quarter) largely survived the city-wide devastation of a 1917 fire. Although the fire started here, the wind swept the flames towards the sea.

THE MEDITERRANEAN

CRETE GUIDE

Circle the largest of Greece's islands

base
CHANIA

Chania (Hania) is the ideal base in Crete thanks to its blend of historic character, enticing food and attractive boutique hotels. The harbour (above) is perfect for evening promenades, while the Old Town has creative shops set in the street level of neoclassical townhouses. Nearby lie sandy shores, mountain villages and hiking in the Samaria Gorge.

activity
HIKING THE SAMARIA GORGE

Hiking the Samaria Gorge (above) ranks as a classic Cretan adventure. This memorable 16km (10-mile) trek winds through limestone cliffs, forests and rugged terrain before concluding at Agia Roumeli, a scenic coastal village. Relax here at a seafront taverna after a refreshing swim in the Libyan Sea. Highlights of the walk include the Iron Gates, where the gorge narrows dramatically, and the diverse array of plants and wildlife you'll encounter, including rare species such as the Cretan kri-kri goat.

beach
ELAFONISI BEACH

Let yourself fall for Elafonisi Beach, where shallow, turquoise waters meet soft sand with a distinctive pink hue courtesy of minute crushed coral and shells. The beach is divided by a narrow lagoon that you can wade across to a small, uninhabited islet. Surrounded by dunes, Elafonisi offers a serene, otherworldly escape – especially in shoulder season when the crowds diminish.

secret
THE INNAHORION

Some of western Crete's most scenic and unvisited mountain villages, the Innahorion (meaning 'nine villages') are spread across the far-western coastal region, surrounded by chestnut and olive trees. The coastal road from Kefali to Sfinari is one of Crete's most beautiful: it winds around cliffs with magnificent sea views unfolding after every bend. For the area's best eating, as well as serene traditional lodgings, head to the remote ecotourism complex of Milia Mountain Retreat.

"This memorable trek winds through limestone cliffs, forests and rugged terrain before concluding at a scenic coastal village"

explore
PALACE OF KNOSSOS

Take your time exploring Crete's most famous historical attraction, the Bronze Age Palace of Knossos. The setting for this grand capital of Minoan Crete is evocative, and the ruins and recreations impressive (though British archaeologist Arthur Evans' unsubtle 20th-century 'renovations' remain controversial). The site encompasses an immense palace, courtyards, private apartments, baths and vivid frescoes. The palace itself features advanced architectural elements, from ventilation systems to sophisticated plumbing.

THE MEDITERRANEAN

→ Beech trees in the 5800-hectare University Forest of Taxiarchis on Mt Holomontas, Halkidiki, home to wolves and wild boar.

↘ A shrine built on limestone outcrops at Portokali Beach, Sithonia – also known locally as Kavourotripes (Crab Hole) Beach.

THROUGH THE NORTH TO TÜRKIYE

Just outside of Thessaloniki, golden sands meet clear waters on the three peninsulas of Halkidiki. Of the two touristic 'fingers' (Kassandra and Sithonia), both known for their diving and watersports, the Sithonian Peninsula is most beloved by families and those seeking a laid-back getaway, with excellent beaches such as Armenistis. Olive groves swathe the north, while pine forests stubble a wild interior, fringing cliffsides that plummet towards coves.

Next up, Ouranoupoli is the gateway to Athos, Halkidiki's final peninsula, home to the semi-autonomous monastic community of Mt Athos (access is granted to male visitors only). Early Christians settled here in the 4th century, and the mountain of Athos featured in classical mythology long before.

Continuing through Macedonia, around the Strymonian Gulf, you'll pass the powerful Lion of Amphipolis, a monument to one of Alexander the Great's generals. For 60km (37 miles), the coastline alternates between rocky outcrops and scenic bays as you approach Kavala, founded in the 7th century BCE by settlers from the nearby island of Thasos. Kavala is often treated as a gateway to the northeastern Aegean Islands, but its draws include the nearby site of ancient Philippi, a 16th-century aqueduct built for Ottoman Sultan Suleiman the Magnificent, and the Byzantine castle and Ottoman buildings of its pastel-hued Old Town.

As you approach Alexandroupoli, eastern Thrace's largest town and the final outpost before the Turkish border, beautiful sandy stretches include Mesimvrias Beach.

know-how

The Vergina Royal Tombs

Alexander the Great (below), born in 356 BCE in Pella, Macedonia, was one of history's most influential military leaders. Tutored by Aristotle, he ascended to the Macedonian throne in 336 BCE following the assassination of his father, Philip II. Alexander's conquests stretched from Greece through Asia Minor, Egypt, Persia and into India, creating one of the largest empires of the ancient world. His efforts spread Hellenistic culture across vast regions, profoundly impacting the course of history throughout them.

The magnificent Vergina Royal Tombs, discovered in 1977 by Greek archaeologist Manolis Andronikos, are crucial to understanding Macedonian history and Alexander's legacy. The royal necropolis contains more than 500 tumuli (burial mounds), including 12 oversized, temple-shaped tombs, dating from the late 4th century BCE. The most significant tomb is that of Philip II, based on inscriptions and the grandeur of its artefacts: incredible frescoes depicting the Macedonian royal family, plus the golden larnax (coffin) and some exquisite golden wreaths, all highlighting the opulence of Macedonian royalty.

RHODES GUIDE

Grandest of the Dodecanese

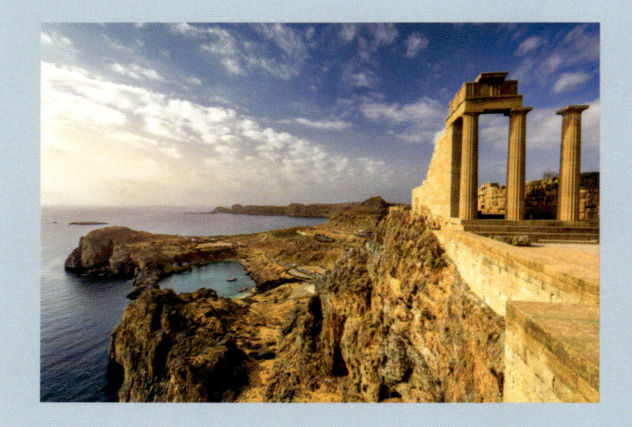

explore
LINDOS

South of Rhodes Town, sugar-cube houses spill down to a turquoise bay at Lindos, the modern town capped by the clifftop, 4th-century-BCE Acropolis of Lindos (above). Once within the battlements built by the Knights of St John, the site's ruins include a Temple to Athena Lindia and a Hellenistic stoa with 20 columns. Visit around sunset when the Acropolis casts a golden glow.

secret
RHODIAN HONEY

Savour the distinct, aromatic flavour of Rhodes' unique honey, redolent of the flora from which it's derived: thyme, sage and pine. Produced through traditional methods (keep an eye out for colourful beehives as you walk or drive along the road), Rhodian honey is prized by those in the know for its rich texture and natural sweetness.

activity
DIVE OR SNORKEL

Book a trip with marine ecotours operator Blutopia Marine Park to dive or snorkel with shoals of thousands of fish – and, if you're fortunate, bottlenose dolphins, tuna and devil rays – in the company of qualified dive instructors. Or opt for a boat cruise to the uninhabited islands of Makri, Stroggyli and Alimia, stopping to swim and snorkel in the cerulean waters.

> "Snorkel with shoals of thousands of fish – and, if you're fortunate, bottlenose dolphins, tuna and devil rays"

beach
PRASONISI

Accessible via a windswept road that snakes for 10km (6 miles) south from Kattavia, Prasonisi Beach extends to form a tenuously narrow, sandy isthmus (which is, in effect, a double-sided beach). This connects to Cape Prasonisi, Rhodes' southernmost point. The Aegean Sea meets the Mediterranean here, creating ideal wind and wave conditions for kitesurfers and windsurfers. Outfitters can help with everything from rental equipment and lessons to overnight accommodation provided in simple surfer hostels.

base
RHODES OLD TOWN

In Rhodes Town, the atmospheric old quarter spirits you back to the days of the Byzantine Empire and beyond, on the far largest and most historically important island in the Dodecanese. The Old Town (below) lies within yet utterly apart from the New Town, sealed like a medieval time capsule behind a double ring of high walls and a moat. Few cities can claim so many layers of architectural history, with relics of the Classical, Byzantine, Knights Hospitaller, Ottoman and Venetian eras entangled in a mind-boggling maze of twisting lanes.

CHAPTER SIX

TÜRKIYE

CREATIVE BOZCAADA ~ **WINEMAKING IN URLA**
CRAFTS IN İZMIR ~ **ANCIENT IONIA ROAD TRIP** ~ **TAVERN CULTURE**
BODRUM'S BLUE CRUISE ~ **BOZBURUN ARCHAEOLOGY**
GULF OF GÖKOVA BEACHES ~ **LYCIAN WAY HIKING** ~ **DINING IN ANTALYA**

ANTALYA

ALANYA

ANAMUR

MERSIN

ANTAKYA

THE MEDITERRANEAN

→ Explore the Mediterranean coast from the Lycian Way, which meanders through this ancient civilisation's landscape.

From serene rural villages to rollicking beach resorts, Türkiye's Aegean and Mediterranean coasts are diverse in flavour, seasoned with thousands of years of history that have inspired stories ranging from the *Iliad* to the myth of Santa Claus. Impressive Crusader castles and Ottoman fortresses stand guard on the shoreline, while older ruins of ancient temples and cities lie silently among rolling hills and atop steep mountain slopes.

Olive groves, wild herbs and the bounty of the sea define the cuisine of the Aegean region, which stretches at length from the Bulgarian border in the north to where the southwestern peninsulas of Bodrum, Datça and Bozburun reach out across the water towards the Dodecanese Islands of Greece. Along the edges of the Mediterranean, the rugged shores of the Lycian Coast in the west and the fertile agricultural plains around Adana in the east stand in stark contrast to the ever-booming holiday destinations of Marmaris and Antalya.

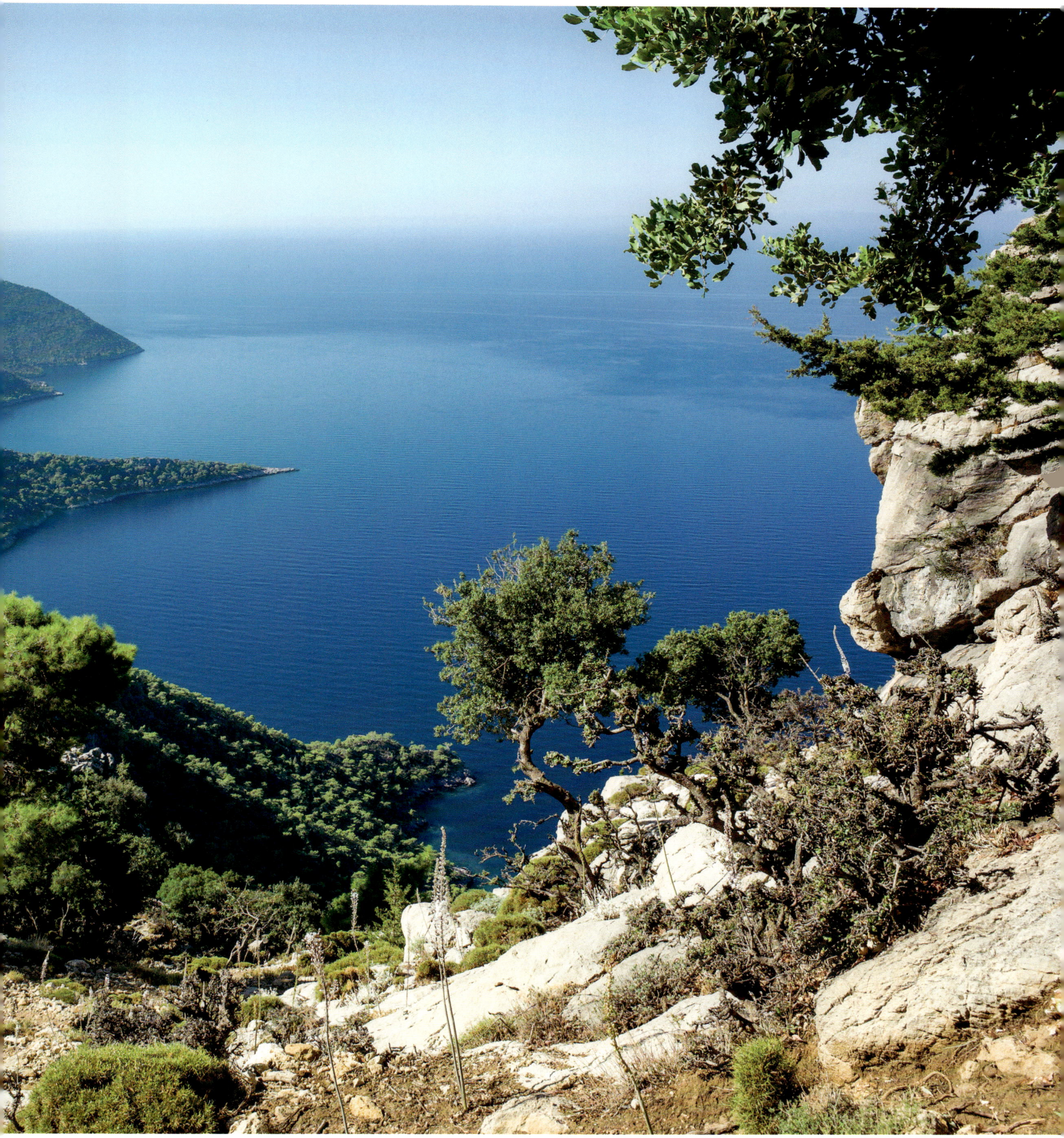

THE MEDITERRANEAN

→ Agamemnon's bust near the site of Troy; he was a king of Mycenae and commander of the Greek forces against the Trojans.

↘ Ceneviz Bridge in the Ida Mountains, which include a protected habitat for Trojan firs, deer, wild boar and jackals.

THRACE AND ANCIENT TROAS

The rural hinterlands of Turkish Thrace collide with history at the Gallipoli (Gelibolu) Peninsula, site of fierce fighting during WWI that helped forge a Turkish national identity persisting to this day. Ferries cross the sea here west to Gökçeada, Türkiye's largest island and a popular destination for windsurfers.

South across the storied Dardanelles Strait, the pleasantly laid-back seaside city of Çanakkale is the gateway to the ancient region of Troas, where ruined temples and bridges hide among wheatfields dappled with brilliant-red poppies. Also known as the Biga Peninsula, Troas' best-known historic site is Troy, where the ruins are more evocative than extant, though a fine museum helps bring the legendary city to life.

Some 30km (18.5 miles) south of here is Geyikli, the departure point for ferries to Bozcaada, the other of Türkiye's two inhabited Aegean islands and a notable wine-producing part of the country. The bucolic coastline then leads past simple beachfront settlements all the way to Babakale, the windswept western tip of the Asian continent, watched over by an 18th-century Ottoman fortress.

Continuing to the east along the Edremit Gulf, pastoral scenes give way to the foothills of the forested Ida Mountains (Kazdağları in Turkish), reputed in Greek mythology to be where the Trojan prince Paris awarded a golden apple to the goddess Aphrodite, setting off the Trojan War. Small villages in the mountains have a mix of Greek and Turkish architecture, their stone homes now sought-after by city-dwellers looking for a peaceful getaway. **CONTINUED ON P190 »**

local angle
New Waves of Creative Inspiration

'Everything about life on Bozcaada is connected to the winds: the way the streets of the old Greek neighbourhood are arranged, the direction in which the grapevines outside the town centre are planted, and whether or not the ferries can run in winter. Professor Rüstem Aslan, the head archaeologist at Troy, once described this region as being a place where "the cultures that have passed through seep into your soul with the winds". While living on Bozcaada year-round from 2016 to 2019, I often felt that the mystical atmosphere I experienced there was due to its rich history.

'Since the political unrest experienced following the 2016 coup attempt in Türkiye, there has been a significant migration from İstanbul to smaller regions like Bozcaada and the North Aegean. This wave has included many people working in creative fields who were seeking alternative spaces; they inspired a variety of new projects such as festivals, biennials, workshops and artist gatherings. Large-scale initiatives from bigger cities began to transform into more diverse artistic productions in smaller towns. These creations blended with local ones to form new cultural identities.

'Bozcaada, having hosted many different cultures over the years, has always been a highly fluid place where each new arrival brings their own cultural influences that combine with the established traditions. The physical limitations of living in a confined space like an island, of constantly seeing the same people in the same places, naturally creates more opportunities for encounters and a sense of belonging.'

Gizem Gezenoğlu, founder of Fermente Events and former partner of the Bozcaada Jazz Festival

THE MEDITERRANEAN

THE NORTH AEGEAN

Lying directly across the water from the Greek island of Lesbos, the seaside town of Ayvalık has a shared history with its Hellenic neighbour. This is readily visible in the restored Greek houses that line winding cobblestone lanes and in the converted olive-oil factories along the waterfront. Though the town retains a village-like feel, new émigrés from overcrowded cities like İstanbul are bringing fresh energy to Ayvalık's creative and culinary scenes. The adjacent Cunda (Alibey) Island is an Ayvalık in microcosm, with quaint restaurants and hotels clustered around the port. Just south of town, the Devil's Table (Şeytan Sofrası), a lava tower formed by a long-extinct volcano, is a popular spot for gathering to watch the sunset.

Some 55km (35 miles) south, a short inland detour leads to the ancient city of Bergama (Pergamon), where a 3rd-century-BCE theatre clings to the side of a precipitously steep hill, and the foundations of a monumental altar sit bereft of the intricate friezes carted away to Germany in the late 1800s. Continuing south along the coast, sleepy Foça was originally named after the area's now-endangered Mediterranean monk seals, for whom a marine protected area has been set up to help the species recover.

Stretching out into the sea west of İzmir, Türkiye's third-largest city, is the Çeşme Peninsula. This summer playground encompasses the vineyards and fine dining of Urla, the chichi windsurfing hotspot of Alaçatı, the more remote and rural Karaburun district, the lively marina in Çeşme town, and a bevy of beach clubs ranging from the family-friendly to the ultra-flash. **CONTINUED ON P194 »**

↓ Ildır Beach on the Çeşme Peninsula, facing the Aegean Sea; the ancient Greek city of Erythrae was sited here, known for its wines.

local angle
Urla Gastronomy

'Winemaking and olive cultivation are a long tradition here: 5000 years old, according to archaeological findings. We have a hot Mediterranean climate cooled by the Meltemi winds off the Aegean Sea, which dry up humidity that can cause fungal disease. Our soil is very special too, similar to Tuscany's, with a high chalk and limestone content. All these characteristics of the terroir make Urla a good location for growing grapevines; the rest is up to our abilities to make the best wines.

'Besides its fertile soils, Urla is also a mixture of many different cultures, from the ancient Luvians and Romans to the Ottomans and the people who migrated here over the last century. All of them have added to our food culture. People from the Aegean islands brought their culture of making wine and their knowledge of edible wild greens, artichokes and seafood. People from the Balkans and Macedonia brought their pastry and lamb dishes. Perhaps because Urla remained a small town in the shadow of more touristic Çeşme and İzmir, people still cook at home and carry on these food traditions.'
Bilge Bengisu Öğünlü, of Urlice Winery and Urla Natural Table Association

THE MEDITERRANEAN

İZMIR GUIDE

An Aegean city of arts and crafts

taste
BOYOZ

Just over a century ago, İzmir was still a deeply multicultural place, full of European merchants and local Greek, Armenian and Jewish communities. Try the street snack *boyoz* (above), a savoury pastry of Sephardic origin, with a hard-boiled egg and a glass of *sübye*, a milky drink made from melon seeds.

nightlife
THE KORDON

Known as the *kordon*, İzmir's long waterfront promenade (above) is the beating heart of the city, especially in the evenings. Locals of all social classes gather here to watch the sunset, whether around a table at one of the seafood restaurants lining the strip, or while sitting on the grass drinking beer or tea and eating sunflower seeds.

buy
HANDICRAFTS

One of the oldest parts of İzmir, the Kemeraltı Bazaar has been a centre of commerce for centuries. Many of its winding streets are full of workaday shops, but artisans still ply their trades here. Look for jewellers, ceramicists, leather- and woodworkers, felt artists, calligraphers and others making and selling their wares in the area's hidden-away *hans* (urban caravanserai), such as the 18th-century Kızlarağası Hanı and Piyaleoğlu Hanı, and the handicrafts market next to the Başdurak Mosque.

> "Locals gather on the grass to watch the sunset, drinking beer or tea"

explore
ALSANCAK

The Alsancak neighbourhood teems with chic restaurants, bars, cafes and shops amid its prosperous residential blocks. Its mid-19th-century train station, one of the oldest in Türkiye, is a symbol of the city, while the area's former cigarette and natural-gas factories have been restored and converted into a museum campus and a venue for concerts, festivals and other cultural events.

culture
ART EVENTS

İzmir played host to its first ever contemporary art biennial in early 2024, but the city's gallery scene had already been growing for some time thanks to an influx of youthful creatives. Exhibition spaces here range from the elegant Arkas Art Center established in a restored seafront mansion to the non-profit Darağaç collective, which organises community-based events in the formerly industrial Umurbey neighbourhood.

THE MEDITERRANEAN

→ A backstreet in Sığacık, a small fishing village turned low-key Aegean resort that is also the location for an Ottoman castle.

↘ A typically rocky shore in the Dilek Peninsula-Büyük Menderes Delta National Park, known for its biodiversity on land and underwater.

THE SOUTH AEGEAN

A long string of beach towns lines the coast south of İzmir, starting in the bougainvillea-bedecked lanes of quaint Sığacık and culminating in the boisterous resort of Kuşadası. A cruise-ship port and jumping-off point for the ruins of Ephesus, Kuşadası has an appealing waterfront promenade that belies the warren of knockoff shops and touts filling its tourist-heavy bazaar area. The 14th-century Genoese fortress on the small island that gives the city its name (Kuşadası means 'Bird Island') has been restored as a public park with superb views.

Kuşadası's real treasure, though, is the 276-sq-km (106-sq-mile) Dilek Peninsula-Büyük Menderes Delta National Park, which juts out into the sea south of the city, almost touching the Greek island of Samos at its furthest point. Rustic sand or pebble beaches shaded by pine trees dot the park's northern coast while hiking trails wend through its hilly and wooded interior, which is home to wildlife including lynx, jackals, foxes, hyenas and wild boar. (The latter are known for coming down to the coast at dusk to forage from picnic leftovers.) On the southern side of the peninsula, the picturesque Greek village of Eski Doğanbey, emptied during the 1923 population exchange, is coming back to life as a tranquil holiday destination.

The lagoons, salt marshes and mud flats of the Büyük Menderes Delta stretch out south along the coast, followed by the resort areas of Didim (home to the ruins of what was once a colossal temple to Apollo) and Akbük, the last major towns before the roads wind up into the mountains. **CONTINUED ON P198 »**

know-how
Meyhane Culture and *Mezes*

Whether at a backstreet *meyhane* (tavern) or a glamorous seaside fish restaurant, evening meals on the Turkish Aegean and Mediterranean coasts generally follow a similar ritual: start with slices of creamy, salty *beyaz peynir* (white cheese) paired with sweet green melon, progress to a selection of cold *meze* (small plates) followed by hot starters like grilled octopus or shrimp casserole, and finish with the grilled catch of the day, served with rocket leaves, red-onion slices and spritzes of lemon, all washed down with *rakı* (an anise-based spirit) or white wine. A fruit plate and black tea typically cap off the meal.

Some chefs show their creativity with special *meze* but these are classics:

Atom Dried hot-pepper pieces and a drizzle of olive oil mixed into thick, garlicky yoghurt to cool the burn.

Deniz börulcesi Tender stems of boiled marsh samphire served with olive oil, lemon juice and garlic.

Girit ezmesi A rich paste of salty and sweet cheeses mixed with parsley, garlic, walnut or pistachio pieces, and other herbs and spices.

Patlıcan salatası Roasted chunks of aubergine and red pepper in a sauce of olive oil, vinegar and pomegranate molasses.

Zeytinyağlı fava Broad beans cooked with onions and lemon juice, pureed into a paste then cooled and served in slices with a drizzle of olive oil and sprigs of dill.

Kabak çiçeği dolması Delicate-orange courgette blossoms stuffed with seasoned rice and served with yoghurt.

Sıcak ot Sautéed local greens and herbs (whatever's in season), topped with garlicky yoghurt and red-pepper-infused olive oil.

THE MEDITERRANEAN

ANCIENT IONIA

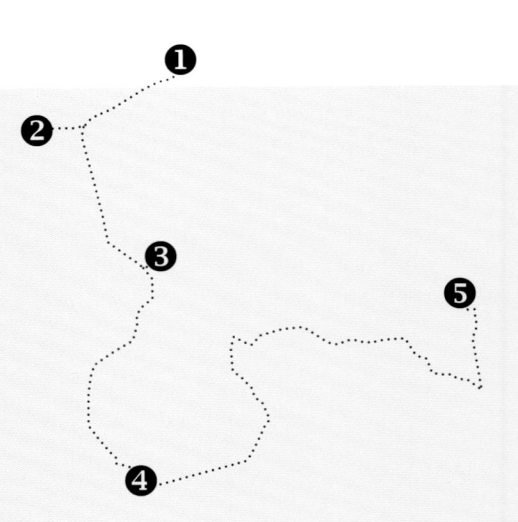

Follow historic routes through the Aegean's rural hinterlands

Distance 102km (63 miles)
Duration Three days
Start Priene
Finish Kapıkırı

❶ Priene
Among pine trees at the base of towering Mt Dilek, the peaceful ruins of this ancient Greek city wend uphill from the farming village of Güllübahçe, about 40 minutes' drive south of Kuşadası. Like the other historical sites in this region (known in antiquity as Ionia), Priene was coastal until sediments from the Büyük Menderes (Meander) River silted up its harbour.

❷ Eski Doğanbey
Spend the night in one of the restored stone houses turned boutique hotels in this old Greek town, to the west at the edge of forested Dilek Peninsula-Büyük Menderes Delta National Park. *14km (9 miles)*

❸ Miletus
A rural road leads south to Miletus, a powerful city that nurtured philosophers and scientists during its 7th- and 6th-century-BCE heyday. Most of the ruins here date to the later Roman period, which produced the 14,000-seat theatre. You can almost hear the roar of the crowd as you climb the stairs inside its entrance halls, passing through tunnels to reach the tiered stone seats. A small museum at the site illuminates the region's history. *18km (11 miles)*

❹ Didim
In antiquity, the people of Miletus would spend four days walking south to the sacred site of Didyma in an annual religious festival, making sacrifices and singing songs along the way to honour various deities. Chief among these gods was Apollo, to whom a massive temple at Didyma was dedicated. Its stately remains are now marooned amid the sprawl inland of the seaside resort of Didim. *20km (12 miles)*

❺ Kapıkırı
The ruins of ancient Heraclea are interwoven throughout the tiny inland village of Kapıkırı, which perches above the shore of Lake Bafa. Once a bay of the Aegean Sea, this brackish wetland ecosystem supports more than 250 different species of birds, including flamingos, pelicans, cormorants and plovers. It's worth spending an extra night in one of the garden bungalows at Agora Pansiyon to better explore the hiking trails and monastery ruins tucked among the dramatic rock formations surrounding the lake. *50km (31 miles)*

TÜRKIYE

↖ Ionic columns of the Temple of Athena Polias at Priene, built around 350 BCE.

↙ A ruined monastery on Kapıkırı Island, near the village of the same name by Lake Bafa.

THE MEDITERRANEAN

THE BODRUM PENINSULA

Bodrum is the most glamorous spot on the Turkish Riviera and its exclusive resorts, glitzy beach clubs and superyacht marinas draw a headline-making crowd of celebrities and their hangers-on. Known in antiquity as Halicarnassus, until the later part of the 20th century this was a sleepy seaside area where the chief economic activities were boatbuilding, fishing and sponge-diving, a tradition with thousands of years of history in the region. A trickle of artsy, bohemian visitors in the 1970s quickly turned into a torrent, and today tourism is Bodrum's raison d'etre.

With olive trees growing amid an arid, scrub-covered interior and coastal settlements dominated by whitewashed villas tumbling down the hills toward the sea, the 689-sq-km (266-sq-mile) Bodrum Peninsula extends off the southern tip of Türkiye's Aegean coastline. The main city, also called Bodrum, sits on twin bays overlooked by a medieval castle (now home to a fascinating museum of underwater archaeology) and is the liveliest place to be in the off-season. The smaller towns scattered around the peninsula's undulating coastline each have their own distinctive character.

Göltürkbükü and Yalıkavak attract the kind of jet-set crowd for which Bodrum is most famed, while tiny Gümüşlük clings to a more boho identity, with rustic beachfront restaurants lit at night by hanging gourd lamps. Workaday Turgutreis and package-tour favourite Gümbet hold down the mid-range end of the resort spectrum; Gündoğan and Bitez are more residential. East of the main peninsula, the compact villages along the Gulf of Gökova remain relatively quiet and undiscovered – for the moment. **CONTINUED ON P200 »**

↑ The city of Bodrum was once home to the Mausoleum at Halicarnassus, one of the Seven Wonders of the Ancient World.

TÜRKIYE

know-how
Birth of the Blue Cruise

The boatbuilding trade began to develop in Bodrum in the 1930s, and over the subsequent decades the manufacture of small traditional sailboats known as *tirhandil* progressed into larger-hulled vessels called *gulet*. Initially valued for their increased cargo capacity, these two- or three-masted *gulet* also had plenty of room below decks for passenger cabins and are today mostly used as pleasure boats for multi-day 'blue cruises' (*mavi yolculuk*) through secluded bays and coves.

An eccentric Bodrum resident named Cevat Şakir Kabaağaçlı – better known in Türkiye as the 'Fisherman of Halicarnassus' – is credited with popularising the blue cruise. Born to a prominent family in Ottoman Crete, Kabaağaçlı became a writer of novels, short stories and essays. He first arrived in Bodrum in 1925 when he was sentenced to three years' internal exile for seditious writing and ended up settling there. (Less talked-about is the previous jail term he served for fatally shooting his own father in 1914.)

In the late 1940s and '50s, Kabaağaçlı began inviting his artsy circle of friends – including the novelist Sabahattin Ali and the painter Bedri Rahmi Eyüboğlu – to join him on his small wooden sailing boat as he explored the Gulf of Gökova. Among these guests was writer and translator Azra Erhat, whose 1962 book about these excursions, *Mavi Yolculuk*, gave them a name that stuck.

→ A traditional *gulet* lies at anchor in the vivid blue lagoon that winds its way past Ölüdeniz Beach on the Lycian Coast.

THE MEDITERRANEAN

→ Whitewashed houses in the Old Town of Marmaris, home to the 18th-century-CE Eski İbrahim Ağa Cami mosque and a bazaar.

MARMARIS, DATÇA AND BOZBURUN
Backed by the green mountains that separate the Gulf of Gökova from the sea, rowdy Marmaris is one of the most popular resort cities on the Turkish Mediterranean. High-rise hotels line its seafront promenade, which runs nearly 10km (6 miles) from the enclave of İçmeler to Marmaris' tiny Old Town, 16th-century castle and busy marina. Activity on Marmaris' bay includes sea taxis zipping to nearby Turunç for the weekly market, ferries to Rhodes, and sailboats cruising the coast and on day excursions to Aquarium Bay and the phosphorescent sea cave at the tip of Cennet Adası (Heaven Island), part of Marmaris National Park.

Marmaris' two remote peninsulas, Bozburun and Datça, could hardly pose stronger contrasts to the city's brashness. Though its more central towns are increasingly taking on the characteristics – third-wave coffee shops, artisan bakeries, chef-led restaurants – of a hip urban neighbourhood, Datça is still proudly protective of its peace and quiet. Long stretches of the peninsula remain wild and undeveloped, dotted with hilltop villages and olive and almond groves in the interior and small, pristine coves along the coasts.

Renowned for its honey, Bozburun is even more rugged and uninhabited, its rocky, mountainous terrain interspersed with pine and sweetgum forests. Its few small towns – like Selimiye, Bozburun and Söğüt – serve mainly as stopping-in points for yachts and *gulet* tours cruising the peninsula's rippling coastline to otherwise inaccessible beaches and bays. **CONTINUED ON P204 »**

TÜRKIYE

local angle
Back in Time in Bozburun

'The Bozburun Peninsula was part of the ancient region of Caria in southwestern Asia Minor. Come the end of the Bronze Age, this whole area Hellenised, but Bozburun remained culturally connected both to the mainland and the Dodecanese Greek islands. Even today, you can see similar house types on the Greek island of Simi as in the abandoned Greek towns around Taşlıca, and you can eat similar food. The only temple in Anatolia dedicated to İlithyia, the Greek goddess of childbirth and midwifery, is here at Phoenix.

'We have discovered more than 50 ancient farmsteads and olive oil workshops that were connected by ancient routes to ports linked with Rhodes, which was one of the most powerful cities in the region in the Hellenistic era. The farmers here produced figs, almonds, barley and, of course, olives and olive oil. The so-called Rhodian wine was actually produced in Taşlıca and spread all over the Mediterranean.

'Later, this area was still rural, and mountainous and separated from the "civilised world" enough for a monastic organisation to be formed – we have discovered more than 15 early Byzantine churches in the area.

'We know there are 10 or 11 ancient sites in Bozburun but there are just three excavations, including ours. You can follow seven or eight different time periods from over 2600 years of history here, because this southwestern part of the Bozburun Peninsula is so untouched. But touristic activities are starting to transform the area; we need to hold back this tsunami of development to preserve this landscape and its history.'

Asil Yaman, founder and director of the Phoenix Archaeological Project in Taşlıca, Bozburun Peninsula

201

THE MEDITERRANEAN

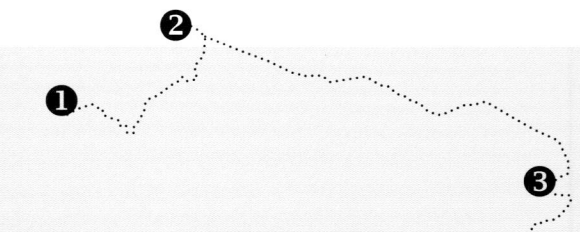

BY THE GULF OF GÖKOVA

A road trip via a pristine island and vast lake towards the Dalyan Strait

Distance 85km (53miles)
Duration Three to four days
Start Cleopatra Beach
Finish Dalyan

❶ Cleopatra Beach
Legend holds that the sparkling white sands on Sedir Island, lying a 25-minute drive north of Marmaris, were shipped in from Egypt to create a paradise hideaway for lovers Cleopatra and Mark Antony. Reachable by boat from a pier in the forested mainland village of Çamlı, the island is lapped by brilliant blue waters and scattered with the remains of the ancient city of Kedrai, including a theatre and a temple to Apollo. This counts as a sublime spot for swimming, although the famous sand itself is off-limits to sunbathers in order to protect it.

❷ Akyaka
Northeast of Çamlı along the Gulf of Gökova, the laid-back beach town of Akyaka is becoming a hip destination for İstanbul chefs, musicians, DJs, artists and yoga instructors who set up shop here for the summer months or longer. Stay in Akyaka's tiny downtown to be in the heart of the action, or to the south in Akçapınar, a kitesurfing hotspot with a more rural setting. An optional detour 40km (25 miles) north takes you to the town of Menteşe, with a preserved historic centre that dates to the Ottoman era. *23km (14 miles)*

❸ Lake Köyceğiz
The tranquil town of Köyceğiz, east of Akyaka, sits on the north bank of Lake Köyceğiz. At 52 sq km (20 sq miles), it's one of Türkiye's largest coastal lakes, with marshy forests and wetlands that attract almost 200 different types of birds, including herons, kingfishers, cormorants and kestrels. Boat tours ply the lake, while the town's farmers market on Mondays draws travellers and locals alike from the surrounding region. *38km (24 miles)*

❹ Dalyan
The waters of Lake Köyceğiz join the Mediterranean via a reed-filled strait in Dalyan, a pleasant holiday town to the south that's dramatically backdropped by 4th-century-BCE rock tombs. Hotels and holiday apartments abound in the town centre, where restaurants and cafes line the winding waterfront. A small car ferry makes the crossing to the ancient city of Kaunos, while passenger boats head through the reeds to İztuzu Beach, a protected sea-turtle nesting area and one of Türkiye's prettiest stretches of sand. *24km (15 miles)*

TÜRKIYE

↖ Cleopatra Beach on Sedir Island; ancient ruins here include a Roman theatre.

↙ The rock tombs of Kaunos; this necropolis mostly dates to the mid-4th century BCE.

THE MEDITERRANEAN

→ The sandy beach at the end of Butterfly Valley, which runs for 4km (2.5 miles) into the base of Babadağ Mountain (1969m).

↘ Tombs of Sidyma's necropolis date from the Classical Lycian, Roman and Byzantine periods and include the mausoleum of a crucial Roman priestess.

THE LYCIAN COAST

Türkiye's western Mediterranean coast is dappled with ancient ruins and hidden coves. Pleasantly lively Fethiye, the largest city on this stretch of the sea, surrounds a wide bay of the same name. Below Babadağ Mountain to the south sits the eerie ghost-town village of Kayaköy, and beyond that the iridescent 'blue lagoon' of Ölüdeniz, a popular beach resort. From near to here, the long-distance Lycian Way hiking trail embarks on its waymarked 710km (440-mile) journey east towards Antalya.

In the summer season, excursion boats run south from Fethiye to Butterfly Valley, where more than 100 species have been recorded. Dramatically cradled by steep cliffs on either side, the small beach here can otherwise only be reached by scrambling down the precipitous (and potentially dangerous) slopes from the village of Faralya. Nearby Kabak has a similar hippie-esque vibe.

Following the ruins of Sidyma, Letoon and Xanthos through the rural hinterland takes you to the golden shoreline of Patara Beach, after which the main highway rejoins the coast, passing the holiday villas of Kalkan and the casually trendy seaside town of Kaş. Further east, ancient tombs carved apartment-style into a rock face overlook modern greenhouses in Demre, home to the 4th-century bishop St Nicholas (the benevolent fellow who inspired the story of Santa Claus). Beyond the agricultural towns of Finike and Kumluca, the wooded ruins of the ancient city of Olympos spill out onto the undeveloped sands of Çıralı. **CONTINUED ON P208 »**

↑ Descending towards the western end of the Lycian Way at Ölüdeniz. Opened in 1999, the trail follows routes used by the ancient Lycians.

local angle
Hiking the Lycian Way

'The Lycian Way trail is spectacularly diverse: it's so magical to be walking through almost alpine landscapes on the steep slopes of Mt Olympos, then at the end of the day you can take a dip in the sea in Çıralı. In the smaller villages, some just a few houses, you can still witness traditional agricultural life. You walk past beekeepers, or shepherds at certain times of the year, or you run into a flock of goats. If we can bring in walkers who stay at village houses and support the local economy, it can contribute to people being able to continue living in these villages and preserving their way of life.

'It's also amazing to be able to walk and see all these traces of ancient civilisations, to stumble upon tombs and houses and towers, some hidden among the bushes and others more excavated. Perhaps I'm romanticising but I fantasise about what it was like here in the old days. People walked more or less on the same trails – since the Lycian Way connects these old routes, you really have this experience of walking on medieval, or even ancient paths. My deepest wish would be to protect it forever.'
Els Hom, programme developer at Middle Earth Travel

THE MEDITERRANEAN

ANTALYA GUIDE

Tour a classically beautiful city

explore
KALEIÇI

The area surrounded by the old city walls is the most historically significant part of Antalya. Known as Kaleiçi ('inside the castle'), its narrow, winding streets are full of prettily renovated Ottoman-era houses. Notable landmarks include the triple-arched Hadrian's Gate, the 2nd-century-CE Hıdırlık Tower overlooking the sea and the 13th-century Yivliminare Mosque.

culture
ARCHAEOLOGY MUSEUM

The expressively carved, larger-than-life statues of a dozen Greek and Roman deities in the Hall of the Gods are the star attraction of Antalya Archaeology Museum, located above Konyaaltı Beach and reachable on the city's vintage tram line. The nondescript building contains a wealth of artefacts attesting to the long and rich history of the Antalya region, from Palaeolithic fossils to Byzantine-era mosaic floors, splendid Anatolian sarcophagi and hoards of ancient gold and silver coins.

taste
PIYAZ

Piyaz, or white-bean salad, is a popular side dish in many parts of Türkiye, but the Antalya version is distinctive. Mixed with a sauce made from tahini, olive oil, lemon juice, apple vinegar, garlic and cumin, and topped with hard-boiled egg slices in addition to the usual onions, tomatoes and parsley, it makes a hearty accompaniment to *köfte* (grilled meatballs). Try the pairing at the no-frills Piyazcı Ahmet or Topçu Kebap restaurants.

buy
LEATHER GOODS

As alternatives to the tourist trinkets on offer at Antalya's bazaars, seek out handmade leather goods by local artisans. Alloro Leather in the Muratpaşa neighbourhood and DicerosCraft in Konyaaltı both specialise in hand-sewn leather bags, wallets, belts and other accessories. Search for more local crafts: in Kaleiçi, İnebolu Ahşap makes rustic wooden home accessories, while Yaz Dükkan is a cute cafe that sells a variety of small ceramic pieces and jewellery by Turkish designers.

"A wealth of artefacts attest to the long and rich history here"

nightlife
THE WATERFRONT

With its long coastline dramatically backdropped by mountains, the waterfront west of Kaleiçi is a popular spot for watching the sunset, whether strolling or eating at one of the restaurants inside Atatürk Park. Perched above Konyaaltı Beach (below), the elegant 7 Mehmet is a local institution, serving a mix of modern Mediterranean and traditional Turkish cuisine.

THE MEDITERRANEAN

→ The 13th-century-CE Red Tower of Alanya, considered a symbol of the city; behind it lie the harbour and the Taurus Mountains.

↘ A fragment of Roman-era aqueduct leads through pine woods at the site of Phaselis, once an exporter of rose oil.

HEART OF THE TURQUOISE COAST
The rugged Lycian Coast begins to soften around Tekirova and Kemer, the westernmost of the stretch of beach resorts surrounding Antalya on either side. Between them sits Phaselis, one of the most winningly sited of Türkiye's ancient cities, with paths winding through pine forests to the ruins of Roman-era gates, walls, columns, aqueducts and a 2nd-century-CE theatre. Originally founded in the 7th century BCE as a port city, Phaselis had a harbour in each of its three bays, now sublimely secluded spots for swimming and sunning. Near the turnoff for Phaselis, a road rises into the mountains to the base station of the Olympos Teleferik, a cable car that sweeps riders 1640m up to the top of Mt Tahtalı, which typically stays snowcapped for half the year.

East of Antalya, past the golf courses and theme parks of Belek, the ruins of ancient Side – including a fine 2nd-century-CE theatre and the remaining columns of a seaside temple to Apollo – intertwine with the streets of the modern tourist town. Inland you'll find the waterfalls, forests and lush canyons of Manavgat, a popular destination for rafting and other adventure sports.

Further east lies Alanya, where a beautifully preserved hilltop fortress dating to the Seljuk era looms over Cleopatra Beach, 2km (1.2 miles) of golden sand. Though Alanya may be best-known for package tours, beach clubs and foam parties, there's rich history and natural beauty to discover on the slopes leading up to the castle, including an 800-year-old shipyard. **CONTINUED ON P210 »**

know-how
Saving Sea Turtles
~~~

Often topping 1m (3ft) in length and 110kg (242lb) in weight, loggerhead sea turtles (*Caretta caretta*) can live for more than 100 years. But along with green sea turtles (*Chelonia mydas*), Mediterranean loggerheads are threatened by human activity: fishing, pollution, climate change and habitat loss, especially of their sandy nesting grounds as hotel development overruns parts of the coast. Volunteer-led conservation efforts are making a difference. Visitors can help by cleaning up their rubbish and not digging in the sand or walking on the beach at night during the May to November nesting season, at these and other key sites:

Anamur Beach This 12km-long (7.5-mile) stretch of sand in Mersin Province isn't just important to sea turtles; its adjacent wetlands are among the most northerly places where critically endangered Nile softshell turtles have been spotted.

Belek Beach One of the largest sea-turtle nesting spots in Türkiye, the soft sand and shallow waters at this 29km-long (18-mile) beach in Antalya Province make it popular among families too.

Çıralı Beach Near the ruins of ancient Olympos in Antalya Province, this 3km-long (2-mile) beach sees growing numbers of nesting turtles.

Patara Beach This 14km-long (8.5-mile) strand near Kaş is one of Türkiye's rare white-sand beaches.

THE EASTERN MEDITERRANEAN

For most visitors, the Turkish Mediterranean may as well end in Alanya: few venture east into the region known in antiquity as Cilicia, where seaside castles, crumbling ruins and rustic beaches are scattered between mountainous slopes and agricultural plains.

The town of Anamur, 120km (75 miles) east of Alanya, is best-known in Türkiye – if you could say it's known at all – for its banana plantations growing a small, sweet local variety of the fruit. But it's also home to the windswept, wave-lashed ancient Roman ruins of Anemurium and the medieval Mamure Castle, which once guarded the coast against pirates. A further 15km (9 miles) east, the Softa Castle peers out across the surrounding landscape from a rocky hilltop perch.

One of the most recognisable symbols of the region is the 12th-century-CE Byzantine fortress known as the 'Maiden's Castle', like a structure from a fairy tale, occupying an island just off the coast of its namesake town of Kızkalesi. In the mountains inland are the Heaven and Hell Caves, a pair of dizzyingly deep sinkholes; and the Adamkayalar (Men Rocks), which are more than a dozen 2000-year-old figures carved into the rock-walls of a canyon.

Between the port of Mersin and the busy inland city of Adana is Tarsus, a provincial capital in the Roman era and the birthplace of the apostle Paul, where temple ruins, a 1st-century-BCE road and other ancient remnants are intertwined with the modern town. Around 50km (31 miles) before the Syrian border, the gargantuan Vespasian Titus Tunnel in Samandağ was carved through the cliffs in the Roman period and survived the 2023 earthquake that devastated much of Hatay Province.

↓ Kırkkaşık Bedesten (the Bazaar of Forty Spoons) in Tarsus was built in 1579 as a soup kitchen, hospice for travellers and school.

know-how

Impacts of the 2023 Earthquakes

␣␣␣␣The city of Antakya, located 25km (16 miles) inland from Samandağ in Hatay Province, has a richly layered history. Founded as Antioch in the 4th century BCE, it was one of the largest cities in the Roman Empire, and later was an important centre of early Christianity; Alexander the Great occupied the area, as did the Crusaders. Until recently it was still a proudly multicultural place, famed across Türkiye for its cuisine influenced by different culinary traditions. Tragically, much of this historical texture was destroyed in two major earthquakes that ravaged a vast swathe of southern Türkiye and northern Syria on 6 February 2023, killing more than 55,000 people in total.

␣␣␣␣Hatay Province was among the hardest-hit places in Türkiye, with the traditional courtyard houses, bazaars, narrow winding lanes and small mosques, churches and synagogues of Antakya's Old Town on the Orontes River largely reduced to rubble. The intricately decorated Roman- and Byzantine-era floor mosaics and other treasures in the Hatay Archaeological Museum escaped serious damage, though the museum building is now undergoing a major seismic reinforcement.

CHAPTER SEVEN

CYPRUS

**WRECK DIVING OFF CYPRUS 〜 PICTURE PERFECT LARA BEACH
A SEA-HUGGING ROAD TRIP 〜 THE NORTH AND SOUTH
ARCHAEOLOGICAL SITES IN PAFOS**

Northern Cyprus

• *NORTH NICOSIA*
• *NICOSIA*

CYPRUS

• *PAFOS*

THE MEDITERRANEAN

→ Kyrenia (Girne) has one of the Mediterranean's most perfect harbors.

Steeped in myth, coveted by conquerors, Cyprus' tumultuous and multilayered past has left ancient riches strewn across this island. Neolithic dwellings, Bronze Age and Phoenician tombs, remnants of once-mighty city-kingdoms, Roman mosaics and mountaintop castles lay scattered throughout the countryside. While strolling the cities you can spot the preserved architectural legacy of the Lusignan, Venetian and Ottoman periods.

Whether hiking between time-warped villages and ruins, over hillsides strewn with Jerusalem sage and wild fennel, or admiring crumbling castle ramparts, Cyprus encapsulates the fascinating history of the eastern Mediterranean, all wrapped up in one bite-sized package.

Sun-soaked stretches of sand are Cyprus' calling card and there's a beach for everyone here, from wild and windswept to family-friendly and packed. As for the food, heavily influenced by Turkish, Greek and Middle Eastern food cultures, Cypriot cooking has some of its own culinary stars, including haloumi (hellim in Turkish) and kebab favourite *sheftalia*.

Just like Aphrodite's ability to lure in the lovers, the island of Cyprus has exuded a magnetic charm on all who've washed up here across the centuries.

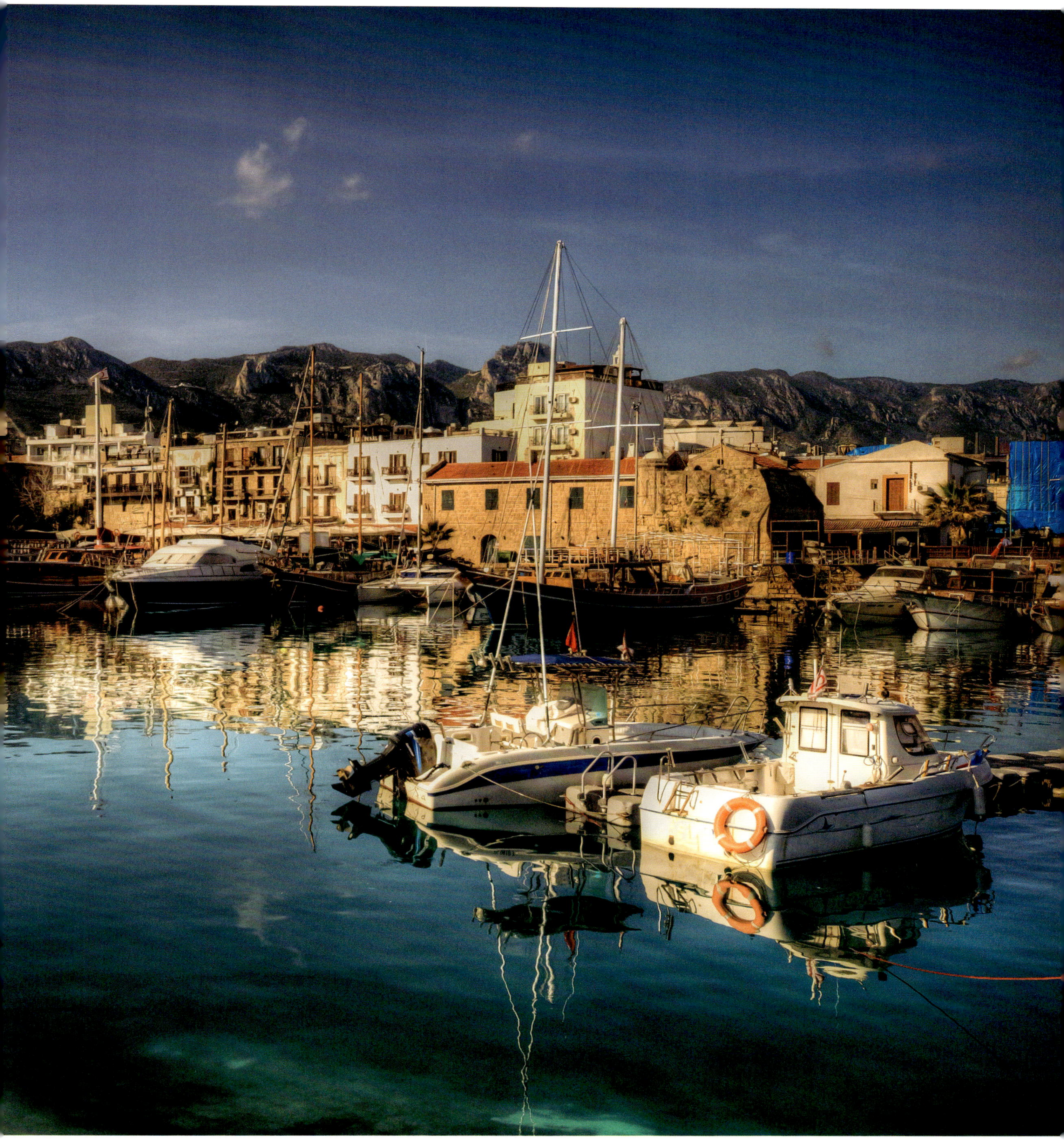

THE MEDITERRANEAN

CYPRUS GUIDE

An island refuge for marine wonders

beach
LARA

The Republic of Cyprus' most spectacular strand is Lara Beach, cupped by limestone rocks and sprinkled with powdery golden sand. Access is via a rough road backed by desert-like, ochre-earthed scrubland, studded with gorse, bushy pines and seasonal wildflowers. This unspoilt beach is an important nesting site for green and loggerhead turtles.

activity
WRECK DIVING

Thanks to silted-up ancient ruins, shallow ports and plain old dodgy navigating, the waters surrounding the Cypriot coastline are a wreck-diving dream. The battered hulks of sunken ships that never made it to port are now patrolled by shoals of flitting fish and the occasional octopus acting as crew. Larnaka Bay's *Zenobia* (above), which capsized in 1980, is rated as one of the world's best wreck dives. Exploring its inner structure, still complete with cargo decks of trucks, is among the island's eeriest adventures.

base
PAFOS

Home to a strip of sea-facing cafes, backstreets dotted with medieval buildings and one of the island's most mesmerising archaeological sites – plus top-notch beaches and scuba-diving sites in easy reach – Pafos (below) dishes up much of the best of the Mediterranean in a single spot. Founded in the 4th century BCE, the city was once the centre of political and administrative life in Cyprus, and today the sprawling shorefront Pafos Archaeological Site safeguards a collection of intricate and colourful mosaics based on ancient Greek myths.

explore
THE GREEN LINE

Since 1974, the United Nations–administered Green Line has split Cyprus in two. Crossing from Greek-Cypriot Nicosia (Lefkosia) into Turkish North Nicosia (Lefkoşa) allows you to gain some understanding of the island's complex and painful modern-day history and experience the two Cypriot communities, living in the south and north.

secret
DIPKARPAZ

Start a sea-hugging road trip to forgotten beaches and tiny villages from Kyrenia (Girne), a town that's always been governed by the sea. Head east on the coast road, passing scattered villages and beaches. At the eastern tip of the Karpas Peninsula, stop at tiny Dipkarpaz (Rizokarpaso) and enjoy the long swathe of sand at Golden Beach, known for wild donkeys munching seagrass amidst the otherwise untrodden dunes.

"The battered hulks of ships that never made it to port are now patrolled by shoals of fish and the occasional octopus"

Gozo VALLETTA
MALTA

CHAPTER EIGHT

EGYPT AND MALTA

EGYPT'S COASTAL HERITAGE ⁓ BIBLIOTHECA ALEXANDRINA

VINTAGE SHOPPING ⁓ EL ALAMEIN'S WWII BATTLEFIELD

MALTA'S GOLDEN BAY ⁓ SEA-KAYAKING OFF GOZO

MARSA MATRUH •   AR RASHID •   PORT SAID

ALEXANDRIA •

EL ALAMEIN •   SUEZ CANAL

ISMAILIA •

EGYPT

THE MEDITERRANEAN

→ The waterfront of Valletta, Malta's capital, which has welcomed visitors since it was founded in the 16th century.

Though this stretch of the southern Mediterranean reveals traces of the history of empires at every turn, left by the Carthaginians through to the German commanders of WWII, foreigners are a rare sight in much of this part of the coast today. Egypt's second-largest city, Alexandria is the best showcase of this bounty of knowledge, with its storied yet faded glory standing in contrast to newer resorts springing up on Egypt's inviting sands.

Africa's fourth-largest country, Libya is alive with possibility, but for the time being, it remains safest explored from an armchair.

The geographical location of the Maltese Archipelago, a few specks in the sea north of Libya, has made it an alluring prize over the millennia. Malta is staunchly Roman Catholic but is home to a beguiling mix of cultures. Its traditional cuisine blends Sicilian and Middle Eastern flavours, and even the fishing boats resonate with the past, their prows painted with eyes like the vessels of their distant Phoenician predecessors.

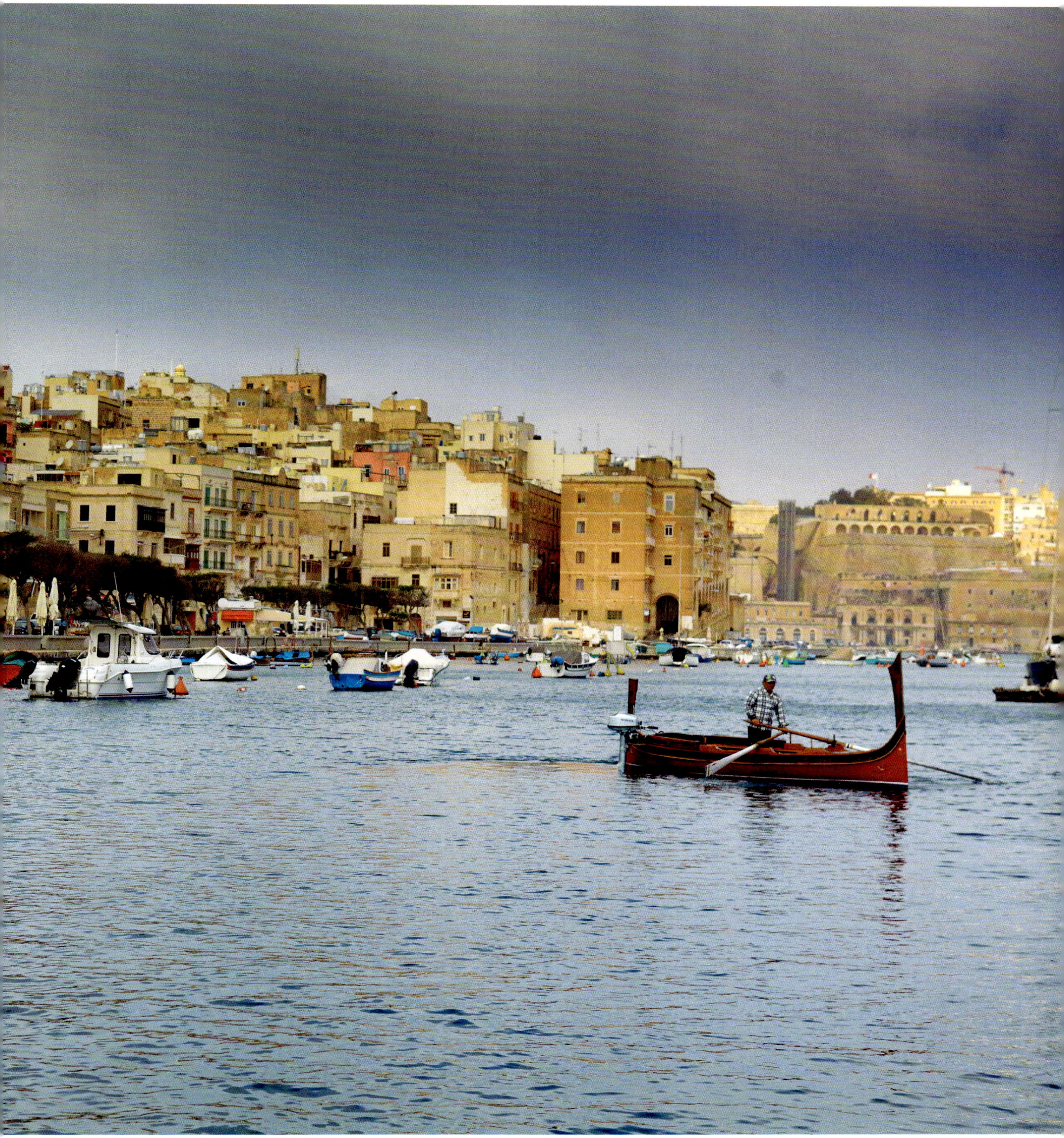

THE MEDITERRANEAN

ALONG EGYPT'S COAST

Drive between epic moments in history, beyond the pharaohs

Distance 283km (176 miles)

Duration 2 days

Start Ismailia

Finish Ar Rashid

❶ Ismailia
Exemplifying Egypt's glorious triumph of engineering over nature, the Suez Canal slices through the sands of the Isthmus of Suez, not only severing mainland Egypt from Sinai but also Africa from Asia. Completed in 1869, the canal represents the remarkable achievement of Egypt's belle époque, an era buoyed by grand aspirations. This period gave birth to the canalside city of Ismailia, whose streets retain some evidence of this fleeting age of grandeur, its distinctive architecture now teetering on picturesque disrepair. Ismailia's historic town centre, with its European-style streets, expansive lawns and late-19th-century villas, is relatively peaceful and pretty.

❷ Port Said
North along the Suez Canal and on the Mediterranean coast is the seaside town of Port Said. The waterfront's once-grand architecture is slowly going to seed, but the yesteryear allure of the centre is enough to prompt a visit. The raised pedestrian-only boardwalk running along the waterfront provides up-close views over the Suez Canal's northern entry point, allowing travellers to admire the passing supertanker traffic. The free ferry that crosses the canal to the languid suburb of Port Fuad is the only opportunity for casual visitors to ride the waters of this marvel of construction. **81km (50 miles)**

❸ Ar Rashid
Snaking along the International Coastal Rd (Hwy 40), the route to Ar Rashid takes short diversions inland and meanders between lakes and expansive desert-like beaches before crossing a branch of the River Nile. Ar Rashid is also known as Rosetta, giving its name to one of the most famous Egyptian artefacts ever discovered: the Rosetta Stone, unearthed here in 1799 and soon taken to the British Museum in London, where it's remained since. The rock tablet has inscriptions in three languages and provided the long-missing key to cracking the code of Egyptian hieroglyphs. About 5km (3 miles) north of town is Fort Rashid, built by the Mamluk Sultan Qaitbey in 1479 to guard the mouth of the Nile – it was here that the Rosetta Stone was discovered. **203km (126 miles)**

EGYPT AND MALTA

↖ The Rosetta Stone was discovered in a wall at Fort Rashid, also known as Fort Julien.

↙ Tugboats pass Port Said on the Suez Canal, which links the Red Sea to the Mediterranean.

ALEXANDRIA GUIDE

Discover Egypt's second city

culture
BIBLIOTHECA ALEXANDRINA

Built in the 3rd century BCE, the original Library of Alexandria was one of the greatest intellectual centres in antiquity. Opened in 2002, Bibliotheca Alexandrina (above) rekindles the institute's spirit of learning and culture. Set in an impressive example of modern architecture, it is now one of Egypt's major cultural venues, home to a collection of intriguing museums.

explore
ANFUSHI

Sitting in the shadow of another of Sultan Qaitbey's forts, Anfushi (above) was the hub of the Ottoman-era city, which lasted from 1517 to 1914. It is formed from a warren of tiny streets, overhung by a few wooden balconies typical of traditional Turkish houses. This neighbourhood is where Alexandria once came to let loose, and where people still flock to seek the best fish restaurants in the city.

taste
SEAFOOD

Naturally, seafood is the focal point for typical Alexandrian cuisine. Expect to buy fish, squid or crab at the Al Midan fish market and have it grilled at a nearby stall along with tomato, onion, chilli and coriander. The city is also known for its tangy vinegar-soaked liver (*kebda iskandarani*), which is usually served in a sandwich and smeared with tahini sauce.

> *"The city's diverse population congregates to live out life's dramas over pastries and a cup of tea or coffee"*

buy
VINTAGE ITEMS

Approaching the western end of Tahrir Sq, the battered yet still conspicuously grand architecture switches to something more intimate as you step inside the city's principal souq district. This is formed of one long, heaving bustle of fish stalls, bakeries, cafes and sundry shops selling every imaginable household item. Vintage hunters are certain to unearth modest treasures while exploring the extensive warren of alleys in Souq Al Attarine, the antiques market here.

nightlife
CITY-CENTRE CAFES

After dinner, it's de rigueur to spend a lazy evening in a city-centre cafe watching the world go by. Since the early 1900s, Alexandria's culture has revolved around cafes, where the city's diverse population congregates to live out life's dramas over pastries and a cup of tea or coffee. Famous literary figures – from Constantine Cavafy to Lawrence Durrell – met here, chattering and pondering the city they could not quite grasp. Many of these old haunts remain, such as Délices and Trianon, and even though the food and drink in many aren't up to scratch, they are living relics of times past.

THE MEDITERRANEAN

EL ALAMEIN AND MARSA MATRUH
West of Alexandria, Egypt's northern Mediterranean coastline runs for another 470km (292 miles) along sandy shores. The sun-soaked beaches and turquoise-hued sea lure floods of Egyptians in summer, and sprawling modern resorts have been built facing the crystal waters. Foreign visitors are rarely spotted.

To delve deeper into this region, take a pilgrimage to the sobering, beautifully kept war memorials of El Alamein, about 113km (70 miles) southwest of Alexandria. Throughout a fleeting moment in 1942, El Alamein commanded the attention of the entire world, as it was here that the Allies won control of North Africa in WWII. Some 26,000 soldiers were killed or wounded in the battles fought between Field Marshal Erwin Rommel, the celebrated 'Desert Fox', and (then General, later Field Marshall) Bernard Montgomery, the leader of the Allied forces. Alamein represented the last defensible position before Cairo and the critical Suez Canal, and the city's war cemeteries are a reminder of the price paid to hold that line.

A few kilometres distant, the desert sands turn into beaches on the northern side of the highway. After 195km (121 miles), Marsa Matruh is the spot to stop and enjoy them. From June to September, it provides a real-deal Egyptian resort-town experience. The brilliant-white sandy beaches and dazzling azure waters are filled with Egyptian families on holiday, and the dusty streets and the Corniche buzz with people well into the early hours. For the rest of the year, Marsa Matruh presses the snooze button and returns to its near-comatose state. **CONTINUED ON P244 »**

↓ The Commonwealth War Graves Commission Cemetery at El Alamein; there are 7240 WWII Commonwealth burials here, 815 unidentified.

↑ September 1942; inspecting a sign set up by Australian troops on the road to El Alamein during the WWII North Africa campaign.

know-how

WWII History on the Egyptian Coast

The 1942 victory at El Alamein was the first time British and Commonwealth forces defeated Axis troops in a pitched land battle, but to begin with, the situation appeared hopeless for the Allies. Rommel had pushed them back to the last defensible position before Cairo, and the Germans were expected in Alexandria any day. Italian dictator Benito Mussolini flew to Egypt to prepare for his triumphal entry into the capital, but the Allies launched a massive counteroffensive. Intense fighting raged for 13 days, causing appalling losses until the Axis line crumbled. Rommel's legions retreated, he was recalled to Germany to avoid the shame of surrender, and 240,000 German soldiers were eventually taken prisoner in Tunisia. The victory ensured Allied control of North Africa, which enabled its forces to launch the invasion of Sicily from Egyptian shores in 1943.

The WWII cemeteries of El Alamein are haunting places with thousands of tombstones standing in a stark desert environment. The Commonwealth cemetery is the largest, with 7342 graves in total; included there are memorials to the fallen Axis forces of Italy and Germany.

MALTA GUIDE

An island nation in the midst of the Med

secret
GOZO'S SALTPANS

Thanks to an area of flat terrain and limestone, Gozo's northern coast is well suited to salt production, and the saltpans just outside Marsalforn are the island's most spectacular ecosystem. Seawater runs into the shallow basins, and the wind and sun do the rest. The saltpans on Gozo date from Roman times and salt is still harvested between the months of May and September.

base
VALLETTA

Valletta (above) is Malta's Lilliputian capital, built by the Knights of St John on a peninsula covering just 0.61 sq km (0.24 sq miles). Valletta's founder decreed that it should be 'a city built by gentlemen for gentlemen', and it retains its 16th-century elegance. Accommodation options include boutique hotels, perfect for romantic sojourns, along with stylish antique-decorated apartments. Stay here for history, culture, and convenient access to restaurants and bars.

EGYPT AND MALTA

activity
KAYAKING

Kayaking is an ideal way to see the coastline of the Maltese Archipelago from a different angle, as you paddle through sea caves and explore hidden inlets. With rock formations eroded into idiosyncratic shapes by wind and sea, Gozo, the smaller island northwest of Malta, is an excellent base for sea-kayak forays. Epic trips kick off at Hondoq Bay on the south coast before crossing the Gozo Channel to the tiny island of Comino.

"En route you pass coastal watchtowers built by the Knights of St John"

beach
GOLDEN BAY

The beaches of Malta tend to be dramatic, rocky and sea-sculpted, with fewer soft and sandy curves of Mediterranean coastline than you might expect. Despite this, the Maltese make the most of every swimming spot. One of the sandy gems is Golden Bay on Malta's northwestern coast. Arguably the country's most beautiful beach, this wide curve of orange-gold sand shelves gently into the dark-blue Mediterranean.

explore
THE XLENDI WALK

To give yourself a taste of Gozo's rugged Mediterranean scenery, tackle the Xlendi Walk, meandering for 12km (7.5 miles) from Mġarr Harbour to the rocky bays around the village of Xlendi. En route, you pass the narrow cove at Mġarr ix-Xini (below), coastal watchtowers built by the Knights of St John in the 17th century, and a vertiginous stairway leading to the compact Carolina Cave.

ALBORAN SEA

ALGIERS
TIPAZA

Strait of
Gibraltar

ALGERIA

CEUTA
TANGIER TETOUAN
         EL JEBHA   MELILLA
CHEFCHAOUEN   SAÏDIA
         RIF MOUNTAINS   MOROCCO

CHAPTER NINE

THE MAGHREB

BROWSING SOUQS IN TUNIS' MEDINA ~ **COASTAL COLOUR IN SIDI BOU SAÏD**
ANCIENT ROMAN HIPPO REGIUS ~ **TRADITIONAL COOKING IN ALGIERS**
EXPLORING THE MOROCCAN RIVIERA ~ **RIF MOUNTAINS ROAD TRIP**
CREATIVE TANGIER ~ **ARCHITECTURE IN SPANISH EXCLAVES**

ANNABA •
HIPPO REGIUS
• EL HAOUARIA
TUNIS •
• HAMMAMET
• SOUSSE
TUNISIA
• SFAX

Djerba

THE MEDITERRANEAN

→ Whitewashed Tetouan, in northern Morocco, lies between the Rif mountains and the Mediterranean sea.

Part of the Maghreb, an Arabic word meaning the place of the setting sun, a trio of North African countries rounds off the southwestern Mediterranean: Tunisia, Algeria and Morocco.

On the east coast of Tunisia, architecture and landscapes unchanged for centuries meet modern tourist facilities, contemporary street-art exists alongside caches of Roman mosaics, and both locals and visitors shop and drink coffee in UNESCO-listed medinas.

Algeria, the largest country in Africa, is a sleeping giant: along the 1200km (746-mile) coastline are remnants of the mercantile Phoenicians who established ports, and of Roman empire-builders whose ruined cities remain remarkably intact. Despite this impressive history, Algeria receives barely two million annual visitors, a fraction of the 14 million that visit its neighbour to the west.

A gateway to Africa, Morocco is a nation of dazzling diversity. Caught between the crashing waves of the Mediterranean and the rough crags of the Rif Mountains, its northern coastline is one of the most charming parts of the country. It beckons with beautiful beaches, adventurous road trips, and creative modern and traditional cities.

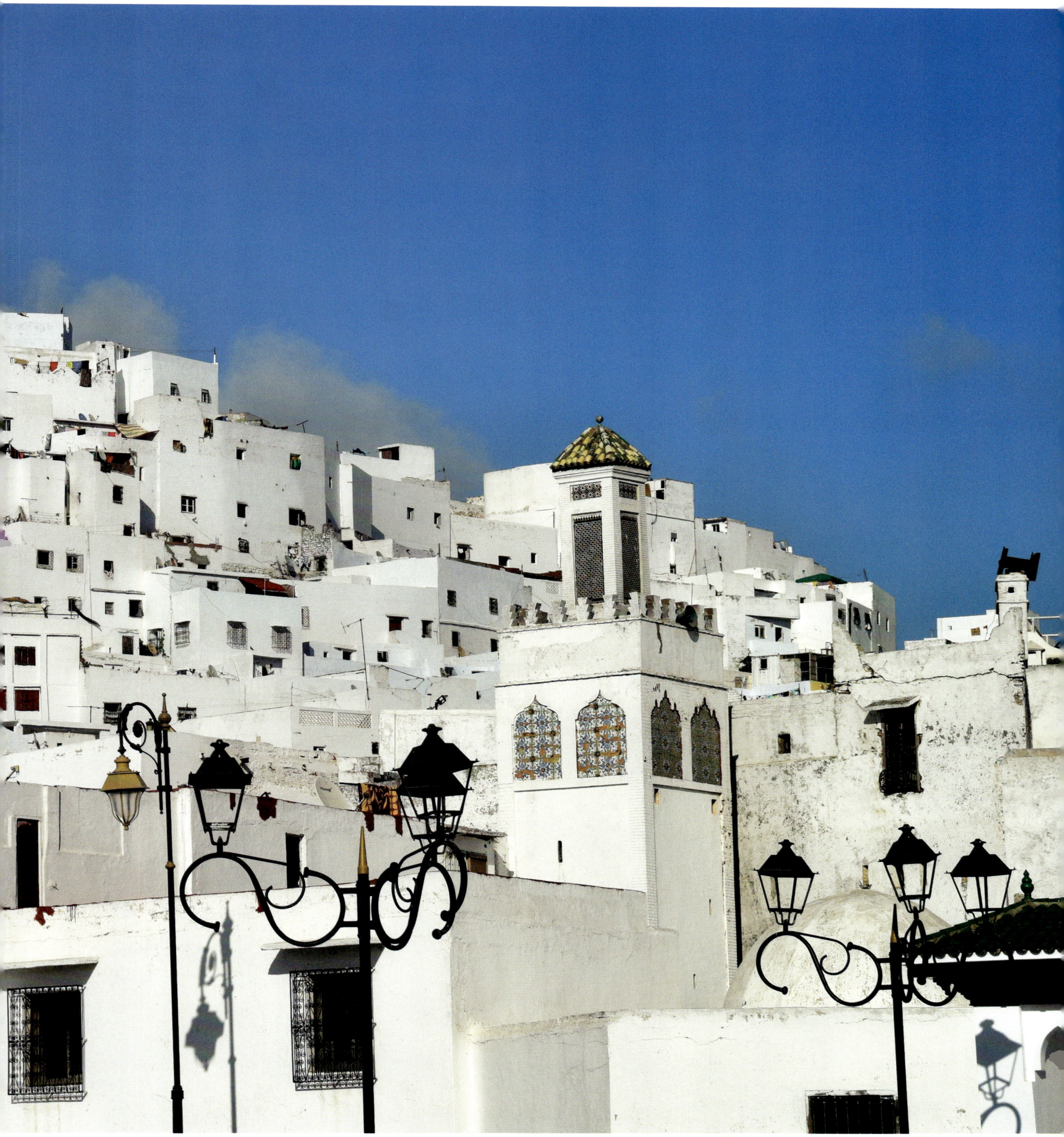

THE MEDITERRANEAN

→ The resort town of Hammamet lies on the edge of the Cap Bon Peninsula, surrounded by groves of orange and lemon trees.

↘ The 8th-century-CE Ribat of Sousse, a fort and resting place for travellers built soon after the Arab conquest of the Maghreb.

TUNISIA'S COASTAL CITIES AND CAPES

Tunisia's small island of Djerba contains the ingredients of many people's ideal holiday: soft-sand beaches, warm Mediterranean waters, varied activities and shops selling an array of local handicrafts. It also sports a maze of cobblestone streets and a history of ethnic and religious diversity more pronounced than in the rest of the country.

Reached along the inwardly curving coast, Sfax presents an opportunity to experience Tunisian life unmediated by the demands of tourism. An afternoon stroll through the medina gives an insight into how the modern and the ancient, and the mercantile and the spiritual, coexist here. Along the coast to the north, Sousse is Tunisia's third-largest city, with three major drawcards: long and sandy Boujaffar Beach; the small but superb Sousse Archaeological Museum; and the UNESCO-protected Aghlabid-era medina, dating from the 9th century.

The protrusion of land into the sea east of the capital, Tunis, is verdant Cap Bon, which devotes most of its efforts to cultivating citrus trees and vineyards. The holiday action centres on Hammamet, the country's first resort town, which has attracted visitors since the 1920s. At the tip of the cape in El Haouaria, falcons and sparrowhawks swoop from the end-of-the-world cliffs on their migration to Europe. The coast looping around Cap Bon is almost one uninterrupted beach, and the peninsula's wild west has a dramatic road that clings to the rocky shore, leading to the faded spa town of Korbous, where a scalding-hot spring spills directly into the sea. **CONTINUED ON P258 »**

local angle
Reviving the Tunis Medina

'In 2013, I opened a seven-room boutique hotel, Dar Ben Gacem, in a 15th-century house in the Tunis medina. Since day one, I wanted to work with micro businesses in the medina, such as street food vendors and artisans. Tunisians traditionally think that tourism is people coming to our beautiful beaches, and we underestimate the potential of our culture.

'Tunisia is almost at the centre of the Mediterranean. We've had migrants from every country around the sea come here. When you sit in my courtyard, in the historical house I've restored, the tiles are Andalusian, the ironwork is Italian and the woodwork is Arab. The food is Amazigh [Indigenous North African]. We underestimate the beauty of the Mediterranean in uniting our cultures.

'Everyone who works at Dar Ben Gacem is from the neighbourhood. Most of them are high-school dropouts. We reinvest our profits into the community and by restoring other buildings, which is how we came to purchase another building to convert into an eight-room boutique hotel in 2019.

'The Mediterranean provided the only travel method before airports. Thanks to the sea, we have this diverse, rich story and an important legacy, but talking about the sea today is not as positive as it used to be. There are lots of economic problems, and that makes me want to restore more buildings, create more jobs and work with more artisans so they can generate employment and give hope. Hope is the most important thing we need to create today in Tunisia, so young people want to stay here and take control of their destiny.'

Leila Ben Gacem, Tunisian social entrepreneur and founder of Dar Ben Gacem

THE MEDITERRANEAN

TUNIS GUIDE

Explore Tunisia's labyrinthine capital

explore
SIDI BOU SAÏD

With its distinctive blue-and-white colour scheme and jaw-dropping glimpses of Mediterranean waters, the clifftop village of Sidi Bou Saïd (above), 22km (14 miles) northeast of the Tunis medina, is one of the prettiest places in Tunisia. Its well preserved architecture is a mixture of Ottoman and Andalusian, a result of the influx of Spanish Muslims here in the 16th century.

buy
GOODS FROM THE MEDINA

A sprawling maze of ancient streets and alleyways, Tunis' medina (above) is one of the most impressive medieval markets in North Africa and one of the country's great treasures. It's home to numerous covered souqs selling all from shoes to shisha pipes, as well as busy cafes, backstreets full of artisans at work and residential areas punctuated by grand, brightly painted doorways. Historic palaces, hammams, mosques and madrassas (schools for studying the Quran) are scattered throughout, many decorated with tiles and carved stucco.

nightlife
THE SUBURBS

Nightlife in the traditional medina and the city centre revolves around slowly sipping coffee or mint tea and smoking shisha in cafes while catching up on the local gossip. To head out bar-hopping, clubbing or late night dining, aim instead for the coastal or northern suburbs – there are plentiful options located off the Av. mer méditerranée in Gammarth and the Av. Habib Bourghuiba in La Goulette.

> "The medina is home to numerous covered souqs, as well as busy cafes and backstreets full of artisans at work"

taste
HARISSA

Couscous is Tunisia's national dish, and *harissa* (spicy chilli paste) is the national condiment, swirled into every meal and commonly served as an appetiser with bread and canned tuna, the country's other gastronomic obsession. In the medina, several upmarket restaurants are housed in exquisite 18th-century mansions and offer extensive menus of local food and wine accompanied by live traditional music.

culture
BARDO MUSEUM

The main draw of the Bardo Museum – the best in the country – is its magnificent array of Roman mosaics, which provide a vibrant and fascinating portrait of ancient North African life. The massive collection, which also includes Hellenistic and Punic statuary, is housed in an imposing palace complex built under the Hafsids (1228–1574), and fortified and extended by the Ottomans in the 18th century.

ALONG THE ALGERIAN COAST

Most settlements on the Algerian coast began as anchorage for early travellers, perhaps Phoenician but possibly even earlier. Northern Algeria's urban hubs by the water make fascinating destinations for adventurous city lovers. In the east, Annaba possesses a pretty seaside melancholy and has a significant ancient Roman site, Hippo Regius. Annaba's excellent natural port, its proximity to fresh water and its fertile farmland drew the Phoenicians here some 3000 years ago; fast-forward a few millennia to appreciate Annaba's city centre, an elegant example of French colonial-era architecture.

West of the capital, Algiers, the town of Tipaza bends along an area of rocky coastline and sits atop deep layers of history that stretch back more than 2000 years. Tipaza's story is shaped by the same forces as other towns in the region, growing by strengthening its ties across the Mediterranean and reaching a peak of wealth under the Severan emperors in Rome, particularly Septimius Severus (193–211 CE), a North African by birth. The city had a brief renaissance under Byzantine rulers, but the end soon became unavoidable. As the ancient town died, many of its stones were carted away to be used in the building of a new city: Algiers.

Nearly 375km (233 miles) further west on inland roads, Oran is a port city with plenty of history, extraordinary 20th-century architecture and an easy Mediterranean vibe – and this atmosphere more than any discernible sights is the real attraction. Admire the imposing French-colonial public buildings, watch giant containers being unloaded in the port, and wander the hazy back lanes, where young men kick footballs, and drying clothes flutter from little balconies. **CONTINUED ON P262 »**

↓ The train station in Oran; services from here run east to Algiers then Annaba, with connections onwards into Tunisia.

THE MAGHREB

↑ The Basilica de St Augustine, with one of Saint Augustine's arm bones preserved inside, rises above the ruins of Hippo Regius.

know-how
Ancient Sites & Christian Saints

The vast ruins of the ancient Roman city of Hippo Regius are among the most evocative in Algeria, stretched across a rolling sheep-grazed site speckled with flowers, rosemary and olive trees, and overlooked by the French colonial-era Basilica de St Augustine. The Numidians (the Indigenous people of what's now Algeria) developed the settlement, but Hippo Regius flourished most under the Romans. Its wealth, then and now, rested on its port – Hippo Regius shipped the wheat that fed Rome.

Christianity first appeared here in the mid-3rd century CE, and Hippo Regius' story is intertwined with that of Saint Augustine, born in Tagaste in Numidia. A teenager of exceptional intellect, Augustine went to Carthage (modern-day Tunisia) to study. He moved to Rome and then, in 384 CE, to Milan, where he was appointed Professor of Rhetoric at the imperial court, one of the most important intellectual posts in the empire. He was won over to Christianity and baptised. In 393, he was elected to the bishopric of Hippo. Under Augustine, and particularly after Rome fell to the Visigoths in 410, Hippo Regis became one of the key centres of Christianity.

THE MEDITERRANEAN

ALGIERS GUIDE

A historic capital built for browsing

nightlife
TEA IN CAFES

Embark on an evening out in Algiers and it soon becomes obvious that tea is the big drink here. It's taken very sweet and with a sprig of mint, and patrons spend hours sipping tea and chatting in the Algerian capital's cafes. Alcohol is not widely consumed in Algeria, although Algiers has some bars, mostly in international chain hotels.

explore
THE CASBAH

The heart of Algiers is its ancient Casbah (above), a steep and narrow maze of streets, staircases and dead ends, its walls painted with murals of National Liberation Front (FLN) heroes like Ali La Pointe, who fought the Battle of Algiers (1956–57). The area has several magnificent Ottoman palaces, most concentrated around Djemaa Ketchoua at the end of Rue Ahmed Bouzrina. The finest is the Dar Hassan Pacha, named after a ruler of Algiers. When the city fell to the French, the house was turned into the governor's winter residence.

taste
TRADITIONAL COOKING

Algerians are generally carnivores, and meat in some form or another (normally grilled) is the centrepiece of most meals. It's often eaten with bread and fresh or pickled vegetables. Along the coast, superb seafood is widely available; look for restaurants on the Rampe de la Pêcherie near the port, as well as in the beach suburbs to the west. Thick, filling and slightly spiced soups are common everywhere. Find restaurants serving traditional home-cooking in the Casbah district.

"Tea is taken very sweet and with a sprig of mint, and patrons spend hours sipping it and chatting in the capital's cafes"

buy
TEXTILES

Shops and market stalls around Algiers are filled with colourful fabrics, garments and woven carpets, along with woodwork, tagine pots, Tuareg jewellery and perfumes. Didouche Mourad is the city's main shopping street, lined with French-era buildings.

culture
NATIONAL MUSEUM OF ANTIQUITIES

The richness of Algeria's heritage is brought home in the National Museum of Antiquities and Islamic Arts (below). The collection of artefacts is drawn from sites around the city and throughout the country. Among the early works are fine ivory carvings and large, totemic Libyan-period warriors on horseback. There is sculpture from the former Roman town of Cherchell, mosaics from Tipaza, a room of bronzes – including a wonderful fragment of a horse's leg and hoof – and a quite extraordinary 3rd-century-CE figure of a chubby child holding an eagle to its chest.

THE MEDITERRANEAN

→ Dwellings in the Medina of Tetouan, a walled inner city where most of the structures remain as they were built in the 17th century.

MOROCCO'S MEDITERRANEAN

For a truly Moroccan experience, beach-hop along highway N16 as it hugs the shoreline all the way from the Algerian border to the point where the Mediterranean meets the Atlantic. The road delivers wondrous sea views while skirting the rocky crags of the Rif Mountains.

Almost within touching distance of the Algerian border, Saïdia has arguably the best beach on this eastern coastal stretch. Increasing development means resorts and watersports keep visitors entertained. Get closer to nature about 200km (124 miles) west at Al Hoceima National Park, scattered with Indigenous Amazigh hamlets where residents maintain a traditional way of life. Thanks to the park's isolation, it helps preserve several at-risk species, from thuja trees to ospreys.

The dramatically corkscrewed highway leads 85km (53 miles) west to the fishing port of El Jebha, which has a picturesque harbour dotted with sky-blue fishing boats and sheltered by mountains. North of Tetouan, Tamuda Bay – the stretch of the coast from Fnideq to M'diq – has been dubbed the 'Moroccan Riviera' for its high-end resorts, complete with mini-marinas, spas and fine-dining restaurants. Moroccan King Mohammed VI summers in a palace nearby.

At the 'end' of the sea, Tangier (Tanger in French) is a meeting place: of the Mediterranean and Atlantic, Europe and Africa, north and south. Its strategic position drew numerous cultures that left their mark: the Carthaginians, Romans, Arabs, Portuguese and British all wrestled for control, giving this gritty port city its unique character. **CONTINUED ON P266 »**

local angle
A New Generation of Creatives in Tangier

↑ The Think Tanger cultural agency wraps together Tanger Print Club (a printing studio), an art residency and the Kiosk art venue.

'In 2016, I started Think Tanger, a nonprofit cultural agency, with the idea of creating a platform where creatives, designers, architects, photographers and artists can come together and take part in the huge shift that's happening in this city. The king wanted to put Tangier on the global economic map, and that process usually takes 50 or 60 years, right? But in less than 25 years, Tangier has undergone this urban transformation. We're seeing new neighbourhoods popping up, the government has been offering free-trade zones for international companies, and Tanger Med is now the most important harbour in the Mediterranean.

'I wanted to create something in my home city because I felt powerless when I saw the tremendous changes happening all around me. Think Tanger's work is mainly about developing opportunities for creatives to be able to do their craft in a city where everything has become driven by economy and industry. One aim of this project is to foster creative public spaces. How can we as artists also transform this city, but in a creative way?'

Hicham Bouzid, creative director and founder of Think Tanger

THE MEDITERRANEAN

INLAND FROM TANGIER

A drive between a legendary port and a blue-hued mountain town

Distance 126km (78 miles)
Duration 2 days
Start Tangier
Finish Chefchaouen

❶ Tangier
This cosmopolitan city keeps reinventing itself while holding on to the free-spirited charm that's captivated visitors for centuries. An investment of billions of dirhams is changing the cityscape like never before, with a new marina, reinvented museums, stylish hotels and sophisticated restaurants. Soak up the atmosphere on the Grand Socco, people-watching over a coffee from the cafe at Cinema Rif. The square has long been a gathering place, joining the old city to the new. From here, you can dive into the medina or discover the Ville Nouvelle (new city).

❷ Tetouan
Between the Rif Mountains and the Mediterranean and famed for its exceptional artisans, this authentic city retains its mix of Andalusian, Spanish and Moroccan influences. First settled by Mauritanian Imazighen in the 3rd century BCE and then by the Romans from the 8th century onwards, Tetouan was the main point of contact between Morocco and Andalucía. Later, it became the capital of the Spanish Protectorate in northern Morocco until independence, hence the Spanish-style architecture. Investment has seen Tetouan rejuvenated; its buildings restored and museums reinvented. Stop by the prestigious Royal Artisan School, where time-honoured Moroccan crafts – including woodcarving, ironwork, brass etching, embroidery and *zellige* tile-making – have been passed down from masters to apprentices since 1919. The building itself ranks as a work of art, with a soaring courtyard that's a riot of painted and carved wood, ornate stucco and tiles. ***63km (39 miles)***

❸ Chefchaouen
Ensconced in the Rif Mountains, Chefchaouen is one of Morocco's prettiest towns. It's no longer an off-the-beaten-track destination for artists and hippies in search of hashish – now daytrippers, Moroccan tourists and Instagrammers jostle for position along its bright-blue medina alleyways. But with its one-of-a-kind colour scheme and laid-back vibe, the 'Blue Pearl' is worth a visit. Muslim and Jewish refugees arrived from Granada in the late 15th century and built whitewashed Andalusian-style houses. The blue hues came later, but exactly when remains a mystery. ***63km (39 miles)***

↖ A traditional enclosed courtyard in the town of Chefchaouen, known for its Berber pottery.

↙ Chefchaouen is in the Rif Mountains, set between the Atlantic and Mediterranean.

→ The Modernista Mezquita Central (Central Mosque) of Melilla, designed by Enrique Nieto and completed in 1947.

↘ Ceuta faces the Strait of Gibraltar; the Phoenicians built a strategic outpost here at the start of the 1st millennium BCE.

EUROPEAN AFRICA

Echoes of the Iberian Peninsula linger in the medieval fortresses and modernist architecture of the autonomous cities of Ceuta and Melilla, the only two European territories of mainland Africa. Sitting on a peninsula jutting into the Mediterranean about 70km (43 miles) east of Tangier, Ceuta represents a compact chunk of Spain: imposing forts and interesting museums, not to mention beer, wine, tapas bars and duty-free shopping. Colonised by the Carthaginians, Greeks and Romans, it was also ruled by Spanish princes, Moroccan sultans and Portuguese kings. Ceuta remained under Spanish control when the 17th-century union between Spain and Portugal ended, and it has been ever since.

Nearly 400km (248 miles) east, Melilla is the other autonomous Spanish exclave on Morocco's Mediterranean coast. At the turn of the 20th century, it was the only trading centre between Tetouan and the Algerian border. As the city grew, it expressed itself in Modernisme, the architectural style usually attributed to the Catalan architect Antoni Gaudí, but spearheaded here by one of his students, Don Enrique Nieto. The result is an open-air museum of magnificent buildings. Modernisme is characterised by the use of curves, asymmetry, rich detail and natural motifs – especially plants. Nieto's work includes the main synagogue and mosque and several buildings for the Catholic church: a handsome demonstration of the city's diversity.

Ceuta and Melilla are magnets for thousands of Moroccan traders, but border guards are focused on stopping migrants' attempts to reach Europe, a pressing issue.

know-how
International Arrivals in Tangier

Tangier's history is a continual tale of foreign invasion, much of it driven by its strategic location at the entrance to the Mediterranean. The city has long piqued the interest of European powers; while the rest of Morocco was colonised by France and Spain, in 1923 Tangier was turned into an 'International Zone' of various sectors. France, Spain, Britain, Portugal, Sweden, Belgium, Italy, the Netherlands and the USA all had a piece of the pie. Expats flooded in, and a wild, no-rules culture broke out, attracting all sorts: socialites, artists, currency speculators, drug addicts, spies, exiles and eccentrics.

Of the many acclaimed artists who passed through, Henri Matisse is the most famous. Enamoured with Tangier's luminous light, he produced canvases – along with sketches – filled with bold, expressive colour. An example is *Window at Tangier*, painted from his room in the Grand Hôtel Villa de France, looking out over St Andrew's Church and the kasbah beyond.

After WWII, Tangier was key to the development of America's countercultural Beat Generation movement, which combined visceral engagement in worldly experiences with a quest for deeper understanding. Writer Jack Kerouac and poet Allen Ginsberg both paid visits, meeting up with another leading figure in the movement, William Burroughs, who had moved here in 1953, having been inspired by writer Paul Bowles.

→ American Beat Generation composer and author Paul Bowles, photographed at his home in Tangier in the summer of 1967.

Index

A
Albania
- Butrint 148
- Durrës 146
- Himarë 148
- Karaburun Peninsula 146
- Ksamil 148
- Llogara 148
- Përmet 147
- Sarandë 148
- Sazan Island 146
- Tepelenë 147
- Vlorë 147

Algeria
- Algiers 240
- Annaba 238
- Hippo Regius 238
- Oran 238
- Tipaza 238

B
Bosnia & Hercegovina 136

C
Croatia
- Bol 139
- Brač 138
- Cape Kamenja 128
- Cres 132
- Dubrovnik 136
- Hvar 136
- Istria 128–131
- Krk 132
- Labin 128
- Lošinj 132
- Pag 132
- Poreč 128
- Pula 128
- Rabac 128
- Rijeka 132
- Rovinj 130
- Split 134, 137
- Supetar 139
- Veli Brijun 129
- Vrsar 128
- Zadar 136

Cyprus 214
- Dipkarpaz (Rizokarpaso) 217
- Karpas Peninsula 217
- Kyrenia 217
- Larnaka Bay 216
- Nicosia (Lefkosia) 217
- Pafos 217

E
Egypt
- Alexandria 224
- Ar Rashid 222
- El Alamein 226
- Ismailia 222
- Marsa Matruh 226
- Port Fuad 222
- Port Said 222
- Suez 222

F
France
- Aigues-Mortes 54
- Aix-en-Provence 58
- Albi 50
- Antibes 72
- Arles 56
- Banyuls-sur-Mer 46
- Camargue 54
- Cannes 72
- Cap d'Agde 48
- Carcassonne 48
- Carry-le-Rouet 58
- Cassis 62
- Castérino 68
- Castres 50
- Collioure 46
- Corsica 64
- Côte d'Azur 66
- Èze 76
- Gaillac 50
- Grussan 48
- Haut-de-Cagnes 72
- Hyères 66
- Îles d'Or 66
- La Brigue 68
- La Ciotat 62
- L'Estaque 58
- Marseille 58–61
- Menton 68, 76
- Montauban 50
- Montpellier 52
- Narbonne 48
- Nice 74
- Nîmes 56
- Orange 56
- Pézenas 49
- Porquerolles 66
- Rayol-Canadel-sur-Mer 67
- Saintes-Maries-de-la-Mer 54
- Saint-Florent 65
- Saint-Jean-Cap-Ferrat 76
- Salin-de-Giraud 54
- Sanary-sur-Mer 62
- Sausset-les-Pins 58
- Sète 48
- Sospel 68
- St-Tropez 70
- Villefranche-sur-Mer 76

G
Gibraltar 10
Greece
- Alexandroupoli 180
- Andritsena 160
- Argolid Peninsula 166
- Athens 163–165
- Cape Sounion 166
- Chalkida 170
- Chania (Hania) 178
- Corfu 154
- Costa 166
- Costa Navarino 158
- Crete 178
- Cyclades 168
- Cyprus 214
- Delphi 172
- Elefsina 166
- Epidavros 166
- Ermione 166
- Evia 170
- Glyfada 166
- Gravia 172
- Gulf of Patra 156
- Gythio 162
- Halkidiki 180
- Hora (Naxos Town) 169
- Hydra 167
- Igoumenitsa 156
- Kalamata 158
- Kalamitsi Bay 158
- Kardamyli 158
- Kassandra Peninsula 180
- Kavala 180
- Kinosura Peninsula 170
- Kyllini 158
- Lamia 170
- Lavrio 170
- Lefkada 156
- Leonidio 162
- Lindos 182
- Litohoro 174
- Malea Peninsula 162
- Mani Peninsula 158
- Marathon 170
- Marathonisi Islet 162
- Mavromati 160
- Messini 160
- Messolonghi 156
- Meteora 172

Monemvasia 162
Mystras 160
Nafplio 162, 166
Naxos 168
Nea Makri 170
Nicosia (Lefkosia) 217
Parga 156
Patra 158
Pelion Peninsula 170, 174
Peloponnese 158-163
Piraeus 166
Preveza 156
Rafina 170
Rhodes 182
Saronic Gulf 166
Sithonia Peninsula 180
Thermopylae 170
Thessaloniki 174, 176
Vergina 181
Volos 170, 174
Vouliagmeni 166
Vravrona 170

I

Italy
    Agrigento 105
    Amalfi 102
    Ancona 112
    Bari 107-109
    Basilicata 106
    Battipaglia 106
    Boccadasse 88
    Cagliari 92
    Calimera 110
    Campi Flegrei 99
    Caorle 118
    Carloforte 93
    Castellammare di Stabia 98
    Cerveteri 94
    Chioggia 112
    Cinque Terre 88, 90
    Elba 94
    Genoa 85-87, 89
    Grado 118
    Herculaneum 98
    Isola di San Pantaleo 104
    La Spezia 88
    Lecce 110
    Ligurian Riviera 84, 88-91
    Marina di Praia 102
    Melpignano 110
    Meta di Sorrento 101
    Monterosso 90
    Murano, Venice 115
    Naples 96
    Noto 105
    Ostia 94
    Palermo 105
    Palinuro 106
    Piano di Sorrento 102
    Pompeii 98
    Portofino 88, 91
    Portovenere 88
    Positano 102
    Puglia 106-111
    Punta Campanella 100
    Ravello 102
    Ravenna 112
    Riomaggiore 90
    Riviera del Conero 112
    Salerno 102
    San Pantaleo Island 104
    Santa Maria di Leuca 110
    Sardinia 92
    Savona 84
    Sicily 104
    Tarquinia 94
    Terracina 94
    Torre Sant'Andrea 110
    Trieste 118
    Ugento 110
    Vendicari 105
    Venice 112-117
    Ventimiglia 84
    Vernazza 90
    Vico Equense 100

M

Malta
    Comino 229
    Gozo 228
    Mġarr 229
    Valletta 228
    Xlendi 229
Monaco 78
Montenegro
    Bar 144
    Bay of Kotor 140
    Budva 142-143
    Cetinje 142
    Herceg Novi 140
    Kotor 140
    Lovćen 142
    Njeguši 142
    Perast 140
    Rijeka Crnojevića 142
    Sveti Stefan 144
    Ulcinj 144
Morocco
    Ceuta 246
    Chefchaouen 244
    El Jebha 242
    Fnideq 242
    M'diq 242
    Melilla 246
    Saïdia 242
    Tangier 242, 244
    Tetouan 244

S

Slovenia
    Istria 124-127
    Izola 124
    Koper 124
    Piran 125-126
    Portorož 126
    Primorska 124

Spain
    Alicante 22
    Almería 18
    Almuñécar 16
    Altea 22
    Andalucía 10-13
    Barcelona 38
    Begur 40
    Benicàssim 26
    Benidorm 22
    Cabo de Gata 18-19
    Cadaqués 40
    Calella de Palafrugell 40
    Calp 22
    Cambrils 34
    Cantarriján 16
    Cap de Creus 40
    Cartagena 20-21
    Castelló de la Plana 26
    Catalonia 34-41
    Ceuta (Morocco) 246
    Córdoba 14
    Costa Blanca 22
    Costa Brava 40
    Costa Cálida 20
    Costa Daurada 34
    Costa de la Luz 10
    Costa del Azaha 26
    Costa del Sol 10-16
    Costa Tropical 16
    Dènia 22
    Elche 23
    Estepona 10
    Falset 36
    Figueres 41
    Formentera 28
    Fuengirola 10
    Granada 16
    Gratallops 36
    Grazalema 12

Ibiza 32
Málaga 10–15
Mallorca 28–31
Marbella 10, 12
Melilla (Morocco) 246
Menorca 28
Mojácar 18
Moraira 22
Murcia 20
Nerja 16
Palma 30
Peñíscola 26
Peratallada 40
Port Lligat 41
Priorat 36
Ronda 12
Salobreña 16
Salou 34
Sa Tuna 40
Setenil de las Bodegas 12
Sitges 34
Siurana 36
Tamariu 40
Tarifa 10
Tarragona 34
Tossa de Mar 40
Valencia 24–27
Xàbia 22
Zahara de la Sierra 12

Tunisia
    Cap Bon 234
    Djerba 234
    El Haouaria 234
    Korbous 234
    Sfax 234
    Sidi Bou Saïd 236
    Sousse 234
    Tunis 234–237
Türkiye
    Akbük 194
    Akyaka 202

Alaçatı 190
Alanya 208
Anamur 209, 210
Antakya 211
Antalya 206
Ayvalık 190
Babakale 188
Belek 208, 209
Bergama (Pergamon) 190
Bitez 198
Bodrum Peninsula 198
Bozburun Peninsula 200
Bozcaada 188
Çamlı 202
Çanakkale 188
Cennet Adası 200
Çeşme Peninsula 190
Çıralı 204, 209
Cunda (Alibey) Island 190
Cyprus 214
Dalyan 202
Datça Peninsula 200
Demre 204
Didim 194, 196
Dilek Peninsula 194
Eski Doğanbey 194, 196
Fethiye 204
Foça 190
Gallipoli (Gelibolu) Peninsula 188
Geyikli 188
Gökçeada 188
Gökova Gulf 199
Göltürkbükü 198
Güllübahçe 196
Gümbet 198
Gümüşlük 198
Gündoğan 198
İzmir 192, 193
Kabak 204
Kalkan 204
Kapıkırı 196
Karaburun 190
Karpas Peninsula (Cyprus) 217
Kaş 204

Kayaköy 204
Kemer 208
Kızkalesi 210
Köyceğiz 202
Kuşadası 194
Lefkoşa (Cyprus) 217
Lycian Coast 204
Manavgat 208
Marmaris 200
Miletus 196
Ölüdeniz 204
Patara 209
Phaselis 208
Priene 196
Samandağ 210
Sedir Island 202
Selimiye 200
Sığacık 194
Söğüt 200
Tarsus 210
Taşlıca 201
Tekirova 208
Thrace 188
Troas (Biga) Peninsula 188
Turgutreis 198
Turquoise Coast 208
Turunç 200
Urla 190
Yalıkavak 198

Photo credits

Front Cover: Igor Tichonow/Getty Images; **Back Cover:** ermess/Shutterstock, Andreas Wolochow/Shutterstock; **9:** Vulcano/Shutterstock; **10:** Stewie74/Shutterstock, Mazur Travel/Shutterstock; **11:** Classic Image/Alamy; **13:** Mistervlad/Shutterstock, Yadid Levy/Lonely Planet; **14:** Mazur Travel/Shutterstock; **15:** Ivo Antonie de Rooij/Shutterstock; **16:** Bahdanovich Alena/Shutterstock; **18:** Juan Miguel Cervera Merlo/Alamy, Marisa Estivill/Shutterstock; **19:** Umomos/Shutterstock; **20:** FCG/Shutterstock; **21:** Shaun Dodds/Shutterstock; **22:** Julia Lav/Shutterstock; **23:** Vivvi Smak/Shutterstock; **24:** Massimo Todaro/Shutterstock, Madrugada Verde/Shutterstock; **26:** Creapubli/Shutterstock, Roman Babakin/Shutterstock; **27:** Riccardo Cirillo/Shutterstock; **28:** Annapurna Mellor/Lonely Planet; **30:** Felipe Santibañez/Lonely Planet, Successió Miró / ADAGP, Paris and DACS London 2025. Photo by Mark Green/Shutterstock; **32:** Annapurna Mellor/Lonely Planet; **33:** Annapurna Mellor/Lonely Planet; **34:** Boris Stroujko/Shutterstock; **35:** Alexander Spatari/Getty Images, Thomas Vilhelm/Getty Images; **37:** Artur Debat/Getty Images, gg-foto/Shutterstock; **38:** Margaret Stepien/Lonely Planet, Alxpin/Getty Images; **40:** Iñigo Fdz de Pinedo/Getty Images, Damsea/Shutterstock; **41:** Charles Hewitt/Picture Post/Hulton Archive/Getty Images; **45:** Ermess/Shutterstock; **46:** Ikumaru/Shutterstock; **47:** Andrew Smith/Alamy; **48:** Wirestock/Getty Images, Boris Stroujko/Shutterstock; **51:** Aurelien KEMPF piksl.fr/Shutterstock, Nata Shilo com/Shutterstock; **52:** Volodymyr Shtun/Getty Images, @Musée Fabre/Montpellier; **54:** Adrienne Pitts/Lonely Planet; **55:** Mutinamatyas_photo/Shutterstock, ArCaLu/Shutterstock; **57:** Rahan1991/Getty Images, Gerhard Roethlinger/Shutterstock; **58:** EyeEm Mobile GmbH/Getty Images, Jon Hicks/Getty Images; **60:** Drabanth/Getty Images; **61:** Hemis/Alamy; **62:** Susan Wildes/Shutterstock, Matt Munro/Lonely Planet; **64:** Jon Ingall/Shutterstock, Alex Treadway/Getty Images; **66:** Roland Bouvier/Alamy; **67:** Lottie Davies/Lonely Planet; **69:** Dufrenoy/Getty Images, Edgar Machado/Shutterstock; **70:** Proslgn/Shutterstock; **71:** Courtesy of Musée de l'Annonciade; **72:** ArtMediaFactory/Shutterstock, Mike Workman/Shutterstock; **74:** M.studio/Adobe Stock, Andrei Antipov/Shutterstock; **76:** Violette Franchi/Lonely Planet, Hannah 13/Shutterstock; **77:** Vue de l'accrochage de la collection permanente | © Succession H. Matisse pour les œuvres de l'artiste | Photo: J. V. © Ville de Nice; **78:** Xavier Bonilla/NurPhoto/Getty Images, Kiev.Victor/Shutterstock; **83:** Matt Munro/Lonely Planet; **84:** AB_Production/Shutterstock; **85:** Roman Sigaev/Shutterstock; **86:** Zummolo/Getty Images; **87:** Andia/Universal Images/Getty Images; **88:** Nathapon Triratanachat/Shutterstock, Alxpin/Getty Images; **89:** Hemis/Alamy; **90:** Justin Foulkes/Lonely Planet; **91:** Courtesy of Bisson Winery; **92:** Den Belitsky/Getty Images, Chloe Frost-Smith/Unsplash; **94:** Dima Moroz/Shutterstock; **96:** Paky Cassano/Shutterstock; **97:** Angelafoto/Getty Images; **98:** Roberto Moiola/Sysaworld/Getty Images; **99:** Antonio Busiello/Getty Images, Andreas Solaro/AFP/Getty Images; **100:** YKD/Shutterstock, Gagliardi Photography/Shutterstock; **103:** Mark Read/Lonely Planet; **104:** Locomotive74/Shutterstock; **105:** Jonathan Stokes/Lonely Planet; **106:** Giuma/Shutterstock; **107:** Magistro & Creativi Associati; **108:** Sopotnicki/Shutterstock, Michael Heffernan/Lonely Planet; **111:** Martina De Pascali/Lonely Planet, Yuriy Brykaylo/Shutterstock; **112:** Matt Munro/Lonely Planet, Arkanto/Shutterstock; **113:** Fotokon/Shutterstock; **114:** Stetiukha Kristina/Shutterstock; **115:** Gabri90/iStock/Getty Images; **116:** Justin Foulkes/Lonely Planet; **118:** robertharding/Alamy; **119:** Bepsimage/iStock/Getty Images; **123:** Ajan Alen/Shutterstock; **124:** Andrew Mayovskyy/Shutterstock; **125:** Juergen Sack/Getty Images; **126:** Justin Foulkes/Lonely Planet; **127:** Courtesy of COB; **128:** Goran Safarek/Shutterstock, Medvedeva Oxana/Shutterstock; **129:** rusm/Getty Images; **130:** lechatnoir/Getty Images; **131:** Tupungato/Shutterstock; **132:** xbrchx/Shutterstock, Creative Travel Projects/Shutterstock; **133:** Jacopo Landi/NurPhoto/Getty Images; **134:** Justin Foulkes/4Corners, niyazz/Adobe Stock; **136:** Roman Sigaev/Shutterstock; **137:** Courtesy of the Meštrović Gallery, photo Zoran Alajbeg; **138:** xbrchx/Shutterstock; **139:** Denis Belitsky/Shutterstock; **140:** Julian Love/Lonely Planet; **141:** Olga Ilinich/Shutterstock; **143:** givaga/Shutterstock, Alexandre.ROSA/Shutterstock; **144:** Ranko Maras/Shutterstock; **146:** Frank Bach/Alamy; **147:** Martin Mecnarowski/Shutterstock, Lukas Bischoff/Getty Images; **148:** Enea Mustafaraj/Shutterstock, imageBROKER.com GmbH & Co. KG/Alamy; **153:** Georgios Tsichlis/Shutterstock; **154:** balounm/Shutterstock; **155:** SCStock/Getty Images; **156:** Florian Augustin/Shutterstock, Georgios Tsichlis/Shutterstock; **157:** Athanasios Gioumpasis/Getty Images; **158:** Valantis Minogiannis/Shutterstock; **159:** Peter Eastland/Alamy; **161:** Leonid Andronov/Getty Images, Evgenii Kiryukhin/Shutterstock; **162:** Georgios Kritsotakis/Shutterstock, Lefteris Papaulakis/Shutterstock; **163:** Czgur/Getty Images; **164:** Alvaro German Vilela/Shutterstock, George Pachantouris/Getty Images; **166:** Heracles Kritikos/Shutterstock; **167:** Courtesy of ArtCinema Hydra, photo Till Völker; **168:** Christos Siatos/Shutterstock; **169:** saiko3p/Shutterstock; **170:** Stratos Giannikos/Shutterstock; **173:** trabantos/iStock/Getty Images, Justin Foulkes/Lonely Planet; **174:** Giovanni Rinaldi/Shutterstock, Myronyuk Vasyl/Shutterstock; **176:** Salvator Barki/Getty Images; **177:** Hilda Weges/Getty Images; **178:** Matt Munro/Lonely Planet; **180:** Konstantinos Tsakalidis/Lonely Planet; **182:** Liubomir Paut / Photographer; **183:** Matt Munro/Lonely Planet; **187:** art of line/Shutterstock; **188:** okanozdemir/Shutterstock, Nejdet Duzen/Shutterstock; **190:** Ibrahim Kavus/Shutterstock; **191:** Marina Cavusoglu/Getty Images; **192:** Alp Aksoy/Shutterstock, boyoz/Shutterstock; **194:** hydm90/Shutterstock, photomobilet/Shutterstock; **197:** Selcuk Oner/Shutterstock; **198:** Leonid Sorokin/Shutterstock; **199:** muratart/Shutterstock; **200:** Efired/Shutterstock; **203:** aricancaner/Shutterstock, Dimos/Shutterstock; **204:** Resul Muslu/Shutterstock, Olena Rublenko/Alamy; **205:** frantic00/Shutterstock; **206:** saiko3p/Shutterstock; **207:** frantic00/iStock/Getty Images; **208:** John Wreford/Shutterstock, Den Tramper/Shutterstock; **209:** Yasemin Yurtman Candemir/Shutterstock; **210:** Mehmet Cetin/Shutterstock; **215:** nejdetduzen/ GettyImages; **216:** Jon Milnes/Shutterstock; **217:** Oleksandr Savchuk/Shutterstock; **223:** Mark Davidson/Alamy, Tony Moran/Shutterstock; **224:** Octasy/Shutterstock, Luis Dafos/Alamy; **226:** Richard Walker Media/Shutterstock; **227:** Popperfoto/Getty Images; **228:** Matt Munro/Lonely Planet; **229:** CoolR/Shutterstock; **233:** TomiV/Shutterstock; **234:** piotreknik/Shutterstock, Andreas Wolochow/Shutterstock; **236:** efesenko/Getty Images, Travel-Fr/Shutterstock; **238:** zaiare/Shutterstock; **239:** Anton Ivanov/Shutterstock; **240:** Habib_Boucetta/Getty Images; **241:** Hak Im/Shutterstock; **242:** tolobalaguer.com/Shutterstock; **243:** Kamal Daghmoumi, Amine Houari; **245:** dsaprin/Shutterstock, Olena Tur/Shutterstock; **246:** Chris Hellier/Getty Images, Sopotnicki/Shutterstock; **247:** Terence Spencer/Popperfoto/Getty Images

About the authors

Isabella Noble writes about Spain for Lonely Planet and lives in Barcelona.

Jon Bryant lives in Nice and covers France for media including BBC Radio and *The Guardian*.

Virginia DiGaetano lives in Rome and is one of Lonely Planet's Italy experts.

Brana Vladisavljevic covers the Balkans and Adriatic region for Lonely Planet. She currently lives in Novi Sad, Serbia.

Alexis Averbuck lives on the island of Hydra and is a Lonely Planet Greece expert.

Jennifer Hattam writes about Türkiye for Lonely Planet and lives in Istanbul.

Lauren Keith has focused on Middle Eastern coverage at Lonely Planet for many years.

Imprint

The Mediterranean
October 2025
Published by Lonely Planet Global Limited
CRN 554153
www.lonelyplanet.com
10 9 8 7 6 5 4 3
Printed in Canada
ISBN 9781837585830
© Lonely Planet 2025
© photographers as indicated 2025

Publishing Director Piers Pickard
Gift & Illustrated Publisher Becca Hunt
Senior Editor Robin Barton
Commissioning Editor Peter Grunert
Designer Adrienne Pitts
Art Director Emily Dubin
Editor Polly Thomas
Image Researcher Claire Guest
Cartographer Wayne Murphy
Print Production Nigel Longuet

Although the authors and Lonely Planet have taken all reasonable care in preparing this book, we make no warranty about the accuracy or completeness of its content and, to the maximum extent permitted, disclaim all liability from its use. All rights reserved. No part of this publication may be reproduced, stored in a retrieval system or transmitted in any form by any means, electronic, mechanical, photocopying, recording or otherwise except brief extracts for the purpose of review, without the written permission of the publisher. Lonely Planet and the Lonely Planet logo are trademarks of Lonely Planet and are registered in the US patent and Trademark Office and in other countries.

Lonely Planet Global Limited
Digital Depot, Roe Lane (off Thomas St),
Digital Hub, Dublin 8,
D08 TCV4
Ireland

Stay in touch lonelyplanet.com/contact

Writers Isabella Noble (Spain), Jon Bryant (France), Virginia DiGaetano (Italy), Brana Vladisavljevic (The Adriatic), Alexis Averbuck (Greece), Jennifer Hattam (Türkiye), Lauren Keith (Southeast Mediterranean and The Maghreb), Jess Lee (Cyprus)

Illustrator Anna Tzortzi (instagram.com/anna.tzortzi/)

Paper in this book is certified against the Forest Stewardship Council™ standards. FSC™ promotes environmentally responsible, socially beneficial and economically viable management of the world's forests.

FSC C021741

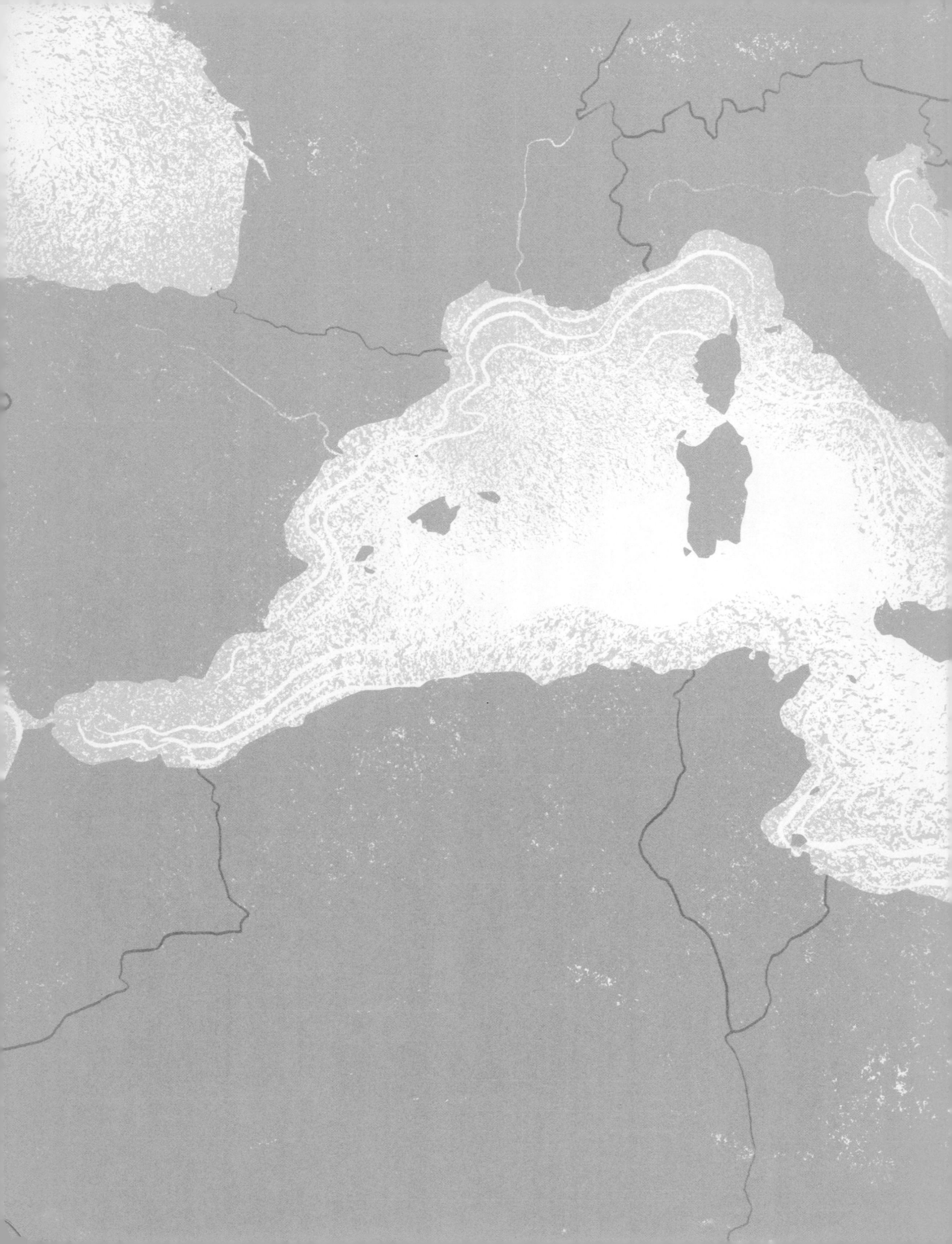